just another little murder

PHIL CLEARY

A Sue Hines Book
ALLEN & UNWIN

First published in 2002

Copyright © Phil Cleary 2002

All rights reserved. No part of this book may be reproduced or transmitted in any form or by any means, electronic or mechanical, including photocopying, recording or by any information storage and retrieval system, without prior permission in writing from the publisher. The *Australian Copyright Act* 1968 (the Act) allows a maximum of one chapter or 10% of this book, whichever is the greater, to be photocopied by any educational institution for its educational purposes provided that the educational institution (or body that administers it) has given a remuneration notice to Copyright Agency Limited (CAL) under the Act.

Allen & Unwin
83 Alexander Street
Crows Nest NSW 2065
Australia
Phone: (61 2) 8425 0100
Fax: (61 2) 9906 2218
Email: info@allenandunwin.com
Web: www.allenandunwin.com

National Library of Australia
Cataloguing-in-Publication entry:

Cleary, Phil.
   Just another little murder.
   ISBN 1 86508 789 0.
   1. Cleary, Vicki – Death. 2. Murder victims – Victoria – Melbourne. 3. Murder – Victoria – Melbourne - Investigation. 4. Keogh, Peter Raymond – Trials, litigation, etc 5. Murderers – Victoria – Melbourne. 6. Trials (Murder) – Victoria – Melbourne. I. Title.
   364.1523099451

Cover and text design by Phil Campbell
Typeset by Pauline Haas

Printed by Griffin Press, South Australia

10 9 8 7 6 5 4 3 2 1

Contents

Acknowledgements	vi
Peter Raymond Keogh (1948–2001)	viii
unfinished business	1
Keogh at large	9
decent women	47
murder changes everything	67
killings of the intimate kind	111
losing one of your own	163
the final insult	199
a noose around a coward's neck	231
Endnotes	257

Acknowledgements

Just Another Little Murder is not a book driven by the irrationality of revenge. It's a political as well as personal tale that attempts to right the wrongs of dispassionate justice. Without the courage and decency of my mother and father, I could never have written it. Every step along the way they are my guardian angels. As a result of the research skills and insights of my sisters, Donna and Lizzie, no stone has been left unturned in piecing together Peter Keogh's early family life. To my brothers Paul and Perry who, like me, bore a special pain, I hope the book says all the things we wanted to say but were never allowed. To my wife, Christine, whose artist's eye translated Vicki's beauty into words and, more than any other person, lived with the story, I trust it's been worth it.

Without the generosity of the family of Judy McNulty, nee Reeves, the story probably would not have been told. Judy's family could have chosen to put the past behind them. Instead, they opened their hearts and their minds to me and relived the pain of those dark days when the killer was on the rampage. As a result of the courage and candour of Judy, her mother and sisters, and her daughters, Terri and Allison, the terror about which so many men dared not speak has been unmasked.

Special thanks too, must go to Julie McAllister. Against all odds, Julie refused to cower in the face of Keogh's onslaught in early 2000. I'm so glad I met her and that she told me what she knew.

My thanks go to all at the DPP, in particular to Bruce Garner and Paul Coghlan QC for opening up their records and allowing me to chew their ears. To my long time mate, solicitor, Tony Hannebery, who listened to my stories and shared a few of his own, I must also say thanks. Although I've rattled the saber at the legal profession, I must thank Peter Berman for his memories of Bob Vernon. So too must I thank defence barristers Ian Hayden and Paul Holdenson QC for so generously sharing their courtroom experiences with the law of provocation. To the inimitable, Detective Ron Iddles, who walked me along the Maria James trail and listened to my theories, thanks also. Likewise to Detective Frank Bellesini and his many colleagues whose recollections feature in the book.

This is a passionate, sometimes fiery book. Without a confidante such as editor Andrea McNamara, it might have been an excruciating experience. Instead, she turned it into a shared journey and was with me every step of the way. Together, Andrea and publisher Sue Hines made me feel like this was an important story. From the moment the cover photo was devised and taken, I knew was in safe hands. Their collective guidance and kindness made it a journey about which to be proud.

My sister, Vicki, was a gift. I hope she understands why her family had to retell all that she endured. So many people loved her. Maybe this book will sweep away the injustice perpetrated on her in the Supreme Court in 1989.

Peter Raymond Keogh (1948–2001)

1948	14 February	born
1960		charged with sexual assault on 8-year-old girl
1961		convicted on 3 separate occasions of shoplifting and larceny
1963	21 September	attacks Constable Bellesini with knife at Northcote Railway Station
1964		faced with attempted murder
1964	17 June	acquitted of attempted murder
1964	10 November	assaults his foreman
1966	3 October	faces assault charges in Bendigo Magistrates court
1967	2 May	loses appeal against Bendigo assaults and gets 3 months
1970		sentenced to one month gaol for assault with a glass
1970		assaults woman in a Coburg flat
1972		assaults and bashes a man in a pool room
1974		found not guilty of assault in pool room

1974	27 December	sexual assault of 9-year-old girl in Canterbury St, Richmond
1975	January	assault on girl at T&G building
1975	26 Feb	sentenced to 5 months for assault on T&G girl
1975	26 August	appeal against T&G assault conviction is dismissed, sentence affirmed
1976	April	sentenced to 18 months gaol for sexual assault in Canterbury St
1977	mid-year	Keogh released from Loddon Prison
1978	18 Sept	charged with theft & unlawful assault on Marilyn Reeves, charges subsequently dropped
1980	autumn	Judy McNulty's sister accuses Keogh of rape
1980	17 June	Maria James murder (Thornbury Bookshop murder)
1981	mid-year	drugs McNulty and children in St David St, Northcote
1981	late	knife attack on McNulty in St David St, Northcote
1982	19 November	sentenced to 3 months for drink driving
1982		sentenced to 18 months for sexual assault on 2 young girls and appeals
1983	October	conviction for sexual assault quashed
1983	November	conviction for drink driving affirmed
1987	26 August	murders Vicki Cleary
1988	16 June	inquest into Vicki's death
1989	6-15 February	R v Keogh murder trial
1991	July	released from Loddon Prison
1993		9-year-old neighbour claims sexual assault by Keogh at Mill Park
2001	3 March	Keogh torches McAllister's home in Tyers
2001	24 June	Keogh suicides

unfinished business

'Dead. Are you sure?' I asked, placing the final piece in the Peter Keogh jigsaw. It was Monday 25 June 2001 when the news came through that the man I'd been tracking for more than a decade might be dead. Suicide? The man who'd murdered my sister wouldn't neck himself. Surely not, I thought, as Julie McAllister relayed what she'd heard. Was it only grapevine hysteria, or had he really gone the way of his mates Watson and Freake? And if he had, did it put Vicki's soul to rest or had the mystery just begun? There were many unanswered questions.

When Julie rang early the next morning, the question became purely academic. 'Hi, it's true. He's dead. Gassed himself in the car,' she said, the relief transparent in the free flow of words.

'Christ! I wanted him alive for that story in the *Age*,' I replied, the real meaning of the event beginning to crystallise in my head. In exactly five weeks Keogh's violent life was going to be spread across the front page of the *Sunday Age* newspaper for him and his drinking mates to see. You bastard, I thought.

For Julie there were no such concerns. 'Sorry, Phil, all I want to do is celebrate. He's out of my life, that's all that matters,' she said with a muffled laugh. Everything Julie said made perfect sense, and she had every reason to be happy. She was free. The problem was my family could never be quite free of him.

Keogh was fifty-three years of age when he died and he'd done it on his terms. Older than his years and ravaged by hate, he was nothing like the girl he killed. Left naked, cut and bruised on a lonely hospital trolley, three months short of her twenty-sixth birthday, my sister Vicki had died a shocking death at his hands. Then a judge I deemed insensitive to my sister's human rights, together with a quisling jury, seemed to have excused away his crime. That's why I had wanted to kill him. Was death by suicide part of the script? I hadn't made up my mind.

Within a few days of Keogh's death, homicide detective, Dave Rae, would recite an interesting tale.

'Keogh told his sister Jenny you were going to expose him in the media over a 0.05 charge pending,' he told me over the phone.

'As if I'd bother trying to publicise some drink-driving charge. He knew I was on his tail. Arson and murder, that's what was on his mind,' I replied.

'Yeah, probably, but in any case we need a statement from you, Phil.'

'A statement?'

'Yes, we've sought permission to take DNA off the corpse and, of course, the Coroner wants to know why.'

It was so typical of the life of Peter Keogh. Someone always had to answer for his violence. A vicious sociopath decides to top himself to avoid public exposure, and before he puts the hose in the window, he tells his sister it's my fault. He knew I was on his trail. You fucking coward, I thought. I'd never met Jenny or any other member of Keogh's family. They were just names on bail sheets and hazy characters in Mum's stories about what happened to Vicki.

Yet, as always, there was a sliver of truth in Keogh's lies to his sister. I had wanted to expose him, and slowly, the Chinese whisper I'd begun the day he torched Julie's home in March 2001 had become a roar in his paranoid twisted mind.

A year before Keogh turned the key in the ignition and brought an end to his violent life, I'd spoken the set of words that would change the course of that life:

'Phil Cleary here, how are you? Look, I've got a story that might interest you. The bloke who murdered my sister will be in the Moe Court in a few weeks facing an intervention order,' I told Melbourne *Herald Sun* police rounds reporter, Phil Cullen. When I explained how Keogh had been harassing his ex-girlfriend just as he'd done to Vicki before he killed her, Cullen knew he had a story.

'Sounds good. We'll send a photographer and give it a run,' he replied.

For now, Rupert Murdoch's tabloid would be my ally in the pursuit of a primitive, swaggering, working-class thug.

At Moe court, Julie McAllister's son Justin was in battle mode. It was now 24 August 2000 and Keogh's devious mind was ticking over. 'I've read this. We know exactly what this bloke's done,' said Justin when he burst into the interview room where Keogh and his female brief were preparing their next move. In his hand was a copy of *Cleary Independent*.

'He went white when I put the book on the table,' Justin would later tell his mother. An enemy was nothing but a 'dog and cunt' when the coward Keogh was bragging. Beneath the apparent look of fright those words would almost certainly have been swirling around his mind.

The very day my book had hit the streets in 1998, Keogh had a copy in his in hand. Buried beneath the story of my four years in the federal parliament was a gruesome chapter that bore the title, 'Murder by any other name'. Here, I laid bare the violence about which his barrister, John Champion, dared not speak at his trial. As Keogh pored over the pages and saw the names and the dates, he soon realised I knew more about his journey than any other person. When I spat out the names Freake and Watson and tracked their role in Vicki's murder, he knew he was never going to escape me. On 8 March 1998, his once closest mate and former housemate, Brian Freake, was found with his throat cut in the very house where the killer had plotted Vicki's murder. Six months later, Brian Watson, Keogh's smiling chauffeur when he stalked Vicki in the weeks before her murder, committed suicide. Was I stalking him? What else did I know and what did I have up my sleeve? Those were the questions he pondered as he waited for me to reappear in his life.

Whenever I was interviewed on TV about how the courts had dealt with him and his women-killer mates, he'd head for Watson's and nervously wait for me to name him. Each time I rolled out his dirty name, he ground his teeth and wondered what memories I might stir among the other victims.

As he sought the safety of his car that day in Moe, a denim jacket protecting his image from a tenacious photographer, Keogh knew I was after him. With his mind befuddled by the descending noose and the immediate demands of adjusting his tie, Keogh forgot about the approach of the camera. As he lifted his head, photographer Nicole Garmston framed his angry countenance in her viewfinder and pressed the shutter. When the flash lit up the front seat, he went berserk and thrust his fist through the partially opened window.

Fourteen years earlier he'd trapped Vicki in her car in a quiet street in Coburg. Now a woman had done the same to him and he didn't like it. With the thought that his image might be destined for the tabloid press, the bully began a burst of vitriol as he frantically attempted to cover his head with the jacket. In the public carpark of the Moe Court, Nicole was a woman he just couldn't touch.

That night he pondered the next move and wondered what spin the *Herald Sun* would put on his appearance at the Court. In the morning he rose quickly and grabbed a copy of the paper. As he thumbed his way through the front pages, the perspiration gathered on his forehead. Peter Raymond Keogh had good reason for not wanting his picture spread across the newspaper. There were any number of women who might remember the violence and another who believed she'd seen him at the scene of a crime. 'Dog and cunt,' he said, dragging the photographer's business card from his wallet when he reached the page and saw the damage.

'What are ya doin' puttin' my fuckin' photo in the paper,' he screamed when Nicole Garmston answered the phone. Although he didn't say so, Keogh knew I'd set it up. Better still, he knew I wasn't finished with him.

In the weeks before his death, I'd rung his watering hole, the Junction Hotel in Preston, and asked to speak with him. I had camouflaged my voice and said I was an old friend. On the first occasion, the bloke had returned to the phone and told me Keogh wasn't in the pub. The next time he had claimed he hadn't seen him for weeks. It was bullshit.

'What's it like serving a murderer?' I had asked.

'Don't know anything about that,' the barman had squealed. Keogh might have been hiding, but the word was filtering back that someone was asking questions.

I really did want to speak with him. I wanted to tell him to keep clear of Julie McAllister and that if I spotted him in the vicinity of any of my family, he'd be in deep shit. The writing was on the wall, but this time he was going to be stopped.

In the aftermath of the separation from Julie McAllister, 220A Mansfield Street, Thornbury had become home. A $60.00 a week bungalow out back of a house, only a brisk walk from the Junction Hotel, it was a fitting place for him to end his life. When he walked through the doors of his old drinking haunt in the months following the arson, he eyed every nook and cranny for a sign someone might be looking. Word was filtering back that friends of Vicki were talking. The decision to drop a match into the wastepaper bin inside Julie's bedroom window was beginning to weigh heavily on his mind. By June 2001 it had come to haunt him.

My campaign against Keogh began long before Keogh set fire to Julie's house. If justice had been done that day in the Supreme Court, my family would have walked away and done our best to get over her murder. Because all we got was injustice, Vicki's murder just wouldn't go away. From that day, in fits and starts, I lifted one rock after another in search of the real Peter Keogh. Along the way I found his victims, read the crime sheets that documented his violence and unearthed the letters that carried his secrets. Nothing was ever perfectly clear and there were always more questions than answers. And just when I thought I had him, he necked himself.

But about one thing I was certain. Vicki had been the victim of institutionalised negligence. An outmoded law, a parole officer who didn't tell all she knew and a string of low-life acquaintances who looked away when Vicki needed them—all had a cameo in the story of a young girl's murder. It took fourteen years, but now I knew the truth.

The morning in 1963 I rushed into the bedroom to tell Mum and Dad about the assassination of President John F Kennedy in Dallas, and the day in 1987 when my brother said, 'The bastard's stabbed Vicki outside the kinder in Coburg'—these were momentous days for me. Monday 25 June 2001 now sat alongside them.

There's an old saying that death comes in threes. It wasn't in my thoughts when I stood in a little church in Foster three days before the suicide. I was there to pay my last respects to 35-year-old Jeff Angwin. Angwin had simply fallen out of bed, dead, leaving two small children and a wife to ponder life without him. The kind of man Peter Keogh could never be, Angwin had been an anchor in defence when I coached Coburg to the VFA premiership against Williamstown, at Windy Hill in 1988 and '89. Without the sheer exhilaration of those premierships, the gloom of murder and a psychologically shattering trial might have strangled my family and me. I never forgot that. Lean and sinewy, Angwin played football like an acrobat dancing above a river of crocodiles. He just stared them down. Yet, as we cried at the loss of one of life's heroes, the weak Peter Keogh, a man we should have dealt with long ago, was telling the bouncer at the Junction Hotel 'I'm gunna neck meself.'

Among the mourners at Jeff's funeral was a sinewy weatherbeaten bloke I knew from years before.

'How are ya, Phil. Remember me?' he said as his bony fingers ensnared my palm.

'Yes, I do. Bill Angwin, isn't it?' We met some years ago. Terrible about Jeff, isn't it?' I replied. He was young Jeff's uncle.

I'd only met him once or twice before, but such was our first meeting that it would always have a place in my memory. We'd talked at length at Johnny Spencer's 60th birthday on Saturday 8 August 1987. Spencer was my dad's great mate and had been his best man when he walked down the aisle at St Ambrose Church in Brunswick in 1951. I remembered the meeting well because Vicki was there with a young bloke she had introduced as Chris Wheeler. He was her new boyfriend. Although one day he'd divulge the anxiety of Vicki's final days, at Spencer's party Wheeler said not a word about the threats Vicki was receiving from Keogh. A new life awaited her, but she had seemed subdued. Two weeks later my sister was dead.

The night at Spencer's had been profound for a number of reasons. In his youth Spencer had been a Marquis of Queensberry pugilist with a quick temper. In his prime he'd have taken to Keogh with his fists and asked questions later. So, too, would have Bill Angwin. He was a deadset knockabout bloke who'd have delivered a simple answer had Wheeler offered us an insight into what he and Vicki were thinking. That night only football was on Angwin's mind. Although I was no thug, nor a boxer like Spencer, I'd earned a reputation as a tough footballer who ran straight and hard at anything between the ball and me. A football legend, they called me. Bill Angwin admired that. Yet, as we talked about my retirement as a player with Coburg and reminisced about those epic Coburg-Port Melbourne games in the riotous VFA, I never imagined we'd be drawn together around the intimate ritual of death.

But there in the Melbourne *Sun,* the day after the murder, nestled among three columns of sorrowful tributes, was Bill's message:

> Deepest sympathies to Phil and family in your sad and tragic loss
> Always remembered RIP,
> Bill Angwin.

The day I shook hands with Bill Angwin at Jeff's funeral, Peter Keogh's demise seemed a million miles away. Yet, just as when Bill and I had met in August 1987, the banshee was calling. This time she was tapping on the window of the bungalow in Mansfield Street, Thornbury.

Cast as a victim of the cultural poverty of the little house above the Merri creek and the violence of inner suburban working-class life, Keogh was an enticing prize to those who made a quid from his lumpenproletarian violence. While his exasperated mother had tried to protect him from a hostile world, young Peter's view of life found its expression in the garish tattoos soon traversing his body. The prophetic 'Death or Glory' was one of them. With yet another inglorious 0.05 pending and gaol looming, he had no option. Death it had to be.

Among Vicki's possessions was a collection of photos that plotted the course of Keogh's life. By the time he was twelve, he was already struggling with the prospect of unleashing a smile on the box brownie. Standing alongside his sisters, in black trousers, white socks, black pointy shoes and floral shirt, the kid from Westgarth was already conscious of his image. Three years later the suppressed smile had given way to a scowl that swept any residual youth from his face. With his sleeves rolled up to expose the biceps that would be his badge of honour, there was nothing of the dandy about Peter Keogh. Fists, not words, would be his calling card. It was a look that acquaintances and enemies alike would never forget.

For the plump 45-year widow in the photo, Keogh was about to become nothing but heartbreak. The loss of her husband in 1960 had added a tinge of melancholy to her demeanour, and she would die with the stigma of rape hovering over the family.

Keogh at large

Spoilt and callous, Peter Keogh had no regard for others. Official records show that he was born at the Women's Hospital on 14 February 1948. Another story as told on a police file is that he emerged from the cot under the hot corrugated iron of the disused wartime US military base, Camp Pell, in nearby Parkville. Whether this was another ruse to bestow victimhood on the boy is a matter for speculation.

Whatever the truth, Keogh was on a path of deceit and manipulation from the time he could talk. On the streets of Northcote and Preston, he was joined by genuinely tough Camp Pell boys who'd been poured from their emergency abodes into flimsy Housing Commission houses and flats north of the city. By the 1960s the local cops derisively labelled the beat 'Little Chicago'. From the mouths of Heidelberg kids came the idiomatic twist, 'Camp Hell'.

When John Thomas Keogh and Mildred Saddington brought the baby Peter Raymond Keogh home to Clauscen Street, North Fitzroy, there were more than a thousand children weathering pneumonia, rheumatic and scarlet fever and the contagious impetigo in the sprawling Camp Pell. With four other children, the eldest only eight years of age, Mildred had her hands full. At 55 years of age, Jack Keogh was 25 years her senior and past tending to the needs of little children. His was the world of the Rubber Workers Union and labour politics. Hers was the home. And so it would be until her death in 1976, when the innocent young boy she brought into the world was incarcerated behind the walls of Pentridge.

My mother had always found it hard not to apportion some blame to Keogh's family for the murder of her daughter. 'If only they'd told me how dangerous he was, it would never have happened,' she'd say. When Peter Keogh was charged with the rape of a young girl in 1974, little sister Jenny bailed him out. And after he killed Vicki, big sister Dulcie was in the court saying her kind and decent brother was abjectly remorseful. Even after the murder trial his sisters stuck by him. 'Don't hurt my brother, will you?' Jenny had implored his somewhat perplexed girlfriend, Julie McAllister, at a Christmas gathering after his release.

It seemed that not even after Julie's house went up in smoke in a brazen arson attack ten months after the separation did Keogh's sisters demand answers. In the weeks before his death they washed and cooked for their violent prodigal brother. From the Cleary's perspective his sisters' words and his family's actions made a mockery of what he'd done throughout his life and showed contempt for Vicki. Was it any wonder we struggled to think well of the Keoghs?

I hadn't laid eyes on Keogh's family until the trial, and I had my first and only conversation with his sister Jenny when I rang her seven months after Keogh committed suicide. There was no rancour in my words. I simply asked if she could help me understand why it had all happened and what had produced such a brother. In between the tears was a sad refrain that captured the hurt and harm this man had done. Peter Raymond Keogh had touched more lives than I'd ever imagined. 'We had a lovely upbringing,' she told me. So why had parole officers painted such a grim picture of life in the family home in Westgarth? By conversation's end, the mystery had only deepened.

When two constables knocked on the door of a house in McLachlan Street, Westgarth around 4 am on Saturday 19 April 1959, there was mayhem. The moment eleven-year-old Peter Keogh learnt that his mate had been roused from bed and shunted off to Northcote Police station, he went into a rage.

A short while before the police had arrived at the door of the single-fronted terrace, they had accompanied a sobbing fifteen-year-old girl from Heidelberg to the Royal Women's Hospital. Here, Dr John Birrell certified that the girl had experienced sexual penetration, but no abrasions, in the vacant block behind Tom Pateras' fish and chip shop in Station Street, Fairfield. A bricklayer's daughter, the young girl told police she'd been dragged from outside the shop after a night at the Northcote pictures with her friend, Noelene.

'Tell anyone and there'll be trouble,' the chief abductor had said as the girl's legs were parted and her body fondled by the men gathered around her. Nearby were the torn pants that had been ripped from her hips by the chief when he'd thrown her to the ground. With her skirt lifted to expose her soft female flesh, she'd become a pathetic figure.

'Shut up, or you'll cop a whack,' snarled the chief, as the rasping sound of his trouser zip pierced the air.

'Can't get it in,' he lamented after five minutes of pushing and prodding. No matter what force he exerted, his warrior's cock could not find a path into the girl's vagina. It was the same with the next. Then came the conquest.

'Got it in, boys,' said Keogh's mate, as he stood to oversee his prize. It was to be short-lived triumph.

In the prelude to the rape, a local tough had fancied his chances with the frightened and confused Noelene. When she heard the sound of his trouser zip and felt the pressure of his hand on her wrist, she soon got wind of what was in store. This and the sight of her girl-friend on her back alongside Tom Pateras' Holden utility sent her into hysteria. When she reached Station Street screaming, 'Help, help, someone!' a cabbie and a local security guard had sensed something was horribly wrong. Suddenly two shots rang out in the lane, followed by a stern command.

'What's goin' on? Don't move!' yelled night watchman Matthew Dunlop, lowering his pistol.

Keogh at large   11

As the hero with the gun made his way through the dark, the girl was whisked away by the boys. Without Noelene's cries and the arrival of Dunlop, it would have been just another gang-bang. In the boys' own Grandview Hotel down the road, the braggarts would have made sure the girl's name was mud. But the appearance of the cops put the spotlight on the boys. Now they'd have to prove she was a damned whore. Francis Patrick Sheehy, a labourer who lived near the mouth of the lane in Station Street, knew which side he was on. 'Leave the boy alone, shitkicker. You got no right to be holding him,' Sheehy had said, unconvinced that a hysterical girl deserved the assistance of a man with a gun. Dunlop had been so surprised by Sheehy's words he allowed the lone boy in the lane to disappear.

When the accused boy from McLachlan Street signed his official statement in front of seasoned Senior Detective Richard John Martin and Constable John Ring at Northcote CIB, he left little for the imagination.

'Was she dragged?' asked the wily Martin.

'No, she was walking, but she was getting dragged too,' replied Keogh's mate.

'What happened next?'

'She was asked to lay down on the ground, but would not so we just pushed her down.'

'Did *you* push her down?'

'I suppose we all did.'

'Did she consent?'

'Yes and no. Well, she didn't scream or struggle.'

'Who was the first person to have intercourse with her?'

'Mick.'

'Who was next?'

'Me. A few others were nearby when Mick was having intercourse.'

Once the rest of the gang was rounded up and told of their mate's confession they fancied they were in trouble. Even in a misogynist court, forcible abduction and rape were no stroll in the park. They hoped the celebrated Catholic barrister, Frank Galbally, would be their saviour. At the committal in Preston on 8 May 1959, the imposing Galbally placed his hands on his hips and eyed the girl in the witness box.

Galbally's forefathers had shared the humble origins of the girl before him. Had she been an Irish colleen set upon by the Black and Tans or a Loyalist mob in Belfast, Galbally's Catholic blood might have boiled. Today, he had a job to do. And as the transcript showed, it seemed that only questioning her character would save the five men accused of forcibly abducting and raping her.

Born at the Queen Victoria Hospital in 1943, Jean was a girl from the wrong side of the tracks. Home was a government house in a bleak housing commission neighbourhood on the edge of Heidelberg. Only four years before Galbally made his way to working-class Preston, Jean's neighbourhood had stepped tentatively onto the world stage. With acres of thistle and paddock to spare, Heidelberg was the ideal site to house the athletes of the 1956 Olympiad. Fresh and clean, the athletes and their houses soon gave way to a less glamorous landscape known pejoratively as 'Olympic Village'. Around the village the locals had settled down to negotiate the anxieties that accompanied a less-than-privileged life. Denied a formal education, and lacking the social graces of the class Galbally's clan now inhabited, the girl from the village should have been a lamb for the slaughter.

Having failed to break her resolve on how she was dragged into the lane by the boys, Galbally moved to what, he fancied, the magistrate knew was the source of the problem.

'Jean, what did you give as your occupation?'
'Trimmer,' she replied, oblivious to the import of the question.
'You normally wear cosmetics, lipstick?'
'Yes.'
'And powder?'
'Yes.'
'You haven't any on today, have you?'
'Yes.'
'What? Have you your normal cosmetics on your face today?'

'No.'
'Why haven't you your normal cosmetics on today?'
'I don't usually wear them during the week.'

With the accused directed to stand trial in the Supreme Court, and gaol now a real possibility, one family offered to sell the family jewels so Frank Galbally could defend their son. An Austin A70 valued at $500 and a house worth $2000 with a $1000 mortgage was tendered as security against their boy's legal costs. With a senior counsel setting his price at $1500, they had no option but to agree to sell the roof over their head if it might save their son.

At crippling cost, Galbally and a team of briefs were commissioned to do battle with the fifteen-year-old victim and her girlfriend. A mistrial in November 1959 left Galbally unavailable when the trial resumed in June 1960. Nevertheless, the struggling families assembled a formidable list of Catholic silks that included Bill Lennon, Mick O'Sullivan QC, Jim Morrissey and Eugene 'Black Jack' Cullity.

Bill Lennon was much sought after by Catholics north of the city. A year after his day in court with a virgin from Heidelberg, Lennon turned his gaze to Susan, a married woman from Brunswick. Unlike the young girl in the paddock, the bruised and bleeding woman who 'cried rape' in April 1961 was a mother who'd mounted a fierce struggle. The man she accused was a local bloke known to her. He'd chosen her home, rather than a desolate lane, to fulfil the needs of his flesh. Lennon's cross-examination was characteristic of the cynicism that confronted women who dared accuse men of sexual assault.

'You often drink at the local pub without your husband, don't you?' asked Lennon.
'I go there with my mother sometimes. We drink in the lounge.'
'I see. And isn't it true that you had an argument with your husband about the attitude of men at the pub towards you?'
'No. Not at all.'
'I see.'
'Is it not true that the men at the pub refer to you as "the body"?'

'Well, not to my face.'

'So they do refer to you as "the body".'

'I suppose they do.'

'Is it a compliment or otherwise?' asked Judge Bourke, stirred by the salacious connotations of Lennon's probing.

'It's a little embarrassing, really,' she replied.

At the Brunswick Baths, a sea of concrete and brick alongside the Upfield railway line, Susan cut quite a figure in a bathing suit. Although the men of Brunswick had said they fought the 'Jap' and the 'Hun' in the name of freedom, she must have wondered what freedoms she had inherited. On a billboard advertising a girdle or a kitchen stove, her shapely body would have been an approved sexual object. In a swimsuit at the Brunswick Baths, it made her a wilful temptress for the man in the dock.

Bill Lennon well understood how a jury looked upon a woman who might have flaunted a voluptuous body. But he knew that her fierce resistance to the attempted rape would ensure his client had a holiday in Pentridge. 'You're a goner,' he told him, once the jury retired. He was right. 'Decent respectable women deserve the fullest protection of the law,' Judge Bourke told the accused before sentencing him to three and a half years hard labour.

But young Jean in a vacant block after dark was different. Wandering through the midnight shadows, her face adorned with lipstick and make-up, she could not so easily hide behind the rites of marriage. A licentious Victory girl who might well have stepped from an Albert Tucker painting, she had some explaining to do for the court.

Towards the end of day one, barrister Lennon explained why Judge Adam should not see the girl in the witness box as in any way resembling a respectable woman. 'So when did you venture out after this dreadful ordeal?' he asked. When Jean announced that she had been to the Arcadia Dance Hall in High Street on Sunday, a mere two days after the alleged rape, he smiled. To the morally upright, a woman who swam at the baths in a liberated woman's swimsuit or refused to sink into unremitting depression after 'crying rape' could never truly have been raped. Only bad girls would occupy the same territory as these men. The accused boys hoped these views dominated the thinking of the jury.

'By the way, are any of your relations or friends sitting in court today?' asked defence barrister Mr O'Sullivan, when Jean resumed her place in the witness box.

'No,' she said, pausing for a moment to reflect on the significance of the question. She might have explained that the dictates of work precluded her parents' appearance, but O'Sullivan wasn't interested in explanation. He wanted the jury to believe this was a dishonoured girl forsaken by her parents for freely engaging in crude sex in a laneway.

'You and Noelene have gone to hotel beer gardens on Saturday afternoons, haven't you?'

'Only once.'

'You have been on other occasions …?'

'No, that was the only time.'

'Who were the girls you used to get to go to some of the parties? There was a girl called Sandy and another called Debbie? Debbie was very popular with the boys, was she not?'

'Yes, I suppose so.'

'And she was a girl of very easy morals and went outside with various boys?'

'Yes.'

'And so did you?'

'No.'

'Not with any single boy?'

'Yes, a boy called Kenny.'

'Did Kenny make love to you?'

'What do you mean? We just kissed.'

'Did you know a girl called "the beetle"? Wasn't she called "the beetle" because she couldn't keep off her back?'

'No, I didn't know her.'

'Did you have a nickname?'

16   just another little murder

'No.'

'And sex was frequently talked about by young people. And you've heard fairly coarse words about sex at parties?'

'Yes.'

'Now you do not refer to the part of your body as your "thing" in conversation with these boys, do you?'

'No, I never talk about it.'

'Do you refer to it as your "box"?'

'No, I have never spoken about that.'

'And the word starting with "c". Is that word frequently used by the boys and girls?'

'Yes.'

'You used to go to the Arcadia dance in High Street?'

'Yes.'

'That was a rough place …'

'Oh, at times, yes, there used to be fights between the boys.'

'And you went out with the boys for a cuddle now and then?'

'No, never.'

'You had a cuddle on the way home?'

'No, we went home by ourselves.'

'Have you used the words "fuck" or "cunt" with boys or girls?'

'No.'

'Do you swear on oath you have never used these words?'

'Not in front of boys.'

'What if there were only girls?'

'Yes.'

No matter how much Mick O'Sullivan tried to tarnish the girl's character she refused to buckle. Although she knew nothing of points of order or of admissibility of questions, about one question she was unequivocal. Jean had never consented to the boy from McLachlan Street and his mates having their way with her.

With O'Sullivan unable to dampen the girl's resolve, Jim Morrissey sought to beguile her with false compassion.

'I suppose you would call us squares in these wigs and gowns. It's a battle between you and people asking you questions, is it not?'

'What do you mean? Trying to tell me that I am trying to change my story?'

'Yes. Now tell me, do you like lawyers?'

'Well, I don't know.'

'I hope you don't dislike me. You realise we have to ask you these questions, don't you?'

'Yes.'

'Your story is true?'

'Yes.'

'You are determined not to change it.'

'Yes.'

Then Jack Cullity began his examination with an odd question.

'You told us you were a single girl, Jean, but you never gave us your occupation. What is it?' he asked, when he rose from his chair early on day two.

'Machinist,' she replied, proudly oblivious to the import of the question.

'At the time of the incident, you were starting to show some interest in boys?'

'Yes.'

'Now, did you object to the boys showing a bit of interest in you outside the hamburger shop?'

'No.'

'You were not unhappy at this stage. Why did you become unhappy?'

'I do not know. As we went around the corner into Wingrove Street, I just did.'

'Now, after the incident, did you think of ringing home or ringing the police?'

'No.'

'Tell us, Jean, who tore the lace off your petticoat in the lane?'

'I don't know. I just heard it rip.'

'And you lost a button off your blouse too. Who did that?'

'I don't know. There was only one other rip. My pants. I only knew they tore them off.'

'Really, your attitude is you are not sure it was Bluey who tore off your pants.'

'It was.'

'Did you see him do that?'

'Yes.'

'Why did you miss the bus?'

'Because Noelene was down at the corner and they had her purse.'

Jean had entered the witness box early on day one. She was asked to step down late on day two. Before she'd taken the stand, Dr John Birrell testified that she had been a virgin before the 'incident' in the lane. At the time of her night in the paddock with the boys, she was four months shy of her sixteenth birthday.

On day four, Mick O'Sullivan chose the privacy of discussion with Justice Adam to place on the record his assessment of the worthiness of the girl. It was a profound snapshot of the thinking of the men in wigs.

> Your Honour
>
> Here is a girl with her background. At the time she was a fourteen-year-old kiddie, going out with boys, drinking beer. The type of girl who is taking a bottle to her own home, fourteen, early fifteen, going off into hotels buying bottles of beer, taking them to the pictures and hiding them down the lane at the back of the pictures. And at half time inviting the boys of the village down to drink beer with them, for twelve or eighteen months before this. I am not blaming the kid, but that is her background and she is a girl who has gone to these rough ballrooms where the police have to break it up. And she has been to these various places and talked amongst her girlfriends in the language she described, and in the permanent company of boys who talk and give lectures on sex. She has to go home and tell her parents she 'went down the lane.' 'What were you doing there?'—'I go there with boys.'

Justice Adam felt no need to caution learned counsel. 'I think I appreciate fully the way that is put,' he replied.

Notwithstanding Mick O'Sullivan's disingenuous disclaimers, it seemed that both believed that Jean had behaved inappropriately. That the girl's hymen was intact before the experience with O'Sullivan's defendant said nothing for the girl's honour. Jean and her friend should not have been out after dark.

Thirty years later, when women marched through the streets of Melbourne under the banner 'Reclaim the Night', the issue was lost on many men of the law.

Jean and Noelene's crime was to have dared to venture out at night from the dog boxes created for them by Prime Minister Robert Menzies and Victorian Premier Henry Bolte. Away from the suffocating, flimsy, prefabricated coffins called home they larked, at the picture theatres and dance halls along High Street. When the stalkers arrived, they tried to pacify them with good humour or played cute. Jean shouldn't have been in that lane. That was true. The problem was, it was the boys who dragged her there.

'Well, Noelene, why did you not go to her help?' asked Lennon, as the evidence of abduction and rape became irrepressible.

'Because I wouldn't have had much hope against five boys, would I?' retorted the girl.

'Even if you screamed out?'

'There was no one there.'

'The hamburger shop was not far away, was it?'

'They wouldn't have helped.'

'How do you know?'

'Because they didn't help when I came down the lane.'

'But they still could have helped.'

'They didn't help later, did they?'

'Please don't ask me questions …'

Please don't ask me questions. It was a retort typical of the men of the Bar. Rhetorical flair from uneducated girls from Heidelberg was not acceptable in a middle-class bloke's court. And when it did appear, bourgeois propriety and legal rule could always be relied upon to subvert a working-class girl's search for the truth.

Fortunately for Jean, Noelene's experience on the streets ensured she was more than a match for Bill Lennon when he sought to belittle her with the noblesse oblige he'd acquired at Xavier College.

At 3.20 pm on Thursday 30 June 1960, after nine days of evidence, the jury of twelve men retired to consider their verdict. At 9.48 pm they returned and declared three of the boys guilty of forcible abduction and rape. The others took a deep breath as they were asked to take their leave. What had seemed like a good idea at the time was now a nightmare for the three convicted boys. Head in hands, they waited to be frogmarched to the prison van for the trip up Sydney Road to Her Majesty's prison.

At 8.30 am on Tuesday 19 July, after nearly three weeks sweating it out in remand, the boys were bundled back into the prison van for a rendezvous with justice. At the court, the tall imposing Allistair Adam was waiting. Whatever Justice Adam thought of the decision, it was incumbent on him to castigate and sentence according to the dictates of the law.

'Had you been older and not affected by drink, the sentence would have been greater than the four-year minimum I am imposing,' he said, the coarse Scottish brogue giving him an executioner's air. Although the judge likened the guilty three to 'a pack of wolves', he couldn't resist the opportunity to fire one salvo at those women who thought the night belonged to all Australians:

> I do take into account also the fact that this young girl, Jean, was, to say the least of it, acting very indiscreetly and unwisely. And that had she known that she was to be subjected to the attacks that were made on her, she no doubt would have acted differently. She did act unwisely with her companion in remaining out after the pictures that night, looking for fun ... it should provide a lesson to many parents ... they have no business to be walking the streets in this mood at this very late hour. It was courting trouble ...

Eight months before the big Scot in the wig and gown presented his pious warning to the girls who scurried across Map 30, twelve-year-old Keogh and a couple of mates pounced upon his first recorded victim. A grade three pupil at Merri Creek Primary where Keogh was now in grade six, the girl was a mere eight years old when he grabbed her and fondled her genitals. For his sexual indiscretion, Keogh walked from the Children's Court with a bond. He already knew the rules. Twenty-nine years later he would be bundled into a prison van and shunted off to Pentridge wearing a sentence no greater than that dished out to the Fairfield rapists. He had good reason to believe he was on the side of the powerful.

While his 'clan brother' was doing time, the stocky Peter Keogh was bristling with confidence and bravado. At Fitzroy High school the gentle of soul feared him. A king-hit man rather than a courageous defender of the disadvantaged, he revealed a deep hatred of teachers and an insatiable capacity for manipulation. Teacher Eleanor Feldman bore a distinctive birthmark on her face that in 1961 had become grist for the Keogh mill. From the rear of the class, where he sat alongside the impressionable Ray Quick, Keogh delivered insults with impunity. Older than his years, he'd reached his diminutive height of 5 feet 5 inches well before his schoolmates. Self-possessed and genuinely nasty, he had few friends.

Jackie Young, an urbane girl from rural Edenhope, who could easily have been a heroine in Edna O'Brien's *Country Girls*, was one teacher for whom he had no answers.

'You and Ray are to sit down straight away,' she once told the pair as they attempted to brush past her for the freedom of the playground. Eventually they did as they were told. She never forgot the look in Keogh's eye.

'He was a criminal who was only going to end up a criminal,' she told me when I went in search of the real Keogh. Having assumed the status of a fully-fledged bully by the time he was twelve, Keogh was already on the path to unremitting violence. With whatever mate he could enlist, he was now robbing and thieving his way along High Street. Soon, he'd come face to face with a loaded gun. For now he was just a young thug.

'You was fuckin' laughin' when the cunt gave me the cuts, weren't ya,' Keogh snarled when he and his mate Eddie cornered their quarry at Rushall Railway Station across the creek from his home. With Eddie pinning the target, Keogh flayed his arms until their man was lying in a heap on the asphalt. That done, they took off. Three years later, Eddie's target would be a girl from the country town of Stawell.

Corralled by Eddie and the boys in the rear of a 1956 Holden in the back blocks of Broadmeadows, she didn't have a chance. 'Cops. Not worried about the cops. We've done this before and haven't been caught,' the driver had laughed as the girl was buried against the back seat. By the time she and her girlfriend made it to a house in desolate Somerton Lane, she was so hysterical she couldn't speak. Eddie went down for rape and copped a mere twelve months in the can. Defence counsel, later judge, Howard Nathan, a man said to care deeply for the disadvantaged, must have scratched his head when the jury returned a generous verdict of 'guilty with mitigating circumstances'.

The bloke who copped a hiding at Rushall Station wasn't interested in the offerings of the law when he came across Keogh a few years later. Now big and handy with his fists, he let the bully have it.

'Phil, you'll be glad to know I gave him a hiding,' he told me with some satisfaction. The hiding came in the form of a thumping fist to Keogh's jaw that left him with no desire to regain his feet or his pride. 'Didn't like him. He was a coward and a deviate. Blokes I knew would have done him in if they'd come across him after he sexually assaulted that girl in Richmond,' he added.

The man who sent Keogh sprawling had no desire to attach his name to the attack on the bully. He'd moved on from those wild days in Fitzroy and didn't want to relive them. Still, I had to ask him one last question. Almost every professional who had dealt with Keogh treated him as a victim. Was he? I asked.

'A victim? He was nothing but a fuckin' arsehole. Most parole officers and middle-class shrinks know nothing about working-class kids,' he said. I was impressed. So, did the boy whose mother fretted about his lawlessness have any redeeming features, I wondered.

'Not a fucking one,' said Brian Sanaghan, a one-time Northcote councillor and sometime drinker at the nearby Commercial Hotel in High Street. An unremarkable establishment owned and run by a gruff publican with an old Irish name, there was nothing endearing about this pub or the Freake-Cole-Chamberlain-Keogh cluster

Sanaghan eyed in the corner of the bar on a Friday night. They were all Keogh had. When they buried him, only 30 people found their way to White Friars chapel in Heidelberg, and not even his kith and kin could speak of their brother's life.

'Better off with him dead, should have done it years ago,' they'd soon say on the street and in the pubs. Dead? I wasn't sure.

There was nothing equivocal about Julie McAllister's response to his death. Not even seven years spent as man and wife could temper her relief and happiness. Like the other women who'd felt Keogh's menacing stare and experienced the chilling threats, she had been desperate to see the end of him. When her house in the Gippsland hamlet of Tyers went up in smoke at twilight on Saturday 3 March 2001, she had immediately understood why my brother Perry had tried to warn her off the relationship. On the night of the fire, she was celebrating her son Justin's wedding in Melbourne. Julie had no doubt whose hand had smashed its way through her bedroom window and placed the match in the wastepaper bin.

'He knew I was at the wedding that night. It's him, for sure,' she told me over a pint at Bridie O'Reilly's in Brunswick. As we discussed the circumstances I thought about what lay ahead. Although the local cop at Morwell had said there was nothing bold about burning down someone's house, I thought otherwise. Yes, arson is hard to prove, and Keogh knew it. But he knew everything would point to him. He had taken out a caveat on his ex-girlfriend's house then burnt it down. Tell me that wasn't mad and bold, I thought.

I wasn't sure what to expect when I agreed to meet Julie and her new boyfriend in Brunswick. Although my own sister had shared his bed, I couldn't free myself from the notion that only a loser would find Peter Keogh an acceptable companion. I had a view about how circumstances and her generosity of spirit had conspired to lure Vicki into his tattooed arms. At 21 she had known nothing of Keogh's world or of his propensity for violence. I felt it should have been different for Julie.

A single mother, she was a mature woman in her early thirties when she agreed to a night out with Keogh. Worse still, she knew he was a convicted killer. With the tears flowing, Keogh had told her how the stabbing of Vicki was an accident and he'd only gone to the kinder to damage the car. That, he said, was why he took the knife. If she hadn't tried to grab it from him, nothing would have happened. So went the Westgarth psychopath's sorrowful story. To complete the lie he claimed to have driven home after the skirmish and to have only learnt Vicki was seriously hurt when he heard a broadcast on the radio.

Tears were the stock in trade for Keogh. At the trial he'd laid them on so thick his garbled account of what happened to Vicki threatened to run forever. Although his memory was clinically selective when he first offered his thoughts in the Homicide interview room five hours after the attack, he had no trouble filling in the details five years later. If, as he told the police and the court, he could remember nothing of the attack after Vicki allegedly swore at him, why did he tell his new girlfriend that Vicki took the knife from his overalls and had been stabbed accidentally in the ensuing struggle?

Why didn't Keogh tell Julie the truth about how he'd cut Vicki's hands and face and been granted a defence of provocation on account of his alleged alcoholism and her provocative language that morning? And why didn't he tell her he could remember nothing after those provocative words? The truth is he knew Julie would never believe the bullshit about suffering amnesia. Nor would she or anyone else have felt comfortable about sharing a bed with a man who could kill on a whim. He remembered what happened. He remembered it, chapter and verse.

So unbelievable was the provocation defence that unfolded in Justice George Hampel's court and so absurd was the verdict, Keogh could never spin it past an ordinary punter. To survive, Keogh had to relate a different lie to her and, as usual, there was a semblance of truth. Vicki had grabbed the knife. As it plunged towards her face in the front seat of the car, she had felt it cut deep into her hand and fingers. Yes, she had tried to take the knife.

Life as a barmaid had brought Julie McAllister into contact with the full spectrum of no-hopers and blowhards whose fate it was to cling to the bar and dribble into the drip-tray. In 1991 she brought a splash of character to the poker machine-littered Junction Hotel and comfort to the men who drank away the residue of plaster and paint and the enduring smell of dead meat. With two sons and a mortgage on a house in Mill Park to support, she wasn't exactly speeding down the fast lane in a convertible with the wind dancing in her long dark hair.

When Keogh emerged from his cabin at Loddon Prison, he was a relatively fit 43-year-old with enough muscle tone and street smarts to attract at least a passing interest from a girl from Melbourne's northern suburbs. He could be polite and courteous when the situation arose. Why not, she thought, when he tapped it on her for a night out. In the prelude to Christmas 1992, Julie had etched her name in the Peter Keogh story and become the last of a handful of women to fall into his web.

A small, shapely woman, Julie was a good catch for the unexceptional Keogh. When I first saw her, I was taken by her physical similarities to Vicki. Like Vicki, she was vivacious and strong-willed. Unlike Vicki, she was unforgiving when it came to Peter Keogh. In a dream many years later, Vicki's mum told Keogh of her sadness and anger at what he'd done to her daughter. Looking on, smiling, was the daughter he'd murdered. 'She'd have forgiven him. That's what she was like,' Mum had thought when she woke to the grim realisation that her daughter wasn't with her. Julie could never forgive him. She and her family could have been in the house when he torched it. She knew just what Peter Keogh could do.

'He was a pussy,' she laughed when I asked whether he'd threatened her in the early days. Julie wasn't cut from the feminist cloth. Men were not the enemy, and glass ceilings weren't part of the vocabulary. Terms like verbal abuse and patriarchy didn't roll off her tongue. A survivor who gave as much as she took, Julie McAllister had no idea of the danger Keogh posed to her and her two boys when she fell for his advances at the Junction Hotel.

When a nine-year-old neighbour's child scurried from her house in Mill Park in 1993 claiming Keogh had fondled her breasts, Julie was temporarily stumped. At the Mill Park Police Station, the local cops were coy. 'He has sexual assault convictions, but we can't give you the details,' they told her. 'Carnal knowledge when I was twelve, Julie,' he said when she went in search of the truth. That was no sin in the world she'd known. His answer was enough to stop her thinking. For the time being, she believed Peter Keogh would never threaten the fabric of her life. And if he did, she'd deal with it.

Peter Keogh was only twenty when Marilyn Reeves, a young single mother, began sharing his bed. It was 1968, and beyond the bungalow in McLachlan Street where the young lovers frolicked, the father of the peace movement, Dr Jim Cairns, would soon bring a hundred thousand people into Melbourne to demand an end to America's war on the Vietnamese. Such sentiments carried no resonance in Keogh's cluttered life. In February, he had thrust a glass into the face of George Vlahos at the Junction Hotel and received a month's gaol.

Had he not carried a brooding contempt for those who embraced fellow human beings, Keogh might have settled down to a normal life with Marilyn. Although a new class of woman was beginning to enjoy the freedom of sex without pregnancy, Keogh's women were cut from the old cloth. Marilyn Reeves was sufficiently besotted with his bravado to bear him a child. In February 1971 they had a son they named Damien.

At La Trobe University, where I began studying politics and sociology in 1972, a sprinkling of working-class kids had begun to open the pages on a new text. The feminist for the times, Germaine Greer, spoke of the liberation of women from the control of men, and others wrote of the violence of war and of capitalism's connivance in the poverty of the suburbs Keogh and I both knew. The formal education denied to men such as John Thomas Keogh began to open in splendour for the post-war children of the old working-class. Boys who'd once run the gauntlet of plod's baton outside the local pubs and dance halls now nailed the principles of law to their defence. It was a powerful mix.

Keogh didn't read from this script. Strength and power was his motto, and a makeshift weapon, not a book, or a hammer and sickle, was his emblem. From the voluptuous cowgirls on his legs to the chain around his neck, Keogh was a moving feast of machismo art. When the police accused her man of attempting to rape a girl in Coburg in 1970, Marilyn stuck with him. 'Dogs and cunts, that's what coppers are,' he told his pregnant de facto.

When it came to the 'wog', Peter Mascia, in the poolroom in Station Street, Fairfield, in 1972, Marilyn was less concerned. A fight was a fight, and her bloke was no worse than the next bloke. Mascia might have left the poolroom covered in blood on an ambulance stretcher, but he had asked for it. That's what her boy said. So convinced was his girlfriend that she dipped into the kitty for the financial surety. No wog or lying copper was going to sever this partnership. Even if Marilyn had suddenly fallen out of love with Keogh, pregnancy and motherhood would have conspired against any retreat.

At the County Court he was as cocky as he'd been a decade before when bulldozing his way through Form One at Fitzroy High. I could just imagine him bragging how he'd put the wind up the wog. When the foreman said, 'Not guilty', the little bloke in the dock ground his teeth with delight. It was 1 July 1974 and nearly two years had passed since the bloodied Mascia had been carted out of the New Australian billiard room. For now nothing, it seemed, could stop Keogh from pleasing himself. His favourite QC, Bob Vernon, had done it again.

Then came the scandal that shook the faith of a little street in Richmond. 'I have no idea where he is,' his besieged de facto had said when Sergeant Noel Francis Ryan, a no-fuss copper from Richmond CIB, appeared on the doorstep of the single-fronted terrace at 44 Canterbury Street. It was the same old story. Whenever the cops came looking, Keogh talked victimisation.

'They didn't get me when I waved the knife at that copper bastard years ago and they won't give up. Once you take on the cops they never forget,' he told her as headed off for the safety of his mother's bungalow in McLachlan Street.

'Mrs Keogh, this is a serious case. The young girl who lives at number 25 claims to have been sexually assaulted by your husband. We need to find him. As you're probably aware, she's only nine years of age,' said Sergeant Ryan when he returned to the house after a fruitless search.

With Marilyn attending a funeral in Sydney, Keogh had been entrusted with the care of their three-year-old boy and his de facto's eight-year-old son from a previous relationship. Nestled in a neighbourhood of tired-looking Victorian houses yet to be reclaimed by the middle-class, Canterbury Street had no airs or graces. On 27 December 1974, a group of children had been playing crocodile in the street. They played with an innocence typical of the times but talked with a frankness that offended the polite.

The trouble started when Keogh's stepson told young Valerie his dad wanted to see her. Under the ruse of thanking the girl for a plum dish she'd given his step-son, Keogh had hatched a vile plot. Within minutes the girl was ensnared. When she couldn't be found, the alarm went up. After a frantic search of the neighbourhood, the girl's mother returned once more to number 44, the house where Valerie had been last seen. After a couple of knocks, the door opened and her daughter rushed past. A moment later, Keogh, dishevelled and nervous, appeared in the hallway. Although Valerie came from a bigger house than her friends did, she found the same rough words to describe what had happened to her.

What emerged in the County Court in April 1976, nearly a year and a half after the assault, was a sad and tragic affair. Once Keogh had the girl in his house, the boys were sent to bed and the girl was forced to undress and sit on his lap. She'd become just another female, humiliated, some professionals would say, as a consequence of the sins of a possessive mother. 'Lick this,' he said, grabbing his victim's head and placing her face against his erect cock, before forcing her into the bedroom. 'Scream and I'll smash your head inside out,' he growled when she began to sob and told him she didn't want to do what we said. 'She was sobbing and spitting into her handkerchief when we got her into the car, and suffered nightmares for months,' her mother told the court.

The moment Valerie took her place in the witness box and began to find the words to describe what had happened, the minefield of sexual assault on a child was laid out bare. He'd tried to penetrate her anus; of that much the doctor was sure. No matter whether the judge decreed that such a fact was legally unsound for the jury to conclude, in a civil court he'd have done his balls. If he'd done it in lawless Belfast, or Crevelli Street, East Preston, where the Camp Pell boys knocked about, he'd have been dead meat. But this little girl didn't have a father or a tribe to bring retribution to Keogh, and he knew it. He always knew where to strike.

When the ordeal was brought to an end by the sound of the girl's mother knocking and shouting at the front door, Keogh had one last act of humiliation up his sleeve. 'Say goodbye to my dick,' he said with a contemptuous smile. Strangely, his parole officer, Margaret Hobbs, conceded he was guilty but said she thought the girl was precocious.

Although he was arrogant about his capacity to beat any cop, within minutes of Valerie's flight from the house, Keogh began preparation for his escape from the tentacles of the law. Within an hour the beard was gone. There was nothing of the remorseful victim of a psychiatric malaise about Keogh. He could do little with his lifeless thinning brylcreamed hair, and nothing to camouflage those narrow troubled eyes. The beard was the one form of disguise open to him. It was the first thing Marilyn Reeves noticed when she returned from Sydney to a tense Canterbury Street. 'Too hot for a beard, darling,' he told her. Whenever the Sergeant Ryan arrived, Keogh was nowhere to be seen.

Alex Goodwin was quite a bit older than Keogh when the secretive 24-year-old labourer with the built-up heels and the tattooed hands took up a general hand's position at the famous T&G building in Collins Street in 1972. After work, they sometimes shared a drink at the South Melbourne pub of Richmond footballer, 'the Whale' Roberts. Goodwin thought Keogh strange, but knew little about him. 'He had strange eyes. During work breaks he'd be down in the lane perving at the girls,' he recalled.

It wasn't until 13 January that Sergeant Ryan found his way to T&G. When he did, Keogh was like a frightened rabbit. As the police car wound its way to Richmond, Ryan prepared to drop the question he believed would ensure a conviction.

'So when did you shave the beard off?' he asked.

'About six months ago, I think. Yeah, six months ago,' replied a worried Keogh.

It was a lie and Alex Goodwin knew it. 'Yes, he definitely had a beard at the Xmas party on the 24th,' Goodwin would tell the court.

With a serious sexual assault case around the corner, Keogh had every reason to be on his best behaviour. But he wasn't. Within a month of being collared by Ryan, the serial rapist was at it again. When an eighteen-year-old blonde stepped from the lift into the desolate T&G basement, she suddenly found herself against the wall, submerged in groping hands and physical force. Keogh had taken a fancy to her. Fortunately her screams were enough to send him on his way. A brazen and merciless man, his journey had hardly begun. On 26 February 1975, at the Melbourne Magistrate's Court, he was sent down for five months. Unimpressed, Keogh immediately lodged an appeal.

While he was fighting the law I was out at the Coburg Football Ground taking my first steps in what would be a long and celebrated career in the then-booming Victorian Football Association. From 1975 until he entered my life so profoundly in 1987, Keogh and I were only ever a page away on a Melways map. Sometimes, we were only a few streets apart. While he roamed Preston inflicting terror on a stream of women, my battles were fought on the narrow confines of the Cramer Street ground, across the road from where he bit the dust after a violent confrontation with local constable, Frank Bellesini in 1963. Although the names of blokes with the form of Preston notables such as the Kane brothers buzzed along the grapevine, Keogh's name never reached my ears. As conspicuous as the much-publicised fight with Bellesini made him, no one ever mentioned the name of Peter Raymond Keogh.

On 26 August 1975, exactly twelve years to the day before he killed Vicki, his appeal against the assault on the girl in the T&G basement was dismissed. It was a grim omen of what was to come. For the next five months he was ensconced in Pentridge Prison. Outside, an innocent young girl prepared to face him in the County Court the moment the gates opened. For all his bravado, he didn't like gaol. There were just too many blokes prepared to give him a whack, and the rape of a nine-year-old wasn't the stuff of armed robbers or romantic criminals. Galbally would defend him, but would that be enough? With the trial due to begin in late February 1976, he chose a handful of tranquillisers and a fake suicide attempt to postpone justice. Regrettably, he survived.

It wasn't the first time tranquillisers had been employed when a crisis hit Keogh's gang. During the Fairfield rape trial in 1960, barrister Bill Lennon had told the court that Keogh's McLachlan Street mate had taken an overdose of sodium barbiturates, and would need a 24-hour adjournment. The court heard that the boy had received the tablets from Mrs Keogh, and that she had used them since the death of her husband. In the eyes of Crown prosecutor, Mr Geoffrey Byrne, it was a calculated attempt to abort the trial.

There's nothing new about working-class mothers protecting violent or lawless sons. To that extent Mildred Keogh was not unusual. However, there was clearly something wrong at 31 McLachlan Street. The absence of a father was a problem. But was that all? The victimhood to which one Westgarth mate aspired in 1960 would be cultivated with absolute rat-cunning by Peter Keogh. Although his sisters stuck with him through the violent sixties, Keogh's rape of the little girl down the street drove a wedge through his relationship with his brothers. So, too, did it spell the end of his relationship with Marilyn Reeves.

There was little time for reconciliation with his de facto when Keogh returned to Canterbury Street in February 1976 and prepared to face the music for the kidnap and rape of a neighbour's daughter. Marilyn had tried to leave him before, but history told her he wouldn't cop it sweet. As she sat in the County Court in a leather coat, listening to Judge Rapke's sermon, she remembered Keogh's words: 'If ya ever try to leave me I'll kill you'. They were words he would repeat many times over the next twenty-five years.

Neither the wizardry of Bob Vernon, who replaced Galbally as counsel for the defence, nor the enthusiasm of his junior, Peter Berman, could save Keogh from another stint in the alma mater. Despite the mountain of evidence against him, the smart arse thug from Westgarth genuinely thought Vernon would save him.

'Identity, that's the key,' he told his client.

Removing the beard after the assault on the girl, then telling Sergeant Ryan he had shaved it off six months earlier was a problem. Ever alert, Keogh had an answer.

'Look, Mr Vernon, when Sergeant Ryan asked me about shaving the beard, I misunderstood him. Yeah, I thought he asked me when I grew the beard. That's why I said about six months ago.'

'Good. Then there's the issue of the tats. Might need you to strip off if she doesn't mention the tats.'

Keogh loved the way Vernon knocked off the coppers.

'I know him,' he'd once bragged to Alec Goodwin when Vernon's name was splashed across the newspaper. What he didn't tell Goodwin was how Vernon had saved him from attempted murder.

'We'll beat this,' he would have thought, after the faked suicide attempt had scored him an adjournment that enabled Vernon to take the case. Suicide was worth a try but the evidence was so compelling the only issue was how long he'd get. 'He's to be pitied,' the girl's well-spoken mother would tell Judge Rapke. Although Rapke said he was 'outraged at the indecencies perpetrated on the girl', and labelled Keogh 'a man of violence', even he chose leniency.

'I couldn't believe Rapke would give that secretive little mongrel only fifteen months. He showed no remorse,' Ryan would later tell me.

Vernon's junior, Peter Berman, wasn't disappointed. 'Could have been a lot worse,' he said. Just how Keogh found the money to pay a silk with Bob Vernon's asking price was a mystery. Cash? Drug money? There were any number of rumours. Whatever the merits of the sentence, Marilyn had decided to call it a day. 'I'm not coming again,' she told him with some trepidation during a prison visit following his mother's funeral. Mildred Dorothy Keogh, the mother accused of firing Keogh's demons, had collapsed of a heart attack in December 1976, age 68, at the very house where her son had come to grief. That son was unmoved by Marilyn's assertions.

'We'll see about that,' he thought as he made his way back to the anonymity of his protected cell. By late 1978 Marilyn would tell police she was terrified of him. Soon another woman would fill her shoes.

Judy McNulty had three young children by the time Keogh began flirting with her at Pampas Pastry in Oakover Road, Preston. At the time she had no idea he'd just done fifteen months for sexually assaulting a little girl. Her eldest, Terri, a girl with a gentle warm face that matched the beauty of her mother, was twelve years of age when Keogh brought his Ford Fairlane to a halt alongside the front fence of 75 Arthur Street, Fairfield. It was early 1980, and Judy's marriage was faltering. As he lifted the latch on the gate, it was the blue ink cobwebs on Keogh's elbows that captured Terri's attention. The girl felt a sense of unease, but calm was restored when her mother backed him down the pathway and out the gate. Beyond Keogh's car was the viaduct that led to the lane where his mates had made their mark twenty tears earlier. Such was the turbulence created by Keogh's relationship with her mother over the next eighteen months, Terri never forgot the day he entered her life.

With the exception of Vicki, each of the women in Keogh's life had fallen into early motherhood. Each, said their friends, was a class above the man who brought such terror to their lives. And each, when the relationship faltered, wondered how they'd so mistaken his intentions. Marilyn Reeves, Judy McNulty, Vicki Cleary and Julie McAllister bore testament to the falsehood of the middle-class sisters' dictum that working-class women were infatuated with violent men. When push came to shove, each of the four women gave Keogh his marching orders. It was then that the real danger had emerged. And when it did, public school boys in wigs, the welfare state and bourgeois justice failed them. That's why Keogh remained at large. And it was why so many other women fell to violent men. Christine Boyce was one of them.

On 19 November 1987, less than three months after Vicki's murder hit the news, Kevin Crowe had pointed a rifle at his estranged wife's face. The moment she grasped her mortality, he calmly pulled the trigger. Christine Boyce fell dead in front of her two daughters, one of whom would tell police, 'Daddy shot Mummy through the neck.' The rifle had been in Crowe's car for a week, and he'd chosen to use it, as he said he would, rather than meet his wife in the Family Court the next day.

'I've shot my wife,' he told emergency services before he set off for the safety of a pub in Brunswick Street, Fitzroy.

At the trial, the killer threw himself on the jury's mercy. 'I wanted to shoot myself but I couldn't do it in front of the children,' he told them. Christine Boyce was a beautiful 28-year-old woman when Crowe first got to her. At 5 feet 2 inches and 119 pounds, she was one pound heavier and one inch taller than Vicki Cleary. In the court a jury of twelve ordinary Australians was cajoled into believing the woman lying in a pool of blood, in a barren lounge room in quaint Kew, had somehow brought her own murder upon herself.

In his first thrust with the knife, Peter Keogh had cut deep into Vicki's lip and chin. If his attempt at murder were thwarted, he'd at least wreak havoc on her face. 'If I can't have you, no one else will.' The words he used in the weeks before the attack had been more than a threat. It was the same with the killer Crowe.

When Dr Richard Collins surveyed Christine's body the day after the murder, he found that two bullets had passed through the dead girl's neck and another through her left breast. Only a blink of an eye earlier, it had been Vicki Cleary's body on the slab in the mortuary. Did he reflect on the terror these women had endured? I wondered. What Dr Collins did know was that Christine Boyce carried gunshot residue on both her hands. At the Department of Public Prosecutions, the word was that she had been begging for her life when Crowe fired.

'The gun went pop, pop, pop,' said the killer. He was never asked what the dead woman said before the first 'pop.' Were she to have survived, Christine Boyce would no longer have so readily been the object of any man's desire. 'I'd wanted to disfigure her,' Crowe told the court. In the eyes of the law, this made him neither mad nor evil. The jury was told by the judge to treat him as an ordinary man.

As Justice Hampel would eventually do with Keogh, Justice Alan William McDonald ruled that it was not inconceivable an ordinary man might, in the heat of the moment, act as Crowe did. Whether McDonald was drawing on the tenets of law or the dour Presbyterianism of his Scottish ancestry when he told the jury it must consider the question of provocation is a moot point. As Keogh had done, Crowe walked from the court with a verdict of 'not guilty of murder'.

Christine Boyce's work as an escort and a collection of nude photos taken eight months before the murder had been manna from heaven for defence barrister Bob Kent QC. Crowe had cheerfully lived off the money she earned as an escort and had requested the photos as a birthday present, and Kent knew it. But that made no difference to the bewigged men and a jury of ordinary Australian men and women. Nor did Crowe's admission to breaking his wife's jaw eight months before he killed her. Crowe was found not guilty of murder and spent three years in gaol. Not one of the defenders of the people said a thing.

In 2001, Kent, by now a judge, would have his own character traduced by his brothers at the bar. A refusal to submit tax returns, not an appearance in scurrilous nude photos, was the source of the moral outrage of his learned brothers. In the newspapers, the pro- and anti-Kent forces waged moral war. Those who knew him were outraged by the character assassination, claiming the character of a man and his capacity to sit in judgement of others bore no correlation to his reluctance to follow the tax laws. He was, they said, a man of compassion and integrity who'd give you the shirt off his back. The problem was he'd broken the law. To compound his problems, in court Kent conceded that he had other outstanding tax debts.

Christine Boyce's mother took the proceedings in with some interest. She remembered how her daughter's character had been sullied in order to help explain away Kevin Crowe's murder. She found it hard not to smile when Kent, with the tax matter unresolved, collapsed and died of a heart attack. Like so many other men at the Bar, Kent would have been in the front line admonishing the Taliban Government for its subjugation of women. Not so when that woman was a working-class girl from Coburg or a middle-class mother from Kew.

In the dingy semi-detached house in Gilbert Road, Preston, in the dying moments of his relationship with Vicki, Peter Keogh had spoken the same language as Kent's client, the killer, Crowe. 'Why don't you get down to St Kilda and earn a quid?' he'd snarled one night after the drink had seeped into his brain. It made a mockery of the tearful man who fumbled with the microphone in George Hampel's court and spoke of his love for Vicki.

On Sunday 29 July 2001, five weeks after Keogh's suicide, the *Sunday Age* carried the article that Keogh never wanted to read. Bearing the unambiguous title 'Public Enemy—the life and crimes of Peter Keogh', it brought to life the real history of the coward.

Fourteen years after he sauntered across Cameron Street, Coburg with murder on his mind, Keogh's tattooed form was finally splashed across the front page of a newspaper. Over the previous two months I'd laid years of research in front of journalist John Silvester. His first paragraph was compelling for the manner in which it disarmed the killer:

> There was something about Peter Keogh that men didn't like. Perhaps it was the way his eyes darted about—never returning a gaze. Perhaps it was the nervous habit of shifting his weight from one foot to the other, as if deciding whether to attack or run. Or perhaps it was the way he would grind his teeth, as though he was only one misunderstanding away from exploding into violence. Even bad men didn't like him. When he was in jail, he needed protection from fellow criminals who could see beyond the tough-guy tattoos to the inherent weakness beneath. He needed a billiard cue, a broken glass or a knife to express his anger and his targets were usually women—or sometimes little girls.

I concluded my thoughts with the following words:

Vicki became my inspiration and my hero. I promised her I'd bring him to justice and tell the world what really happened outside that kindergarten and thereafter in a Melbourne court.

Now the last of 'The Boys' responsible for Vicki's death—Freake, Watson and Keogh—is dead. It's not the way Vicki would have wanted it but then she loved everyone.

Writing Opinion pieces for the *Age* newspaper, outing him in a book, and naming him on ABC TV wasn't the same as splashing his dial across the front page of the Sunday paper. Protected by those professionals that looked no further than his lies, he never had to face up to his violence and misogyny. Now those who shared his company around the bar would have to tell their mates why they thought he wasn't a bad bloke.

'If he doesn't like it, he can have his day in court,' Silvester had said as we assembled the pieces of the Keogh jigsaw. Never for a moment did I imagine he'd be dead before the article hit the streets. Keogh knew the noose was tightening. He'd felt my breath on his neck and wondered what would come next. Frightened and isolated, he couldn't face another day. By the afternoon of Sunday 24 June, he'd had enough. I just wished he'd been there in Mansfield Street, Thornbury with the paper spread across his barren table. After all he'd done, he should have been alive to read his obituary.

A few days after the article appeared, Christine Boyce's sister Carmel, fired an email:

Phil

Thought I'd drop a line to congratulate you on the article in the *Sunday Age*. It takes courage to do something more than just cop injustice. In my experience not many men are courageous at all. And yes, systems that reinforce that working-class men are obsessive, and kill, and this is OK, reflect nothing but an outrageous abrogation of moral authority or a cute middle-class boys way of explaining away emotion that cute middle-class boys have no handle on. Confusing hate with love, fury with passion, and vengeance with pain.

Carmel

I'd met Carmel in the aftermath of the trials that brought such grief to our families. Fourteen years later, she'd lost none of her contempt for the institutions and the people that protected the likes of Keogh and Crowe. Murder does that to you.

The Queen v Crowe is just another file, a bundle of papers in a box in the Office of Public Prosecutions. Open the box and it's all so familiar. Photos of a weapon, the dead woman and endless manipulative and demeaning words designed to cleanse all men of their violence. At the trial, Carmel was relentless in her attempt to defend her sister's character. 'She left because she feared …' Carmel had begun to explain, before 52-year-old Justice McDonald cut her off midstream.

'Just a moment, Madam,' interrupted the exceedingly serious former Geelong College boy on the Bench. Carmel wanted to tell the court what every woman really knows: men who kill aren't ordinary, and women who leave them do so for a reason. A woman's fear isn't something men in wigs want to hear about in their courts. They call it hearsay. What they mean is, 'dead women don't speak.'

Like Keogh after him, Kevin Crowe's act of cold-blooded murder had been transformed into that of a man searching for justice. When the moment arose to debate the admissibility of the nude photos of Christine Boyce—destitute woman turned escort—defence barrister Mr Bob Kent captured the morality of the courts:

> We would submit it is a proper and valid argument to say it is relevant to know that the person who is deceased in this case was an attractive woman both in face and body and was in fact the wife of the deceased man. And that in those circumstances a juror might say, 'an ordinary man in this man's situation may well have acted, lost control and acted in that way (the photos show) … she is somebody whom we could understand him having a great passion for …'

'It might go to the attack on her character,' Crown prosecutor Parkinson had replied.

'I can't see how that would go further than that. She was a prostitute. I can't see how photographs would be seen to attack her character,' said the judge.

Eventually the Crown withdrew its objections to the novel Christine had been writing, and the nude photographs, being tendered as evidence. It was beyond the men of law to understand how prejudicial it was. Had Christine been fat and ugly, would the defence have tendered nude photos to show that no ordinary man could have been so engulfed by passion as to lose control and kill her?

> No one hurts me or hates me. These are ordinary guys. They appreciate me. I feel like a proverbial bride.

In the sad writings seized upon by the defence, Christine revealed the trauma and unhappiness of her life with Crowe. Dux of the Catholic Sienna College, Christine Boyce, a caring and sensitive woman, had been forced to sell her body to escape his brooding violence and the poverty he'd foisted on her. It would only strengthen the legal argument that she was not a respectable woman. 'It is not beyond the realms of imagination for a human being to say they can understand that a man who was married to a very beautiful and intelligent woman might be more likely to react the way this man did', Bob Kent, had told the judge. A murdered woman with blood pouring from her neck had been transformed into a naked femme fatale. She was now a worthy target for Crowe's gun. In his heart, Kent must have known the killer didn't lift the gun because he was infatuated with his estranged wife's beauty and wanted to protect his children. Crowe killed his estranged wife because she refused to live by his barbaric rules.

It was the man due to represent him in the Family Court, solicitor Keswick Steel, who emerged as a witness to the killer's sorrow. Steel had acted for Christine during the break-up of her first marriage. After a few hours of drinking in Brunswick Street, Fitzroy, Crowe attempted unsuccessfully to contact Steel. Around 9.30 am the next morning, the two men met in the staff room of Steel's liquor store in Essendon.

'It was about an hour and a quarter—a very emotional conversation ... He indicated that he was going to scare her and possibly disfigure her by shooting her in the breast ... At one stage we were both weeping ...' Steel told the court after Bob Kent asked if Crowe had said 'why it was his wife had been shot'. In 2002, Steel told me how before the murder, Crowe had said he wanted to disfigure Christine. He said he didn't believe him. Tell me the parables of Christine and Vicki are any less barbaric than so-called honour killings attributed to Islam by the hand-wringing western gentry.

When its turn came to sit in judgment, Rupert Murdoch's Sunday tabloid had no illusions as to who deserved sympathy. Above a tawdry, brutally chauvinistic account of how Christine Crowe's prostitution caused her husband to kill her, the screaming headline, 'Love pulls the trigger', told what the dispassionate men presiding over Christine's corpse thought.

A few months later the director of Public Prosecutions, John Coldrey QC, sent a kind letter to Carmel's family saying he understood their sense of injustice but could do nothing about the verdict. On 17 March 1989 he sent a similar letter to me.

Imagine if that old colonial hanging judge, Sir Redmond Barry, or some pompous, philandering contemporary, had been banged by the mistress, I thought. Would provocation have been on offer for the aggrieved women? Where was the preening, strutting, master of the hypothetical, Geoffrey Robertson, when you needed him?

Heather Osland wasn't starring in a television hypothetical or sharing a bed with a judge. By 1991 she'd been on the end of thirteen years of primal lust and torture from her husband, Frank. Heather tried to tell people of her fears, but it didn't quite work out. Terrified that they were about to be murdered, Heather and her son defended themselves. In the mayhem a grave was dug, Frank was drugged and David, crashed a pipe into his step-father's head. It was an act that would have mystifying consequences.

In 1995 mother and son were charged with murder and sent to trial concurrently. Like Shakespeare's Lady Macbeth, Heather Osland was bestowed with the murderer's heart and found guilty. The jury couldn't decide on her son's guilt, so he was sent for retrial. Condemned as an evil and wicked mother, Heather went down for 14 years. David was found not guilty.

Heather Osland's crime was that she scoffed at the laws of patriarchy, tossed the victim's badge on the scrap heap and chose counter violence. When she did, Andrew Bolt and feminist recruit Jill Singer rose in the tabloid pulpit to remind women of their responsibilities. So outraged was someone at the *Herald Sun* when Heather sought a pardon, they plastered the savage 'This killer got justice' above Singer's response. I wondered what the feeling might have been had Frank Osland been an Arab. But Frank Osland was her lawful husband according to western law. That gave him rights.

I wasn't thinking about Jill Singer, Heather Osland or Julie McAllister when I took off with my wife for Clifton Hill on the evening of Saturday 3 March 2001. Entertainer Mary Kenneally was turning 50 and she and husband Rod Quantock had thrown open the house for a bit of music and good cheer. I hadn't expected to see Jill Singer that night, but she just happened to turn up with children's rights lawyer and republican, Moira Rayner.

'Jill, I can't believe you'd do the bidding for the "Hun" on Heather Osland,' I'd said, once the pleasantries were out of the way. I hadn't planned to be so forthright, but somehow the words had a life of their own.

'What do you mean?' she replied, rolling her eyes.

'Well, I reckon it doesn't help when an avowed feminist runs a line that condemns a woman to life under the heel of a monster like Frank Osland.'

'You obviously don't know the case. She planned the murder and even got her son to do it. He's an emotional wreck because of it.'

'So it's her fault that her son smashed the pipe into Osland's head. She's just another Lady Macbeth?'

'Well, yes, she was conniving. You need to find a better case or a more deserving one.'

'What was she supposed to do? Just cop it sweet? Frank Osland was no different from a Balkans rape camp commandant.'

'Oh, come on. How can you make that comparison?'

'Easily...'

'She should have gone to the police. That's what I would have done if I lived with a violent man.'

'Osland did call the police and they didn't help.'

'Come on...'

'Jill, your boss, John Kiely, wouldn't even run the article on Osland I sent to him. But he was happy to give it to you and have you comment on it selectively in the paper. Was that professional?'

'He didn't tell me that.'

'Really?' I said as the conversation was brought to an end by some bemused partygoers.

These days Jocelynne Scutt is Tasmania's Anti-discrimination Commissioner. A barrister of unbridled courage with an intellect to match, she has been one of the most profound critics of the hypocrisy of the courts in their dealings with women. So critical was Jocelynne of Jill Singer's position in the 'Hun', she refused to be interviewed by her when the ABC TV's '7.30 Report' covered the case. Jocelynne Scutt had taken Osland's appeal to the High Court, where Justices Kirby, McHugh and Callinan, ruled against her in a split decision.

In Justice Michael Kirby's view, there was nothing inconsistent in the verdicts of 'guilty' for Heather and 'not guilty' for her son. Beyond that, he said the need to uphold the sanctity of human life was too compelling to grant Osland freedom on the grounds of self-defence. She should have found a way out that avoided the taking of her husband's life. Justices Mary Gaudron and Bill Gummow were less timid. They supported Jocelynne's arguments.

As Jill and I downed Chardonnay and tested our theories of violence within the confines of middle-class Clifton Hill, the fire brigade was already combing the embers of McAllister's home in the town of Tyers in eastern Victoria. Taking a leaf out of Jill Singer and Michael Kirby's book, Julie McAllister had sought a legal solution to Keogh's harassment. On 24 August 2000, she had secured an interim order at the Moe Court that prohibited Keogh from being within 200 metres of her home. He had responded with a caveat on the house.

'Looks like arson, Mrs McAllister. The water was turned off and it seems the fire started in a wastepaper bin in your bedroom,' they said. Once the news sank in, she became the last of a string of women who'd imagined death at the hands of Peter Raymond Keogh. 'I didn't do it,' he would soon tell solicitor Peter Lamer, of Cain and Lamer. I don't know whether Lamer believed him. The man Justice George Hampel had sentenced to a brief holiday at Loddon Prison Farm for the killing of his last girlfriend was a serious menace to women. The problem was, no one seemed to have noticed.

A few months before the fire, Judy McNulty's daughter, Terri, had spotted Keogh in the poolroom of the Clifton Hill Hotel. Just on twenty years had passed since the day she first laid eyes on him a few blocks away from the hotel, in Arthur Street, Fairfield. Contemptuous of all that he had done to her family, Keogh stumbled towards her without a worry in the world.

'I know you, don't I?' he asked.

'I don't want to talk to you,' she had replied, the awful memories flooding back. Only when her friends told him to piss off did he take his leave.

After leaving the party on what I would later call 'the night of the fire', I paused for a moment and eyed the hotel. Wedged on a busy corner in Queens Parade on the edge of Map 30, it was no palace. The night's activities were coming to an end, and a gorilla with a bow tie was showing excited revellers their leave.

'Should go and have a look for him,' I thought.

As I prepared to head for the door, my wife caught the attention of a passing cab. A few weeks later, the killer would tell insurance investigator, Jack Jacobs, he'd been drinking at the Clifton Hill that night. I still wonder if he was there.

As if to warn me of the impending danger, a burst of letters and phone calls came my way in the latter half of 2000. When a sad, handwritten letter documenting a girl's murder by her de facto husband arrived in July, it fired my interest yet again. Like so many mothers who'd lost a daughter to a violent man, Sandra Smart carried a heavy, aggrieved heart. Her daughter's killer had been sentenced to a minimum two years gaol by Justice George Hampel. The girl's parents had been told that a pre-trial agreement reducing the charge from murder to manslaughter would result in Mark Bottriell receiving between eight and ten years gaol. Bottriell had battered Debbie Smart from pillar to post in the years before her death.

I fancied it was time to test the mettle of the Victorian Attorney General, Rob Hulls:

Dear Rob

... over the past decade I've written and made numerous public statements regarding the inconsistencies in the criminal justice system ... Whilst it's true that the killing of my sister in 1987 and the subsequent granting of a defence of provocation by Justice George Hampel was the impetus for my position, it is the inconsistencies in the law that concern me. My contention is that Justice Hampel was wrong to allow a defence of provocation in my sister's case. I did not accept then and still believe Justice Hampel to have been wrong in drawing on the killing of Zerrin Dincer by her Turkish father in 1981 to support defence counsel's right to plead provocation in my sister's case.

Attorneys General have a great opportunity and indeed a responsibility to further the goal of equality before the law ... just as we expunged prejudicial forms of cross-examination from rape cases, so too should we explore the kind of assumptions from which too many judges proceed in cases involving the murder of women.

However, as I argued in relation to the trial following the killing of homosexual Keith Hibbins in the Fitzroy Gardens, similar assumptions operate in other settings.

I look forward to talking with you about this issue.

Had he been alive, Keogh's long-time mate, Brian Freake, wouldn't have quite understood my letter to Rob Hulls. There were no women in hijabs in Freake's world and a bloke took what he could get. Amphetamines had blurred their judgement. Homeless street kids, boys and girls, could always find a spot in Freake's bed. That was until someone took a knife to him in 1998. Just who cut his throat was a matter of speculation on the streets. Even after a local bloke was charged and later convicted, not everyone believed it.

Freake knew the verdict of manslaughter and the sentence dished out to Keogh was a joke. He didn't romanticise the killer or believe he was some alcoholic depressive. 'Keogh seemed to be coming to grips with the separation. Wasn't drinking much. Seemed all right. Ate a pizza before we arrived home,' he told the Court when asked about Keogh's movements in the weeks and the night before the murder. Later he would add a crucial piece to the story.

'I've got thing's on him,' he told Kevin Chamberlain as soon as the trial was over.

'What do ya mean?' he asked his mate.

'He told me what he was gunna do to Vick. Waved the fuckin' knife before he went,' Freake replied.

Even in the shifty world inhabited by a petty crim, low-level drug pusher, they knew something about free will. Freake knew Keogh was an arsehole, but had other reasons for enduring his company. Was this why Freake was found with his throat cut in early 1998? Was the knife-man responsible? Some thought he was.

decent women

At 21 years of age, Vicki was no match for the streetwise petty crims who'd ingratiated their way into her life in late 1982. Born in 1952, I was nine years older than Vicki and wasn't in her circle when Keogh's mob arrived on the scene. Vicki was Mum's first girl after four boys. Christened Vicki Maree, she followed Paul, born in 1956, and Perry, born in December 1959. Another boy had died two days after his birth in 1958. Vicki arrived after only two hours of labour on 21 November 1961 and was already at peace with the world. When Mum rang home to tell Dad they finally had a girl, Ron Cleary cried into the phone. Although he spent his entire working life slicing his knife through carcasses of red meat, Dad wasn't made from the same stuff as Peter Keogh and the tattooed men who streamed from the abattoir at Oakover Road, Preston, into the drinking holes along High Street. Nor were his sons.

Their daughter was a quiet girl at first. So serene was she, Mum wondered if life might be too arduous for her. In time, that serenity was emboldened by a spirit and an empathy that was unconstrained in its love of fellow humans. At the farm in Broadford that had become the Cleary home in 1981, Vicki would lie on the floor while her nieces threaded their tiny fingers through her long rich brown hair. These days my daughters still remember it with great affection. Unlike the acclaimed Frank Galbally, who stood before juries to explain away the violence of working-class thugs, Vicki genuinely cared for the underdog. She would never have voted for Liberal Prime Minister John Howard, or turned a blind eye to a quisling Labor opposition. She'd have defended refugees and children. My sister was a woman of courage and compassion. When she told her mother that such was the state of Keogh's deteriorating back, she might have to nurse him in later life, Lorna felt deep anxiety. Although she bit her tongue at the time, in her heart Lorna didn't believe him worthy of such devotion.

The preparedness of women to mother him was something Keogh had exploited throughout his life. This, coupled with her youthful innocence and her fundamental decency, made Vicki an easy sting. Peter Keogh could never be like her. Instead, he milked her for the warmth the gods had bequeathed. Then when she could take no more, he cast a pall of despair over her.

Thirty-four-year-old Julie McAllister should have been a different kettle of fish. Julie had worked in bars in the northern suburbs all her life and had an effusive and confident manner. Separated from the father of her children she was resourceful, yet imbued with a strong sense of propriety. She was no one's fall girl.

By the autumn of 2000, she wondered how he'd slipped under her guard. It was all too familiar. If his aversion to intimacy and sex hadn't sent her over the edge, his indolence would have. He and Julie knew it was a relationship going nowhere. 'I want you out of here,' she told a stoical Keogh in March. Keogh reacted as he always did. There was no animation or acrimony as he grabbed his belongings and left her little brick house in Tyers. That was the end of it. Or so McAllister thought. Although he was a bad drunk, the man she lived with for seven years slept like a baby and gave not the slightest suggestion he might do her harm.

The next day it was a different story. The nonchalance had given away to aggressive words that would soon be transformed into dangerous threats. Peter Raymond Keogh was back in action. Already he was planning to torch her house.

First came the unsigned letter to her son from Keogh, dated 13 April 2000. Bristling with lies and paranoia, it was the killer to the bootstraps.

> Dear Justin
>
> Just writing to let you know the real reason why Mr. Keogh and your Mother broke up. As things ar'nt (sic) always as clean cut as she leads you to beleive (sic). I beleive (sic) that you should know the real truth, and that is your Mother was caught in their bed with another man by Mr. Keogh. Who happens to be one of your brothers (sic) best friend's father, who also has a family of his own.
>
> And ask yourself what type of person is your mother. It's a known fact that Mr. Keogh has been imprisoned for stabbing before. Your mother must have nine lives to get away with this for so long. Maybe this time she has bitten off more than she can chew. One can only hope. A Mother should be honest with her children, instead she chooses to lie to you.

It was a telling picture of the obsessive Keogh and the dangerous Oedipal forces that drove his outrages. The words 'A Mother should be honest with her children' leapt off the page. From childhood, Keogh had dined on the myth of his mother's possessiveness and the secrets of McLachlan Street. Forty years after parole officer O'Sullivan blamed Keogh's mother for her son's violence, another mother was in the frame. Around June 2000 an anonymous man rang Allianz Insurance and said he had some secret information of relevance to the company. A woman in Cedar Court by the name of Julie McAllister had paid someone to torch her house, said the caller. More than eight months would elapse before the mysterious arsonist would actually torch Julie's house.

Police have little doubt that man was Peter Keogh. Only he and Julie knew the name of the insurer. He was right about one thing—someone was preparing to torch the house. Only he was silly enough and impulsive enough to so comprehensively expose himself to suspicion by carrying out his threat.

decent women 49

Keogh's lies about McAllister being in bed with another man resonated with words he had used in the Supreme Court in 1989. Careful not to demonise Vicki and so frame her murder as an act of revenge, he cried as he described her as a 'cold, distant rejectful (sic), deceitful woman', seeing another man but lying about it. So, just as he had done to Vicki Cleary, he now cast his ex-girlfriend, Julie McAllister, as a liar and a whore. Worse still, she was a bad mother. In reality her crime was identical to Vicki's—she'd refused to come to heel. And as in 1987 he was now talking violence. Free of the dictates of the court, the knife-murder of Vicki could now be flaunted as a sign of his power. He was preparing to strike again.

As if to mock his sexual crimes, Peter Keogh wasn't big on sex with the actual woman in his life at any given time. Sex with a child or a subjugated woman was so much easier for him. Some wondered whether he wanted a mother, not a lover, in the marital bed. When the days of abstinence slipped into months, Julie looked for an answer. Was there something wrong with her? Had he been sexually abused in gaol? A shrug of the shoulders then a defiant 'No one touched me in gaol' was all she got from him. The suggestion that some bloke had forcibly thrust his cock up his arse wasn't going to be met with anything but the strictest denial. How different it was when it was Keogh's appendage engaged in the assault!

Just why he wasn't excited by intimate sex remains something of a mystery. It had been the same with Vicki. 'We hardly ever have sex. And don't worry about children, he's had a vasectomy,' she told her mother early on in the relationship. Although Lorna Cleary was relieved, she worried that a girl who so loved children might be left without them. Just why she stayed with this unremarkable man, our mother couldn't fathom.

'What did you see in him?' I asked Julie, in the aftermath of Keogh's suicide.

'I don't know really. The first time we went out, he drugged me. I woke up not knowing what had gone on.'

The words 'drugged me' fell like hand grenades. How did this savage find his way into our lives, I thought? And how did we let him dud us?

'So what did you say to him?' I probed, still looking for the answers.

'I told him that if he ever did that again, he wouldn't see me again.'

I had no idea whether he'd ever drugged Vicki, but there was a familiar ring about Julie's tale.

A once vibrant, timber-producing town only 45 minutes up the Hume from Melbourne, by 1987 Broadford was in decline. With the paper mill no longer thriving, work was at a premium. Only football brought a semblance of life to the place. Vicki hadn't wanted to live in Broadford but Keogh had taken no notice. In February 1987, they had moved into a neat weatherboard house just off the freeway in White Street, only a couple of miles from our parents' farm. It was a disastrous move. Separated from her friends in Melbourne and with Keogh ensconced in the local pub, Vicki knew what had to be done. On a Saturday night in early May, she told him it was over.

Keogh responded as he always did.

'Think you can leave me, do you,' he roared, as he threw her to the floor and pressed his arm across her throat. Sex was a lot easier for the killer when it was taken by force. The more she screamed, the more he enjoyed the conquest. Satisfied with his work, Keogh locked the doors and hid the keys.

'What are you going to tell your mother?' asked Keogh the next morning, when she said she was leaving.

'I'm going to tell her everything,' she replied.

That afternoon Vicki did tell her mum it was over with Keogh. Seated on the cane couch wearing her blue mohair jumper and jeans, she calmly recounted a bizarre story that traversed the previous night and the past years. The black eye she had explained away a year earlier, his refusal to let her leave the kitchen table until he gave permission, and the aggression were laid out bare.

'All right, just leave all that behind you and move on,' Mum had said. Although she was genuinely stunned that Vicki had hidden so much from her, Lorna Cleary saw no point in dwelling on the bad times. She was just so happy it was over.

The next day, before they left for the football, Mum told Vicki not to go near Keogh. On the way home from the game, she could hardly believe her eyes when she cast a glance up White Street. It was the beginning of the troubles. 'Ronnie, I think we should go back to the house. I think that's Vick's car,' she told her 61-year-old husband. Ron and his childhood sweetheart, Lorna, had been married for 36 years. They were a loving couple with no grasp of the drama that lay ahead or the events that had transpired only minutes before their decision to stop at the house.

As Vicki sobbed in the bedroom and stared through the front window Keogh dealt a hand of patience and waited. Under the guise of wanting to 'have a talk' he had lured her to the house then struck. Alone and scared, my sister wondered whether she might be saved. Twice in consecutive days she had feared for her life.

Then came the knock at the door.

'What's going on?' asked her mum, once she sensed the tumult into which she'd found her way.

'She's got another bloke. I'm upset,' said Keogh.

'Well, you don't own her, Peter, and she's told you she wants to leave. Don't you understand that?' Dad replied.

Ron Cleary was no man of war. What if he plays up? he'd thought, as he waited for the next move. On the table behind Keogh, mum noticed a large knife. She'd seen it before. At the trial it would reappear as photo 28 in a collection of 34 photos that captured the aftermath of 26 August 1987. Four inches of black handle and eight inches of blade, it was a real knife. But Mum didn't dwell on the knife. All that mattered was the terror in a daughter's face. As Vicki steered her Ford up the gravel road towards the farm, her younger sister took in all that had happened. Crying and distraught, Vicki cut a desperate figure. It was the beginning of a baptism of fire for fourteen-year-old Elizabeth Cleary.

After our brother Paul, who lived with his wife and three sons in a house on the farm, heard about what had happened, he decided to front Keogh. When he and his mate Tony Batham called at the house, they found a repentant man who swore there was no problem and that it was all a misunderstanding. Oblivious to the terror Keogh had visited on women throughout his life, Paul believed it would be the end of the drama. In hindsight, we all now know that counter-terror was the only effective weapon against him.

Unaware of what others knew, our family was simply thankful the relationship was over. How could any of us have imagined what was brewing in his mind or where that mind had been? Only Vicki knew that. Ashamed by all that had happened, and protective of her family, she chose to ride it out and put her fate in the hands of those unable to protect her. It cost my sister her life.

When I met Julie McAllister after her house went up in flames, I found it hard to escape the grim reality that she and other women had actually chosen to spend time with Keogh. More than ten years had passed since the trial, and now I knew so much about the killer. None of it fitted snugly into the neat neo-Marxist theory of class that I'd once used to explain the monopoly working-class kids held on gaol beds. Eight days in the Supreme Court in 1989 had offered me a profound insight into how the boys from the other side of town colluded with the bourgeois state to protect violent, cruel working-class men, such as Peter Keogh. He was no romantic criminal at war with an unjust state, and never could he find poetic words to describe his life. Nor was he a victim. But his war against working-class women and girls was far removed from the men of law. Sadly, my sister was one of those women.

Some professionals said his father's illness left him without a role model. Others blamed a domineering mother. So what was the truth? Both his father and his grandfather had married women more than twenty years their junior. Were they rakish, sexual predators who taught the Keogh boys that a woman was nothing but an object to be taken by force? When twelve-year-old Terri McNulty overheard Keogh describing the bed he shared with her mother in St David Street, Northcote, as 'the work bench', she knew there was something wrong with him.

Pat Cole, the guardian angel who plucked Keogh from Reservoir, delivered him to the solicitor before the blood had dried on his runners. At the solicitor's office she waited as Keogh prepared to place the victim's crown upon his ugly head yet again. For years I thought about Cole's actions that day and her evidence. Another good woman conned or a stupid working-class woman mesmerised by men of violence? I wasn't sure.

At the time of the murder, I knew nothing about the woman who'd taken Keogh to solicitor Robert Digala's city office. Nor did I know that a month earlier, Keogh had told Digala he wanted to send a letter of demand to Vicki in relation to her car. If only the little bastard had sent that letter. If only Keogh had shown his hand and asserted his vexatious claim to the car, we'd have seen the game he was playing. He owned not a single hubcap of the 1984 Ford Vicki had purchased with a loan from a Broadford bank. Keogh knew he had no right to the car. It didn't stop him delivering a vitriolic diatribe at Vicki on the Monday before he killed her. 'You'll be hearing from me and my solicitor,' he bragged. Bastard, I thought, when I found out.

When I finally caught up with Pat Cole, after Keogh's suicide, she told me she was in a state of confusion when Chamberlain told her what had happened to Vicki and then asked her to pick Keogh up. 'Kevin rang and said Vicki had been stabbed and Keogh was in our house in Reservoir. He asked me to drive him somewhere. I didn't know what to do,' she told me over the phone. An English migrant, she'd taken up with Kevin Chamberlain in her late teens and had been with him thirteen years when they visited Keogh the night before the murder. When she and Chamberlain bedded down on Tuesday 25 August he wouldn't have been surprised to know Keogh was hatching a murderous plot.

'If she don't pull up, I'll neck her,' Keogh had growled as he stared into a stubbie of Victoria Bitter at Cramers Hotel a few weeks earlier.

'What's the drama, Pete?' Chamberlain had asked.

'She's talking about going me for half the house,' Keogh had replied. At the trial Keogh denied that Vicki had ever said anything about the house.

No sooner had the police dumped Keogh at Pentridge after killing Vicki than Cole and Chamberlain, Freake and the cloying Watson were lined up at security for a visit.

'Jesus. All we need is for them to get word he was here after he stabbed Vicki and they'll be after blood,' Chamberlain had replied.

'What'll we do, then?' asked Cole.

'Get a fuckin' gun, that's what!' he replied.

'A gun!'

'Listen. If they find out Keogh said he was gunna neck Vicki, and I did fuck-all, how's it gunna look?'

The possibility that the incriminating evidence to which Freake and Chamberlain were privy might reach the ears of those close to Vicki had both men in a panic.

Fortunately for them, we were in a state of shock when they delivered their statements to the police, and so never thought to ask what they knew. Nor did the police ever bother to explain how Cole and Chamberlain had lied about Keogh's respite at their Reservoir home that morning. To my eternal regret, I never got to confront Freake, Watson, Cole and Chamberlain in the aftermath of the murder. By the time I discovered the real truth, Watson and Freake were dead and too much time had passed.

The wake, held at the Coburg Football Club on the Friday, was terrible. While the stench of defeat hung in the air, here and there men talked revenge. Capital punishment wasn't the answer, but justice did not preclude retribution. Keogh had scoffed at life and society, terrorised Vicki then taken her life. And now as we grappled with the trauma, Keogh sat in the Pentridge Remand yard only a mile away, plotting a course through the maze. Already the gaol was buzzing with the word that the bloke who knocked Phil Cleary's sister was inside. It spelt danger.

Eventually I would discover that a cluster of people in the clubroom knew first-hand of Keogh's history of terror. Like characters in a Thomas Hardy novel, they'd doffed their hats as they passed in a pub or on the street, without speaking the words that might break the impasse. At the Eltham Hotel, Vicki had told an old friend,

Des Powell, she was lying low to avoid a bloke who was annoying her. Two weeks later he and I were shaking hands at her funeral. She hadn't seen Powell for some time before the conversation in Eltham, and had no idea of his detailed knowledge of the man about whom she spoke. In fact, Des had offered Judy McNulty protection when Keogh was stalking her. If only Vicki had uttered the words, 'Peter Keogh', who knows what might have happened? As he looked into Vicki's ebullient eyes at the pub that day, Powell had no idea she had lived with the man whose violence he'd seen.

We were all wise after the fact. As I heard the stories and felt the warmth of the girl who had larked with the crowd beneath the smoke-stained ceiling after we thrashed Frankston in my 200th game on 6 June, I could only regret. In the *Age*, an article had appeared the week before that game. Under the heading, 'Wise man of the VFA', I was portrayed as someone who knew and understood the fabric of the great Australian game. If only I'd seen that Vicki was in danger. If only that kind of wisdom had been thrust upon me. That's what I thought as we made small talk in the social club after the burial.

As the morning moved on, solutions came thick and fast. Some angry men had found an answer to Keogh's arrogance.

'Could get him knocked in the can, or hire Gangitano when Keogh gets out,' an old friend had said without so much as a blink of an eye.

'You think so?' I asked.

'If we can raise the money the job's done,' he replied.

'Won't solve anything,' I said, leaving the conversation in the hands of a couple of friends of my sister. It was not the last time the matter would be raised.

Alphonse Gangitano had appeared in the Coburg Social Club during 1986. An acquaintance of a bloke who laid bets with our SP bookmaker president, Allan Tripp, he was already carving out a name for himself. A few years earlier, Tripp's debt collector, Brian Kane, had been gunned down in Brunswick's Quarry Hotel. Known as a tough man around the northern suburbs, Kane had cut his teeth in Crevelli Street with swarms of kids from Camp Pell. At the Planet Theatre he was not a man to be messed with. I never met him.

A decade after his name was flagged as a potential assassin of Peter Keogh, Gangitano was shot dead at his home in Templestowe. At the Inquest, the Coroner identified another northern suburbs boy, Jason Moran, as among those involved in the murder. Disgraced barrister, Andrew Fraser, had once acted for Moran and, it was alleged, had named him in a telephone conversation. Fraser had been gaoled only a month earlier for his part in a massive cocaine-importing scheme. When he had his knees-up at the cocaine mecca, the Botanical Hotel, a couple of years earlier, the legal fraternity were there with bells on.

Gangs have always been a feature of life in the northern suburbs. But my flirtation with the physical force men was brief and salutary. From the Merri Creek, east to Darebin Creek, the children of working-class families, many with fathers afflicted by the war, embarked on their rites of passage. Education was still the domain of the rich, so most boys left school at fourteen and went labouring or, if they were lucky, into a trade.

While ambitious daughters of the middle-class spread their legs on the casting couch or the bed of a University lecturer, working-class girls offered themselves to tribal warlords in the back of Packards and FJ Holdens. It might have drawn ridicule in a bourgeois court, but on the block it brought adoration. Watching a warlord panting in orgasm was enough for one girl to liken herself to Queen Cleopatra.

'The power of the pussy,' she remarked, when asked why she'd offered her jewels to a succession of men in one sitting. Only through sex could a girl subdue the wild beast, and be afforded protection from other predators. This was crude patriarchy at work.

For one year of my life I eyed the path trodden by 'the boys'. I couldn't stick a glass in a bloke's face or line-up for a fuck, but the need to flex my muscles was very real. For me, football became the theatre of war. Not so for many of 'the boys'. From the fists, it was only a short step to the broken glass and the pistol. And while it wasn't exactly the Wild West in the housing estates around Pentridge Prison, there were some bad men. Crammed into domestic chicken pens, many blokes looked for creative ways to escape the drudgery of factory labour and overcome the alienation.

When I first laid eyes on Peter Keogh I thought I knew where he'd come from. I imagined that he had left behind the machismo reflected in the tattoos and found another life. I just wished it wasn't my sister who was sharing his bed. Never did I imagine that he was a killer. Peter Keogh might have knocked around but he didn't mix with men like Gangitano, Moran or Brian Kane. He knew the risks of terrorising someone experienced in physical force. Single women, and men without a love of violence, were easy pickings. In the cesspool of Her Majesty's Remand section in 1987, Keogh soon learnt there was trouble brewing.

In the preceding couple of years I'd made a number of sojourns into Pentridge for sports days, organised by the bush lawyer, convicted murderer, Peter Lawless. Lawless had been in for nearly fifteen years and bore some infamy as the last man in Victoria sentenced to death. It was never carried out. The news that the bloke who killed my sister was inside had travelled fast. Keogh was told to look out. Before long he'd been shunted off to the barbed wire zoo they called Jika Jika. He was terrified.

Keogh remembered those days in Pentridge in the weeks after he sent Julie McAllister's house up in smoke. If he was charged, he knew he'd have to run the gauntlet once more. But how dangerous was he? Enough for me to tell Julie to take care, when we met in Brunswick. That done, I got on the phone.

'I'm ringing about an arson attack and its ramifications for the woman who owns the house,' I explained to someone from the Police Ethical Standards who took my call a couple of days later.

'It's not really our area,' she replied.

'I think it should be. If the arsonist is her former partner, do you regard the owner of the house to be in any kind of danger?'

'That's a hypothetical I can't answer,' she replied. It was as if we were playing a game.

'Hypothetical? If a man with a history of violence towards women, including the killing of my sister, is responsible for this arson, then it's not hypothetical,' I said, my frustration rising.

'It's a subjective judgment.'

'Subjective? Not at all. This man has a record of violence against women. It's a fact. All right, I'll record this conversation and if anything happens to this woman I'll make it public. Does that suit?'

'Mr Cleary, the people to deal with this are the local police in charge of the investigation.'

'They haven't even interviewed him yet,' I replied.

It was a conversation going nowhere.

It was no wonder Keogh had been able to act with impunity, I thought, as I laid the phone to rest and contemplated the next move. I wasn't prepared to have him think he could do this again. When Vicki had sought protection against him in May 1987 it was the same bureaucratic screen that confronted her.

'An intervention order won't stop him killing you. You need a lawyer,' a young clerk at Kilmore Court had said when she went in search of an intervention order. The clerk of courts, Laurie Corboy, was on sick leave the day Vicki called. Sadly, his junior's response was typical of the times.

'It could well have exposed his priors,' Corboy would tell me some years later. This time there'd be none of the equivocation that led to Vicki's death.

If the mollycoddled little prick was in his full-moon phase, we needed to act. Unfortunately neither the *Herald Sun*, which had sent a reporter and photographer to Moe Magistrate's Court for the hearing into the intervention order, nor the *Age* newspaper, would run the story about the arson. Didn't want Peter Keogh to miss out on a fair trial should plod ever lay charges. If he could do it to McAllister's house, then what about my place in Brunswick? I thought. And what if the bastard hires someone to do it? There was a lot to consider. At night I'd listen for a sign he might be creeping down the back lane. Sometimes I'd imagine he was about to walk through an unlocked door. In his little cranny he wondered when I'd appear. It was a game of cat and mouse.

Julie McAllister, the insurance investigator and the Morwell police all believed Peter Keogh was the man who had torched the house. They had good reason. On the night of the arson he was nowhere to be found. Better still, the gods had played mistress with the boy from Westgarth.

'Jesus,' thought Keogh as he heard the sound of brakes and waited for the thump in his rear end outside the Grandview Hotel in Fairfield. Although he'd once been a regular at the pub, tonight was business and he was on the wagon.

'Christ, just what I need! I'll have to exchange names,' he mused as he opened the car door, cast a glance at his old drinking haunt and walked back to inspect the damage to his back bumper bar. A quick check of his watch showed that it was 5.30 pm.

'I'm so sorry. You seemed to stop all of a sudden,' came the explanation from the female driver.

'Bloke in front hit the brakes,' said Keogh scribbling the name Peter Keogh, 6 O'Donnell Street, Rosanna, the address of his sister Dulcie, on the piece of paper provided for him. Keogh never gave his real address. He never knew when the cops or some woman's bloke or brother might be on the warpath.

As he eyed his-long time drinking hole, he must have remembered his great sexual conquest of twenty years earlier in the autumn of 1980. When he was on a rampage, Keogh always remembered the conquests. Judy McNulty and her sisters, all ten of them, were known for their beauty. One, a single mother, resided in a flat not far from Judy, who was at that time living with her husband in Arthur Street. Winter was just around the corner the night Judy's sister rugged up her toddler and walked to the phone box outside the hotel to make a call. With the phone occupied, she decided to try the phone inside the hotel.

The predatory Keogh had met her when Judy had begun flirting with him earlier in the year. The moment he spotted Judy's sister, he would have felt a surge of adrenalin. I experienced it when some bloke was between the football and me. He felt it when a woman stood between him and gratification.

'Stay for a drink, why don't ya?' he asked when she appeared in the lounge. She declined and, having made the call, took off home. As he watched her leave the pub, he considered the next move.

'Must go, on a promise,' he quipped to his drinking mates as he ordered six long necks and went in pursuit of her a little while later.

When I spoke to Judy's sister in 2000, I was taken by how vivid was her recall of the events and how candid she was with me. Although Keogh would tell a different story, it wasn't hard to finger the liar.

'I'd put my daughter to sleep and was on the couch watching the "Don Lane Show" when there was a knock at the door. I knew it was him. For a split second I contemplated not opening the door, but I didn't want any trouble. I didn't like Keogh at all, but I didn't know what to do. So I opened the door,' she said.

'Thought I'd just call in for a beer,' said Keogh, moving inside and placing his six-pack on the table.

The moment he perched himself on the three-seater couch, Judy's sister knew there was going to be an impasse. After he'd downed a bottle, he slid alongside her and fumbled his way around a kiss.

'Don't do that, Peter. You know it's not right. You're going out with my sister.'

'Don't worry about that.'

'I don't want to do anything with you, Peter.'

'Listen, no one stooges me,' he snarled, grabbing the empty bottle and banging it against her head.

'Not in there, please, not with my baby,' she implored, as Keogh began to drag her to the bedroom where her child slept. It was to no avail. This was sex, as Peter Keogh loved it. In the background Bert Newton was spinning the Wheel of Fortune and telling gags that had middle Australia laughing.

As Keogh took his leave, he paused to place his arm around his conquest and lay one final kiss on her lips. It was exactly what his rapist mate had done in the lane a couple of blocks away, back in 1959. Like him, Keogh believed rape was just part of the landscape, and something a woman secretly desired. It was a myth that sustained him until a woman finally shut the door on him. Then he smashed it down. By the time she got her sister on the phone at Pampas Pastry, Keogh's victim was hysterical. As always, the serial liar and bully had another story. 'She asked me for it,' he would tell Judy. Sadly, she believed him.

Keogh was no cleanskin when he passed his old haunt on Saturday 3 March 2001. And make no mistake, his appetite for terror was as voracious as it had been on that autumn night in 1980. With Tyers only two hours away via the Eastern Freeway, Springvale Road and the South Eastern, everything was ready.

'Arrive at 8 pm, case the site for half an hour, park across the paddock, flick the match at 8.30 and disappear into the night.' It was a breeze: or so he thought.

'Stick that and your fuckin' intervention order where it fits,' he thought as he scampered along the path, the flames beginning to lick the spouting of the little house he'd once called home. No one in Cedar Court or at the sportsground saw a thing. By the time they spotted the flames, the arsonist was on his way home. Better still, he now had an alibi. And once he altered the time of the accident, bingo!

'I was in Melbourne that night. Had an accident outside the Grandview Hotel. The publican knows me. He'll vouch that I was there,' Keogh told insurance investigator Jack Jacobs over a coffee at the Northland Shopping Centre in Preston. It had taken Jacobs a couple of weeks to track Keogh down. But after a series of calls to his sisters, an edgy Keogh finally took the bait. Desperate to know what spin the police were putting on the fire, he agreed to a meeting. Northland was a place where he always felt comfortable. Although he wouldn't speak with the police, he desperately wanted to know what they thought. A chat with Jacobs, he thought, would put him a step ahead of the cops. It would prove a flawed strategy.

Keogh's first mistake was to furnish the investigator with a dodgy alibi. He should have shut his mouth. The problem was he'd stuck a caveat on the property, and he wanted to know how the fire might affect his claim to a financial interest in the house. That meant he needed to talk with Jacobs. But how to deal with the caveat and his financial claim while not saying anything incriminatory, he wondered.

The more he talked, the more he dug a hole. Soon it was obvious he was as guilty as sin.

'What time was that accident, Peter?' asked Jacobs as they sipped their coffee and made small talk.

'She ran up me arse at 6.30 pm,' he replied.

'And the publican at the Grandview? He's known you for twenty years, has he Peter?'

'Yeah, about that long. I was at the Clifton Hill after that. The bloke there knows me too. Pool table Pete, the security guard calls me. I'll be on the surveillance cameras. Got tested at a booze bus in East Coburg on the way home,' he added, squeezing a last puff from the rollie perched between his thick fingers.

As Keogh related the lies, Julie McAllister's father, Don, listened quietly. Deceived by the manipulative Keogh's bullshit, he had taken his side after the separation. As bizarre as it sounds, he believed the man who was now a prime suspect in the torching of his daughter's house was a good bloke. And nothing his daughter said was going to change his mind. For now the two men were like father and son.

In the recesses of his mind, Keogh carried an image of Jacobs. As Keogh took his leave, he thought about the name and the face. Jack Jacobs had been a detective when Maria James was murdered in 1980 and had worked on the case. It would have left Peter Raymond Keogh with plenty to think about as he waited for the coppers to call.

Little did Julie's father know that Keogh was digging a hole from which there was no escape. The names of drivers who blow below the legal limit are not recorded at booze buses and hotel surveillance film is destroyed after a few days. The cunning career criminal knew that. Although the possibility that Keogh would drink all night and not blow 0.5 was enough to make Jacobs and me laugh, it didn't prove Keogh lit the fire. But lying about the time of the accident and naming witnesses who didn't see him on the night was plain stupid. Soon the police were at the door.

'Mr Keogh, you'd be aware that the house you've had a caveat on in Cedar Court, Tyers was burnt down on Saturday 3 March around 8.30 pm,' began Detective Peter Allen.

'I've been told by an insurance investigator. That's all I know.'
'Where were you on the night, Mr Keogh?'
'Next question.'
'Can you tell me where you were?'
'That's my business. I can't help you, Detective. I've got nothing to say.'
'Mr Keogh, you gave a set of answers to Jack Jacobs that leave me wondering about your movements on the night.'
'Really?'
'You seemed to get the time of that accident outside the Grandview Hotel, Fairfield, wrong and named a number of people who either don't know you or didn't see you on the night. The publican at the Grandview says he hasn't seen you for years and the bouncer at the Clifton Hill Hotel says he doesn't know you.'
'I've got nothin' to say, mate, nothin' to say.'
'Mr Keogh, you can expect to see us again. There's a good chance you'll be charged.'

'Sure, mate.' Keogh's nonchalance had a nervous edge that left Detective Peter Allen convinced his man was the man. But could they pinch him? Allen thought there was a chance.

As with the decision to kill Vicki, burning the ex's house down would have seemed like a good idea at the time. But with a seriously tarnished crime sheet and provocation not on offer this time, he was in deep shit. And I was going to make sure the lid was on the bucket— the posse would never have the final say on the matter. As if to mock the woman who had paid with her life and those who had endured his terror, the brooding stalker chose his own path. For this, at least, Julie McAllister was thankful. As the circle tightened, the man Julie had feared might re-enter her life with fatal consequences had become a victim of his own malice and cowardice.

When Detective Steve Smith appeared on Keogh's doorstep asking questions about Brian Freake's 1998 murder, he saw first-hand Keogh's paranoia.

'Did Phil Cleary give you the address? He won't leave me alone. Keeps hassling my girlfriend. Thinks he's important, 'cos he's an ex-politician,' he'd told the detective. The bully didn't like being stalked, and I knew it. That's why I worked him over and set the dogs barking. Nothing was going to bring Vicki back, but he was going to pay.

Rarely a day would have gone by without him thinking about where I was and what I might have in store for him. The moment the verdict rang out in George Hampel's court my relationship with Keogh was cemented. Soon I was the man who knew too much. Every time I put pen to paper on Vicki's murder, I banged out those three words: 'Peter Raymond Keogh'. When I appeared in 'Guns and Roses', an award-winning ABC TV documentary on family violence, on 13 December 1990, Keogh sat alone in his cell at Loddon Prison Farm and listened to every word I uttered. Worried that my condemnation of his violence and the injustice that saved him might jeopardise his application for early release, he couldn't get to the parole board fast enough. Seven months later he was free.

And when I featured on the ABC's '7.30 Report' special on the law of provocation, it was more of the same.

'What did you watch on the TV last night?' Keogh had asked, as he sized up the attractive barmaid on the other side of the bar in the Junction Hotel.

'Didn't see anything,' she replied.

The last thing Keogh wanted was for anyone to know the truth of what he did to my sister.

By December he and the barmaid, Julie McAllister, were an item. When 'Four Corners' featured me in a program aptly titled 'Excuse for Murder' on 10 May 1993, Keogh took off for the stalker Watson's house in Gilbert Road.

'Why did Phil Cleary say it was a violent relationship?' Julie asked when he returned to her Mill Park home.

'He's a liar. That's bullshit. I never done anything to her,' he replied.

Keogh was not a remorseful man. He was a low-life bastard who would say and do anything to survive on his terms. He knew what he'd done and he knew I wasn't going to stop until the truth had been

decent women   65

told. Yet not once did I try to speak with his girlfriend Julie McAllister prior to the separation and never was I afforded the chance to embellish the vitriol I'd delivered as I passed him after the verdict came down in the Supreme Court.

On his police file there are scribbled a host of notes from arresting police. At the tender age of sixteen, there was one telling entry. 'The defendant is an habitual liar,' the cop had written. It would be his signature sign and his epitaph 37 years later. 'G'day, it's Phil Cleary here. I was looking for Peter Keogh. Is that you, Peter?' I asked, one night in 1997.

'Sorry, got the wrong person. No, no, there's no Peter Keogh here,' the man with the trembling voice replied, as he settled his finger on the receiver and continued with a mock conversation. Never again did I speak with the miserable little coward.

'What's the problem, Peter? You're as white as a ghost,' Julie said, lifting her head from the Christmas presents she was wrapping.

'Nothing. That was Phil Cleary.'

'Phil Cleary! Why would he be ringing you? You said he was a scumbag.'

'Just wanted to see how I was.' A liar and a coward was our boy, Peter Keogh.

murder changes everything

When Keogh was released from Loddon Prison Farm near Bendigo on 18 July 1991, no one in authority bothered to advise the Cleary family that he was back on the streets. Three months after the screws dumped his clothes at the front gate, a former inmate broke the news to us. Three years, ten months and twenty-two days had passed since the morning he took off to kill Vicki. Only two and a half years had elapsed since George Hampel had sentenced him.

Hampel knew that eight years with a minimum of six meant that Keogh might well be incarcerated for less than four years. Three years and eleven months for taking a young woman's life—it was hard to accept that a judge in a civilised democratic country could offer such a man a sentence at the bottom of the manslaughter scale.

Nothing, not the killer himself or his acquaintances, had been changed by the murder. At the gate of the prison was the driver, Brian Watson, a pimp who should have been dealt with. Back home he'd catch up with Freake and an old friend from Pampas Pastry by the name of Ken Bailey. Bailey who, unbeknown to me, lived only a couple of blocks from my home, had been a regular visitor at Loddon. During and after the gaol term, he gave Keogh regular updates as to what I was saying on the radio or the TV. Must be some kind of bloke, I thought, when this bit of intelligence came my way.

At cosy Loddon, Keogh, as always, was a protected prisoner. Every morning at 6.45 am a young bloke who'd known Vicki watched as Keogh was led from Unit One in the minimum-security section to the gate, for work duties. It was the only time anyone in the gaol saw him. Shit-frightened of being bashed as a payback, he had a screw by his side night and day. When the grey-haired convicted murderer, Peter Lawless, arrived from Pentridge, Keogh went into a panic. He had reason. Lawless told people he knew me.

Locked away under the control of the Justice Department are the documents that chronicle the reasons for Keogh's 'protected prisoner' status. Consistent with his life, the information in the files is beyond the teeth of the Freedom of Information Act. Although I've never laid eyes on the files, I know that Keogh named Peter Lawless and notorious armed robbers Peter Clune and Teddy King as the blokes assigned the task of fixing him up. I'd met Lawless before and after Vicki's murder, but have never spoken with him or the others about Keogh. From the time he was imprisoned in 1975, Keogh needed protection. For a bloke who could wield a weapon against the unprotected and brag about his conquests, he wasn't particularly brave when the gates were shut behind him.

After my election to the federal parliament in April 1992, I temporarily forgot about the killer. The excitement of capturing former Prime Minister Bob Hawke's seat in a by-election, and the national drama this created, left me with little time to contemplate the movements of the insignificant Peter Keogh. When I lost the seat at the 1996 general election, I soon found the scent again. A lot of water had passed under the bridge, but soon my eyes bulged as I scoured his documented life. I began to fully understand the extent of the miscarriage of justice that had been perpetrated on my sister.

The arrival in April 1995 of the 480-page transcript of The Queen v Peter Raymond Keogh had been the catalyst. How considerate, I thought, when Justice Hampel's office told me they'd waive the photocopying fee and send it gratis. Soon I was reminded how bad those eight days in the Supreme Court in 1989 had been. It's amazing how much you forget when shock overtakes you. Did George Hampel really say that, I thought, as I rediscovered the words and remembered the sound of his voice.

Night after night, I discussed the murder trial with my mother and revisited George Hampel's words. I had no idea that only a few weeks earlier, Keogh had been convicted of drink-driving and sentenced to two months gaol. Nor did I know that one of his brothers was six months into a twelve months gaol sentence for his part in a fraudulent $164 000 building scam.

'What were you thinking, George?' I asked myself. Soon I was poring over Keogh's police record and hearing stories that left me in disbelief. The more I learnt, the more I became convinced that the investigation and the prosecution were riddled with flaws.

Eventually I came to grasp the dimensions of the crime. And when I cried it was with a mixture of sorrow and anger. Then I happened upon ambulance officer Ivano Forte's description of Vicki's last moments. 'The girl said, "Please don't let me die." I remember it so vividly', Forte had written in a statement tendered to Magistrate Jillian Crowe.

As the stories came my way, the desire to finger Keogh and find out just what Cole, Freake, Chamberlain and Watson knew—but hadn't told—escalated. By now Keogh was miles away in rural Tyers. If he hadn't been there, I'm sure I'd have gone looking for him.

On one occasion in 1997, before we broadcast a VFA match from Traralgon, I drove into Cedar Court, Tyers, to see if I could spot him. Would I have jumped from the car? I don't know. Murder does strange things to you. As the facts of his sordid life emerged, my desire for revenge escalated. As the handwritten letter that arrived a few weeks later showed, the friends of Vicki were obviously thinking about him too:

> At a gathering of people the other day I overheard a conversation that you and your brothers would like to know the whereabouts of a certain Peter Keogh the man that caused you and your family a terrible

heartache. Lot 6. Ceder (sic) Crt, Tyers, 3844, 0351-918-469. He has lived there for about 3 years.

(From a friend)

By the time I'd unearthed the unabridged Peter Keogh, I wasn't the least bit surprised to find a woman by the name of Linda Gleeson on the phone. It was July 2000 and Julie McAllister, a woman I'd never met, had given her boyfriend his marching orders.

'Phil, I'm hoping you can help me. Peter Keogh is harassing my friend, Julie. She separated from him a couple of months ago, and I'm worried about her safety,' Linda said.

'You know, Linda, my brother Perry warned her about him. Tell Julie to get an intervention order,' I said. It was the battle I'd been waiting to wage against him. Now I had good reason to go after him. He was about to feel the noose around his coward's neck.

When Julie rang, it was so horribly familiar.

'Hi, Phil. I know I should have listened when your brother rang ages ago. But I didn't think he was a problem. Now he's hassling me. You know? Phone calls where no one answers. Scratches on the car, crank calls and threats. I'm worried,' she'd said.

'Yes, I wanted to speak with you, but I had this horrible thought that you must have been like him and wouldn't listen to what I said. Julie, you must get an intervention order, tell the police and take care. He must be exposed. It's the only way to deal with him,' I told her.

While Julie related her story I laid out the photo of the killer taken on the day he killed Vicki. Eyes downcast, his head framed by the shadow from the flash and his thick hands a patchwork of freckles branded with scars from the removal of tattoos, he looked a pitiful figure. How easy it should have been to stop this man, I thought. There was nothing of the muscle or the physical form of the hard-working labourer about this killer. His narrow shoulders clad in a Nike tracksuit top and his jeans, sloppy and formless, he was no tough bloke.

On the front left thigh of his blue jeans was a discernible dark patch of dried blood. Not even the protection of yellow overalls could impede his work being laid out for all to see. I imagined how he'd planted that leg around Vicki's body, pinned her with his left hand and struck the blows that sent the blood spurting from her chest and stomach across his camouflage, leaving a trail of red spots alongside the zip of his Nike top. Now it was here for the world to see. Arrested yet again he was a pathetic figure. Yet he was alive and Vicki was dead. How could a decent woman from Preston live with this monster, I thought, as I considered the next move.

Despite all he'd done, I had tried so hard not to hate him unreservedly. Even after Julie McAllister brought the news of his death, I drifted momentarily into thoughts bordering on sympathy. A tragic lonely soul, Keogh was dead at 53 years of age. Was he that bad? I wondered. But when I heard the words 'tragic and lonely' roll off Detective Dave Rae's lips in June 2001, I blanched, remembered the terror, and rearranged my sensibilities. Dead in the backyard of a house in Thornbury, flat out on his back alongside his car. Dead, the bastard was dead! He can't be, I'd thought.

Just as the psychiatrists had predicted their client might do when they lined up to explain why he couldn't stop himself from murdering my sister, he'd chosen to poke a tube into the window, lie back and reflect on a troubled life.

'Suicide is common in such people,' the shrink in the bow tie and the funny hat had told Justice George Hampel fourteen years earlier. So were they right in explaining his violence by way of 'traumatic episodes in his childhood'? Were they right and was I too hard and vengeful when I said he was 'nothing but a mollycoddled little prick'? And was it depression—even remorse—that had sent him into a nosedive that Saturday night? Bullshit! History had caught up with the bastard. 'Scared, that's why he did it,' I told my mother. I had no illusions.

Dr Bernie Bignell, who had a practice on the corner of Plenty Road a block from where Keogh had lived with Vicki, wasn't conned by the shifty bloke with the tats. Asked by the defence to provide character evidence at Keogh's trial, Bignell's reply was hardly reassuring.

'He was an aggressive little bastard with a spurious Workcover complaint. That's probably not what you want to hear,' said Dr

Bignell. John Champion QC chose to look elsewhere for some professional support.

I'd always fancied that some day I'd stare into those rotten eyes and resolve the impasse. In a compassionate moment, I imagined sitting and hearing his version of what happened. Then I realised how silly that was—he was a bastard. 'This one's for Vicki, you fucking murderer.' That's what I really wanted to say.

'Fucking murderer.' That's what I called him when our eyes went close to meeting in court on Tuesday 14 February 1989, his 41st birthday. They couldn't meet because he chose to bury his face in those evil hands in a thanks-be to the god of middle-class male justice, that saved him from what, in another time, would have meant the gallows.

My sister, Donna, was pregnant when she spotted him at a table with an attractive woman and her young son in the Reservoir Hotel in April 1993, less than two years after his release. What is a decent, good-looking mother doing with a known killer? I wonder if she knows how dangerous he is, she'd thought, turning to avoid his line of vision. So distressed was Donna that she had to go outside to calm down.

It was hard to believe that only a blink of an eye after the foreman stunned Court Three with a resounding 'not guilty to murder', Keogh would be back picking up an unsuspecting woman in his old stomping ground. For a bloke who ran to the authorities with stories about how Phil Cleary was after him, grabbing a counter meal at the Reservoir seemed somewhat injudicious. 'Let's give him a whack,' the bloke who'd been at Loddon with him had said. After some discussion, the blokes decided that Perry Cleary should have the call on that matter.

When my brother picked up the phone and heard the words 'Keogh's in the Reservoir Hotel,' he began shaking almost uncontrollably. By the time he made it to the pub, Keogh had gone. With the trial so fresh in his mind and the anger unabated, there's little doubt Perry would have taken to Keogh with whatever force he could muster. Fortunately for the coward, he'd taken his leave. As Keogh headed back to Julie McAllister's house in Mill Park, he was oblivious to the car trailing him. Now at least the friends of Vicki Cleary knew where he lived. The problem was, he was preparing to escape.

It was an edgy Chamberlain who listened as I brought the news of Keogh's death. Although he steadfastly avoided divulging what he knew of Keogh's intentions, his revelation at the Committal Hearing in June 1988 was a bombshell. When the words 'Keogh said he'd neck Vick if she didn't pull up over the house' rang out through the little courtroom in Hawthorn, a deathly silence enveloped us.

'Neck her' was macho for murder. It was an undiluted death threat that should have reached the ears of someone close to Vicki. It was no wonder Chamberlain was nervous in the days after the murder.

Following the attack in Cameron Street and a settling coffee in Sydney Road, Keogh had been reacquainted with the man privy to the threat. At Chamberlain's house in Rosenthal Court, he dumped the box containing the knife, the overalls and the masking tape. The issue for Chamberlain and Cole, was that they lied to police about Keogh's flight to their home. To this day I still don't know exactly what happened after Keogh arrived at the house. At the trial the foreman noted that there 'appeared to be an hour's discrepancy' between Keogh's 9 am arrival and Cole receiving the phone call that resulted in her picking him up. Unfortunately neither was asked to explain. Bit by bit, facts emerged that cast a clearer picture of their attitude to what Keogh had done. While I was far from happy about Cole and Chamberlain's role after the murder, it was Watson and Freake who were the prime culprits. How I wished I'd found Watson before he necked himself, or discovered what Freake knew about Keogh's intentions when he left his house at 6.40 am that morning.

'He's taken the knife and gone after Vicki,' the small-time drug dealer relayed down the phone to former girlfriend Pam Duggan the minute Keogh had stormed out.

'Do something! You need to ring Vicki,' she'd told him. Faced with the chance to be someone, Freake was a failure. By the time Keogh had dispensed with Vicki and was in the Chamberlain house, frantically preparing his case, word had travelled. It was now 9 am. A series of phone calls were made and Cole, Freake and Chamberlain agreed that there would be no mention of Keogh having been in Rosenthal Court.

Soon a different story would emerge.

'No,' said Cole, 'I spotted him up the corner and picked him up.'

'No, he was never in the house,' said Chamberlain.

'Now, Mr Chamberlain, you say that your dog found the box with the knife and overalls,' asked Constable Barry McIntosh.

'That's right.'

'So you never saw Mr Keogh.'

'That's right.'

'Mr Chamberlain, I'd suggest you try to remember exactly what happened that morning. It seems Mr Keogh has a different account of events.'

'Look, I'm worried sick about this. All right, he was in the house. But I didn't want him there and knew nothing about the box and the knife till the dog pulled it out. I got him out as fast as I could. Vick was a friend of ours.'

Although Cole admitted to picking Keogh up in the street, her evidence, too, bore the stench of complicity. Eventually she would emerge as a witness for the defence.

Kevin Chamberlain didn't drink at the Junction Hotel. He'd met Keogh when the taciturn bloke with the darting eyes joined his school of drinkers at the Grandview Hotel in 1981. Later they drank together at the Commercial. It was here that Vicki met him. The moment she stepped through the doors one night in late 1982, looking for her barmaid friend, Kerrie, Keogh was on the prowl. For the young barmaid—daughter of Lorna Cleary's close friend and neighbour, Gloria Tyler—it was to be a dubious honour. Born only days apart, Vicki and Kerrie enjoyed an enduring friendship until Keogh drove a wedge through it.

Perched at the bar, he gave not a hint that a few blocks north at 48 Fyffe Street, Northcote, yet another woman and her de facto husband were engaged in heated debate about him. According to the woman's ten-year-old daughter and her girlfriend, Keogh had fondled their breasts and run his hand up their legs. On 20 November 1982, he was convicted of sexual assault, and sentenced to two years gaol. As always, he appealed. With this appeal, and another pending against a 20-day gaol conviction for drink-driving, Keogh knew it was going to be difficult to hide the charges. As the Appeal approached, he chose to bring Vicki into his confidence. Soon, she would tell people he didn't do it. Not once did she tell her family.

Apart from Keogh's low-life mates, every person who met Vicki and Keogh together wondered how he'd manage to win her. Janet Benstead, a technical assistant colleague of Vicki's in the microbiology laboratory at Melbourne University, was one friend who never understood the attraction. Brought up in a comfortable family in Waverley, Janet thought him scary, dark and brooding, completely at odds with her free-spirited, sublimely generous friend.

'Janet, Vicki's friend is the only person you've brought into this house I haven't liked,' her father had remarked after her 21st birthday in June 1985. Janet didn't see the tattoos on Keogh's arms. She didn't need to. None of the girls with whom Vicki worked felt comfortable in his company. They sensed that deep down he was at war with them. When Janet's mother rang her in Queensland two years later with the news that Vicki had been killed, she didn't need to name the killer.

'Peter Keogh...' she replied without so much as a prompt.

When I unearthed the views of parole officer Margaret Hobbs, and psychiatrist Thomas Oldtree Clark, I was no longer surprised that Vicki fell for Keogh's lies. In April 1983 Clark would write, 'I frankly find it difficult knowing him not to believe his story'.

Unlike Clark and Hobbs, my sister had no idea Keogh had been convicted in 1976 for the sexual assault of a nine-year-old girl. Yet not even this could dissuade Dr Clark from accepting Keogh's claim that he'd done nothing wrong to the girls: 'He says he has had body contact with these children whilst playing sport or in everyday activities...' With Hobbs and Clark on side, Keogh would embellish his victim's narrative until Vicki believed everything he said.

murder changes everything   75

Vicki and Kerrie didn't know about a series of letters written by professionals over the preceding years which had cast a pall of doubt over the man now in their company. As a parole officer specialising in treating sex offenders, Margaret Hobbs had first met Keogh in 1975 after the Richmond outrage. Jim Goulding, who had pioneered a distinctive brand of psychotherapy and regarded Hobbs as one of his best pupils, never forgot the damning assessment of Keogh she delivered to him in June 1980.

'Margaret was brilliant. She understood these deviates. She said he was no good,' he told me twenty years later. It was so at odds with the glowing endorsement Hobbs had given Keogh in a document dated April 1983 I just couldn't bring myself to tell Goulding what I knew.

While Keogh was conducting a reign of terror against his estranged girlfriend, Judy McNulty, Hobbs was beginning to like what she heard from the tattooed man in her rooms in Box Hill. So convinced was she by his intentions, throughout 1981 she implored McNulty to bury her misgivings and accept Peter Keogh's desire to expunge the demons forged in childhood trauma.

'I loved him so much I got this tattoo,' he told Hobbs, pointing to the rose and cross with the words 'Dear father'. Today, Judy McNulty's sisters are as mystified by Hobbs' relationship with Keogh as they were then.

In the inner circle, Keogh ridiculed Hobbs' myopia.

'She thinks she understands me but I've got her wrapped around me little finger,' he told Lorna Cleary when she asked about Hobbs.

Keogh couldn't resist the chance to display some bravado. It was also part of a game. By bringing his girlfriend's mother into his confidence, he gave the impression he was honest and open and had nothing to hide.

As with almost everything Keogh did, there was always that flicker of truth. He did have her wrapped around his finger. But she knew things that might bury him if they were divulged. And she had said things about him to others that would have enraged him. The problem was he turned the ignition before I found the Hobbs letters that revealed just what a danger this man posed to women.

Lorna Cleary always wondered about Keogh's relationship with Hobbs, but had no idea what really brought the pair together. The three-month sentence for drink-driving dished out on 19 November 1982 in the Northcote Magistrate's Court was no secret. What wasn't revealed to Lorna was that four days earlier in the same court he'd copped a minimum of eighteen months gaol for the sexual assault on the girls. It wasn't something Vicki could easily tell her mother. And anyway, he'd said he was innocent. And so did the Appeal Court.

'Living with you and Vicki, is he? Oh, oh, that should be all right,' Hobbs remarked with a stutter, when my sister Donna announced during a visit in 1983 that she and Vicki were sharing a house with Keogh. At Keogh's recommendation, Donna had sought Hobbs' advice on a personal matter. Hobbs didn't breathe a word about Keogh's past or the grave reservations she'd expressed between 1976 and 1980 about his attitude to women. Hobbs had treated Keogh when he was on a rampage. More than anyone she should have known the dangers Vicki faced.

So why did she not tell all she knew? And what might she have said if Donna had recounted the story of Keogh appearing at the end of her bed in the dead of night? 'Oh, yes, he told me that. He sleepwalks sometimes,' Vicki had explained when Donna nervously described what had happened. There were just so many signs. All we needed was for someone to translate them.

The relationship between Hobbs and Keogh was the furthest thing from Vicki's mind as she waited for the results of a series of tests in March 1983. As he climbed the St Vincent's Hospital steps, Keogh remembered the night in 1963 when he'd arrived in an ambulance after a torrid battle at Preston Station.

'I was here once. Hurt my knees playing when I was a kid,' he'd told Vicki. Later, in the heat of the separation, he would relate the real story about his stay at St Vincent's.

When I visited her at the hospital after football training, I experienced my one and only sighting of the mob. Gathered around her bed was a collection of cronies who skylarked with the young girl as if they owned her. I noticed her embarrassment and wondered what it all meant. Like a child kidnapped by a fanatical religious sect, Vicki needed to be rescued.

'Who is this mob?' I asked Mum the next day. I sensed it did not bode well. Mum agreed but had no solution. Little did I know that Peter Keogh had begun moving his belongings into the spare room in the house that Vicki shared with Kerrie Tyler. A short while later, he and Vicki would be an item. In the early days, Vicki hid the relationship from her family.

Amazed by his luck, Keogh showered Vicki with flowers and attention, in the hope that his young partner wouldn't tire of him. Older men, Vicki told her sister, Donna, didn't need a woman with the beauty of the Madonna in their bed, and they didn't notice if a girl's skin had less than a porcelain finish. For now, the nagging insecurities were subsumed in a seemingly uncomplicated relationship. Soon it would all change.

Dad had never been happy about the relationship, but whenever he expressed his reservations his daughter would have nothing of it. So for now, everyone held their peace and a mob of no-hopers became a constant in my sister's life. And although I was mystified by her choice and couldn't stand the thought of him being part of my family, I said nothing.

I never thought to ask Harold Martin what he knew about the bloke sharing a house with Vicki. On the football field, Martin was the quintessential big bad man. He'd been an institution with Preston in the old VFA before transferring to Coburg as coach in 1982. It was to be yet another coincidence in the drama that was unfolding around me.

In a football jumper, Martin was a fierce man who took on all comers. In the 1978 VFA grand final against Prahran, he'd slammed a pounding left and right combination into the head of former Kangaroos legend, Sam Kekovich. Slammin' Sam's knees buckled, and he swore that Martin was one of the toughest blokes going around. It remains one of the most talked-about moments in Martin's eventful football history. Away from football, Harold was a teacher of intellectually impaired children. In the late seventies, he'd taken a teaching position at Pentridge Prison, where he was to become a confidant of Peter Lawless.

Harold Martin had grown up in Thornbury. His brother Tommy, smaller but thickset, with black curly hair, was no slouch either. They were regulars at the Junction Hotel. In the company of another local institution, Arthur Pugh, they regularly crossed the path of some of the hard men of the north. After a game against Coburg at Preston in 1981, a bloke from the Coburg Housing Commission taunted him, his wife and brother Tommy with a loaded gun. In the absence of the pistol, Harold would have sat the bloke on his arse. When Keogh went to Pentridge for drink-driving in 1983, he spotted Martin but never identified himself. The bloke with the gun did. 'Could have knocked ya that day, Harold,' he said as the big bloke wandered by.

Despite my friendship with Martin, Keogh's name never found its way into our conversation. A cunning criminal Keogh had too much to hide to risk allowing me a glimpse of his life. I first saw him when I called in to see Vicki at their place in Beauchamp Street, Preston, one night in late 1983 on my way to a football presentation at the Junction Hotel. He nodded, but remained inconspicuous.

'Like a cat on a hot tin roof, that bloke,' I'd remarked to my wife. In yet another remarkable irony, the only time I ever ventured into the Junction had come after that brief meeting with him in the house he shared with my sister. It was one more signpost to the tragedy that lay ahead.

Sadly, none of us read those signposts until it was too late. Neither Vicki nor her girlfriend, Kerrie, was privy to the accusations being thrown at Keogh when he moved in with them in 1983. It was no surprise that he didn't like Vicki being in his company at the Commercial Hotel, or that Kerrie would soon leave the house. Wiser on such matters than Vicki, she sensed trouble.

'Keogh, isn't it? My missus reckons you raped her and put her up the duff before I met her,' an agitated meat worker had told Keogh when he spotted him in the lounge at the Commercial Hotel in early 1983. 'Bullshit. Nothin' to do with me, mate,' Keogh had replied, stubbing his cigarette butt in the drip tray and nervously lifting the stubbie of Vic Bitter to his lips. Kevin Chamberlain had looked on, waiting for the next move. 'Went to water,' he would tell me in 2001.

It was not the first time Chamberlain had heard a bizarre allegation against his drinking mate. Only a couple of months earlier, Keogh had scrambled from the poolroom at the Curry Family Hotel in Collingwood, with a woman in pursuit. 'You, ya fucking child molester bastard. What are you doing here?' she screamed.

'Jesus, why didn't you tell me you were going there,' Keogh had said when Chamberlain joined him in the car, where he'd taken refuge from the plump 40-year-old woman howling for his blood.

The Junction Hotel was one place Keogh did feel at home. Like a dog to a bone, he headed there the minute the Loddon Prison gates closed behind him in July 1991. Here he made small talk with the White brothers, Jim 'the Pom' Pentelow and a bloke known as Billy.

'Don't trust him, Julie I'm telling you, he killed that woman,' Billy had told Julie McAllister.

'I know all about that. It was Phil Cleary's sister. It was an accident. He was found not guilty,' she explained. Although Billy was adamant she shouldn't go near Keogh, and kept muttering about him having 'killed that woman' the killer had already spun his tale past Julie. For now she believed him.

After the arson in Tyers, whenever I drove past the Junction Hotel I'd give it the once-over in case I might spot him. I never did. I imagined him there on a stool, rolling a fag and regaling some loser with his triumphs.

The night he and his mate set upon a hapless 'wog', Peter Mascia, and the epic with the copper on the Preston Railway Station were the crowning glories. 'Don't fight wogs. They'd stick a knife in your guts as soon as look at ya,' he'd told a copper after bashing Mascia at 152 Station Street, up the road from Tom Pateras' fish and chip shop.

Whatever the sense of solidarity manifest in the Rubber Workers Union of his father, racism wasn't yet expunged from the thinking of these boys. Keogh didn't like immigrants. He was the rock-solid embodiment of White Australia. The 'wog' Mascia was unprepared and outnumbered when Keogh slammed a billiard cue over his head then stuck the boots in at the New Australian Pool Room in October 1972, sometime after midnight

When off-duty cop Constable Dennis Harrison mustered the courage to suggest Keogh put down the billiard cue, he was confronted with the full-strength thug. With his smart-arse sidekick, Ted in tow, Keogh reminded Harrison who was the boss. 'Say nothin', that's what my lawyer, Bob Vernon, told me. He'll get me off this,' Keogh quipped to his mate as they waited for the cops to burst through the door.

'Whatever you say, sir. I didn't hit anyone with a billiard cue, only with my fists, sir, in a fair fight,' said Ted.

'Did Peter Keogh?'

'No, sir, I never seen Peter hit anyone with a billiard cue,' his mate told Constable Gavan O'Neill.

The boys loved the ambiguous, 'yes sir, no sir,' rejoinder when dealing with the cops. There'd be no incriminating statements from the boy Keogh. If his mate from McLachlan Street had shut his mouth after the rape down the road, they might have beaten the charges.

'This one's for you, Bellesini,' he surely thought as he belted the cue over Peter Mascia's head and slammed the boots into his body. Keogh never forgot that a bloke with a wog name had brought him down a decade earlier.

Constable Frank Bellesini was nearby in the Divvy van on the night of Saturday 21 September 1963 when he got word that one of the locals was on the warpath at Northcote Station.

'Looking for a dark-haired teenager in a white jumper. Suspect is drunk and dangerous. Has boarded the train at Northcote headed for Preston Station,' came the message.

'Will intercept, over and out,' he replied, planting the foot.

The wail of the siren in Cramer Street was nothing new, but what followed added some preliminary excitement for the bodgie mob heading for the dance at the Town Hall. The appearance of the paddy wagon was the cue for a dramatic sequence of events.

'The coppers are after you!' yelled Larry, his mate from Plant Street, when he caught sight of the men in blue.

'Jesus,' thought the young Bellesini when the belligerent fifteen-year-old scaled the small fence and began his charge.

'There's the fuckin' copper bastards. I'll kill the cunts,' screamed Keogh through cupped hands, before drawing a knife from his belt.

Prior to boarding the train at Northcote, Keogh had plunged his spinning head in a bucket of water. An unfruitful crack at erasing the effects of the sherry he'd downed over the course of the previous hour and a half, it only sharpened his aggression. All things being equal, a round of mayhem at the Preston Town Hall looked a monte.

'Have you got a ticket?' asked porter John Morley.

'I'm not buying a fuckin' ticket,' he replied, placing his fingers around the handle of the knife wedged in his belt.

'Look, if you don't get one here they'll want one at the next station. And anyway you're not allowed on without a ticket.'

'I'm not buying a fuckin' ticket,' he repeated, before drawing his weapon.

Undaunted, Morley grabbed the boy's wrist and told him to drop the knife.

'Come on, Pete, the train's coming,' cried Larry as his belligerent mate grappled with the railway porter. Weakened by the sherry and surprised by Morley's determination, Keogh couldn't dictate the outcome of this skirmish. When the knife hit the concrete, Morley stuck out a foot in a vain attempt to send it onto the lines. Suddenly, Keogh was on the train and Larry had the knife in his hand. As the rattler headed for Preston, Morley eyed the blood on his hand and wondered whether he'd see the young bloke with the strange eyes again.

Before the porter's appearance on the Northcote Station platform, Keogh offered a snapshot of the thoughts that lay in his twisted mind. 'Get ya fuckin' clothes off,' he had said, pressing the blade against a young woman's stomach.

Was this a motif in the Keogh household? The Rubber Workers were a union that called a spade a spade and had little time for theory or fancy ideas. Was this the way of his father, John Thomas Keogh?

Morley had only his bare hands when he took on the bully. Constable Bellesini was a different matter. He had a .32 colt revolver in his holster when he felt the blade slide across his hand. This bloke means business, he thought. As he stepped back, the drunken youth followed. There was only one solution. The baton had to give way to the pistol.

As the first shot skidded between Keogh's legs, a burst of sparks danced along the track sending frightened commuters in all directions. Fuelled by alcohol and rage, the rogue boy was unmoved. Down he went in a screaming heap when the next slug ground into the flesh and bone around his left knee joint. But in an instant he was on his feet again, the knife flashing in his wonky hands. The cop with the gun never considered planting one in his body. 'No competition, this one,' he thought as he took aim and sent a second slug into the boy's right knee. Keogh had been kneecapped. As Bellesini and Constable Alec Wallace bundled Keogh into the Divvy van, Larry and his mates delivered some menacing assessments of the battle.

Keogh's mates didn't step forward to reclaim their comrade. Unlike the legendary Kelly girls under the Warby Ranges in June 1880, all Keogh's mob could rescue was a lying, small-time suburban thug. The Kelly girls, at least, had a couple of brothers about whom to be proud. With the damp morning mist subdued by the pungent odour of smoke and death across the line from the Glenrowan Railway Station, Maggie and Kate Kelly showed what courage really was. No uniformed 'trap' was going to confiscate the bodies of young Dan Kelly and his mate Steve Hart.

For all his sins, Ned Kelly had gone to war because a local copper had assaulted his sister. In contrast, Peter Keogh, writhing on the bitumen, a useless knife by his side, was a pathetic figure. He desperately wanted to be someone. Mohammed Ali, even Brian Kane or a serious standover man would do. But God had conspired against him. The boy from Westgarth was no Kelly from Greta. The Irish ancestry and hatred of coppers aside, the two men had nothing in common. Keogh was a coward.

In the Preston lock-up, the wounded boy was full of bravado and showed no intention of moral surrender. 'My uncle's a gunnie, he'll fix ya, ya fuckin' copper bastard. You'll be dead in forty-eight hours,' he roared as the men of law dropped him onto a canvas stretcher and radioed for an ambulance to take him to St Vincent's Hospital. 'Look at my tats. Must be tough, hey!' he shouted. It was the cry of a pathetic and insecure boy. It was different when they ripped the armour from the delirious and bleeding Ned Kelly. The bushranger accepted his defeat. He'd made his point and didn't need to convince anyone he was tough or courageous. Even the traps knew that.

Keogh had dispensed with the bravado by the time Dr John Chew ran a gentle hand over his wounds. Sometime after 9 pm the doctor decided the boy's right leg would need to be set in plaster. It was a bad night for Keogh. Winged by a 'wog' he was now about to be repaired by an Oriental. Still he'd have been amused to hear Chew's prognosis.

'The injuries sustained would not cause any further deterioration of the rational mental processes of the patient,' Chew had advised the Crown Solicitor in a brief, neat, handwritten letter. Had the Constable fired less true, the irony of those words would never have troubled anyone.

'I was young and compassionate but, in any case, it didn't improve his humour,' Bellesini caustically would explain many years later.

Following a police interview at St Vincent's the next day, Senior Detective D B Ritter handed fifteen-year-old Peter Keogh a statement and asked him to read it aloud. The three-page account of events on the Epping line the night before concluded with the words:

> I didn't even know that I was injured until the police were putting me in the divvy van then I noticed my knee hurt. I'm sorry for any trouble I caused or if I have hurt anyone. I will definitely give the grog away.

Underneath, in tortuously constructed capital letters, Keogh had scratched:

I HAVE READ THIS ALOUD IT IS ALL TRUE Peter Keogh 22-9-63

'Need a hundred quid to get me out on bail, Mum,' the son had told his mother. It was a lot of money for a widowed mother of six. As always, she found it. Whether the humiliating shooting at Preston and the damage to his knees were the catalyst for the war Peter Keogh carried on over the next 40 years is something about which I'll never be sure. Maybe there was another story? Even before Bellesini banged three slugs into his knees, Keogh was a dark spot on the Merri Creek landscape.

Sexual assault, bullying and theft had become his modus operandi long before the cop pointed his pistol. Even before his invalid father died, the female body was something for Keogh to rough up. It was as if he always seemed destined for a bad end.

The years immediately before and after her husband's death were gruelling for Mildred Keogh. Forced to take outside work to hold the family together, Millie must have wondered what had befallen her. In the space of a year she'd lost her husband and her mother, and two sons were already well-known to the local police. Moreover, no sooner was one son in trouble with the law than her youngest was staring down an attempted murder on a policeman. Things couldn't have been worse.

To rub salt into her wounds, professionals seemed to be white-anting Millie's frantic attempts to halt the slide. Parole officer K J O'Sullivan had a tale of strange import for the court. O'Sullivan had been called by Bob Vernon to produce a report that might persuade Justice Monahan to deal gently with his client after he waved his knife at Constable Bellesini. In a Children's Court psychiatric report tended in 1960, O'Sullivan found the right set of words:

> Mother is an overpowering woman who is very possessive and keeps far too rigid a watch on Peter. She nags a great deal and, in her own words, 'is always on his back.' Peter has little peace. Mother feels rather sorry for herself, both because of her recent loss (of her husband) and also because of her present illness (hernia) and appears rather skilled in manipulating everybody in her environment and getting them to do the things she wants. However, mother has insights into her attitudes, and is willing to co-operate with us.

Written when her youngest son was on a rampage across Northcote and his close mate had gone down for rape, it was typical of the welfare apologists enlisted to study young Keogh. Just what O'Sullivan believed Mrs Keogh should have done with her son remains unclear. It wasn't hard to imagine the little liar buttering up some shrink. It would be his signature sign for the rest of his life.

During the rape trial that rocked McLachlan Street in 1960, Justice Adam had bemoaned the lack of order in the lives of the teeming uneducated masses along High Street. His message was simple. Families must keep their daughters off the street at night, lest they tempt men like the 'Fairfield rapists'. Now, having followed his instructions, the mother of a boy who'd rape a girl as soon as look at her was being ridiculed for keeping an eagle eye on a wayward son.

So often, Peter Keogh and the boys of his milieu were freed of any need to take responsibility for their brutal conquest of women. Such were the forms of cross-examination allowed under the rape laws of the time it was a brave woman who 'cried rape'. The assault behind Tom Pateras' shop, and the trial, were typical. Fortunately for Jean, the cultural prejudice that resulted in many women being blamed for rape didn't win the day. But Keogh understood the message. Women were to blame. That was the lesson Keogh learnt when the girl from Heidelberg was dragged before the men of propriety. The criminal justice system was a willing and culpable ally in Keogh's thirst for terror. While the serial bully laughed at them, a stream of interlopers excused his violence.

When Mildred Keogh died, her family delivered a story at odds with the utterances of the professionals:

> A wonderful mother who devoted her life and her love to the whole family. You will be deeply missed and always loved.
>
> Always loving, thoughtful and kind.
>
> Dear one, my pleasure was having known you
> You will always have a special place in my life.

I can find no police records in relation to the death of a boarder in the bungalow at 31 McLachlan Street in the years immediately after John Keogh's death. 'I killed him. It was an accident, but he'd been bashing us,' Keogh had told Lorna Cleary in 1984. As was always the case when the killer needed sympathy, the trademark tears welled in those dangerous eyes. Lorna Cleary had no idea of the history of systematic violence that lay behind the feigned sorrow.

Nor did she know that Keogh's brother, Barry, had related this and more sinister tales to Judy McNulty's distressed sister following her 1980 rape. So was it true that Keogh killed a man? Although their sister Jenny told me it never happened, why did Peter Keogh and his brother so freely tell people about the event. It remains a mystery. If Barry Keogh could tell Judy's sister that his brother was dangerous, why couldn't he ring the Coburg Football Club and tell me?

Brian Watson, a bloke who'd heard all the stories, was under no illusion as to what drove Keogh. A tallish, fidgety redhead, Watson was wary of Keogh's propensity for violence. But he and Keogh shared a past and some secret predilections. Rohypnol, the date drug, was their stock in trade. In the weeks leading up to her death, Watson had been at the wheel, laughing as they eyed Vicki's Ford Falcon a short distance ahead.

'Pull up alongside the bitch,' Keogh had ordered, as she brought the large square car to a halt at the traffic lights on the intersection of Bell Street and Plenty Road, Preston.

Driving to the kindergarten—a job that had been her dream—was to become a nightmare for Vicki. In September 1986 she'd seen an advertisement in the *Age* for a kinder assistant at the centre and excitedly sent off an application.

> I believe that I have an honest and cheerful disposition and enthusiasm, especially where children are concerned because I have been associated with them since the age of twelve through my own family environment and because I find their company both enjoyable and rewarding.

When the news came through that she'd been successful, she was over the moon. There was no going back, and soon Keogh would be out of her life. From the beginning she loved her new job and everyone loved her. But instead of 1987 being a year of joy for Vicki, Keogh and his mates ruined it.

'It was so frightening,' she told co-worker Pam O'Grady, before breaking into a stream of hysterical utterances one day at the sink. The stark revelation to O'Grady that the police knew Keogh because of a shooting convinced her friend of the danger.

Whether Vicki imagined the fate he planned for her I'll never be sure. Why, two months before she died, did she tell our youngest sister, Lizzie, that she could have her belongings if anything happened to her? After the separation in May 1987, Vicki was a woman under siege. The man who stared contemptuously through the passenger window of Watson's car should have been dealt with. Had Vicki gone to the police, it would have been the same old story. There was only one solution. My brother Perry and I lived nearby and could easily have disposed of Keogh, Watson and Freake. It remains our greatest regret.

It's hard to explain how much it hurts to know what the three dead cowards—Freake, Watson and Keogh—did to our sister. Their deaths haven't erased the pain. When Keogh was led down the corridor within reach of us at the Committal, I saw first-hand the depth of a brother's anger.

'Come on, Perry,' I said, throwing my arms around him as he shaped to hit the killer. Keogh said nothing. He knew he was safe and that an attack would only enhance his victim status and his claim to need protection. My brother would literally have killed him. Having to restrain him and suppress my own desire for retribution was one of the hardest things I've ever had to do. Had Vicki told us in June 1987 what she told O'Grady and Fabian Gatt, there would have been no such restraint.

Fabian Gatt lived across the road from the kinder. During work breaks, Vicki would head for the safety of her house. From the upstairs room of number 42 Cameron Street, she'd peer through the curtains for a sign that the stalker might be on the prowl. On a gloomy afternoon in June, they eyed Keogh lurking alongside a tree outside the front gate to the kinder.

'Look at him ducking his head. He's a bad man, Fabian. They think I'm just putting it on at the kinder. If only they knew,' she told her gently-spoken friend.

'Do you want a lift home?' asked Fabian.

'No, my car's over there,' replied Vicki, pointing to the carpark where she'd eventually meet her death. Fabian Gatt loved the vivacious teacher of her children. She was genuinely worried about Vicki, and wondered whether the kindergarten authorities understood Vicki's fear.

In the privacy of number 42, Fabian and Vicki spoke intimately about their lives. Before long, Fabian came to understand how much Vicki wanted to escape Keogh. 'He'd kill you as soon as look at you,' Vicki had said one day, when Fabian announced that she'd go and speak to the man hiding near the kinder.

'Really, so you wouldn't consider going back?' asked Fabian.

'I hate him. I'd never go back. He's disturbed and sexually depraved,' replied Vicki.

The truth was Keogh couldn't get his penis up and he had a vicious streak. Whether due to alcohol, or a subliminal dislike of women, the bloke now terrorising my sister was unhinged. Like Judy McNulty before her, Vicki had tried to help him. 'He needs me,' she had told Fabian in the early days, but by June 1987 it was well and truly over. My sister was never going back.

The day Keogh struck, Fabian was engrossed in her children only twenty metres away in her mock Spanish-style house. She didn't hear a thing or see the man in yellow overalls in the driveway next door at number 40. Deep inside number 32 Cameron Street, young John Carfi heard the screams. So too did Maria Seirlis and her children next door at number 30A. As the chaos took hold, Maria and her son rushed to the bay window in time to see the blood-stained knife glistening in the sunshine. Oblivious to the struggles of her friend, Fabian could only lament the loss.

'The world lost a beautiful, loving teacher and I lost a friend,' she said.

Keogh's appearances at the kindergarten after the separation and the phone calls that left Vicki in tears created confusion for director, Maree Matthews-Jessop, and her staff. Maree had attended Mercy Convent, Coburg with Vicki and was surprised by her choice of companion. Dealing with a suburban thug was not her forte. 'I was scared,' she told the persistent defence barrister, John Champion. Although the evidence was unequivocal that, on one occasion in June, Keogh had forced open the door and demanded to see Vicki, Champion had a job to do. The nervous director had to be transformed into a hostile witness.

'You didn't like him, did you?' he asked.

'Tell him you thought he was a fucking lovely bloke who wouldn't have done anything wrong if you and Vicki and every other woman in the world just let him have his way,' I wanted to bark from our little enclave against the courtroom wall. More importantly, I wanted the prosecutor to challenge the appropriateness of the question. In pre-trial discussion, Justice Hampel had made it clear what he thought.

'Nothing unusual about the defendant wanting to see the girl and being angry when he can't,' he assured Champion when the barrister suggested the kindergarten director's evidence might be prejudicial.

Maree Matthews-Jessop was the most nervous witness to take the stand. Fair-haired, quietly spoken and exceedingly proper, she attended without notes or specific records of Keogh's visits. By the end of her moment in the box, there was so much confusion as to when Keogh had been at the kinder even the judge wanted an explanation. Fractured by Vicki's death and the grim realisation that Keogh's appearances at the kinder had been a prelude to murder, Maree did her time in the box very hard. She was fodder for Champion's cause. But what did it matter if she couldn't specify the exact days, I thought. Sadly, it was all part of blaming someone else. A dead girl who left a dangerous man, and a devastated young kindergarten director were on trial. That's how the blokes liked it.

Although Keogh's handful of appearances at the kinder and his numerous phone calls created anxiety and tears, nothing apart from screening his calls was done to counter him. A community of women was no answer to Keogh. Instead of putting him under the spotlight and calling the police or the family, management asked that their employee resolve it. Family violence and stalking had yet to find its way into enlightened public discourse.

'You'll need to sort it out, Vicki. We can't have this man coming to the kinder like this. The parents will start talking. Maybe you should take a few days off,' Vicki was told. Pride and confusion conspired against Vicki's challenging the orthodoxy. On a mild, warm Wednesday in late August 1987, hindsight would come flooding across Cameron Street, leaving all of us in its wake.

The footsteps of Peter Keogh are dotted all over page 30 of the Melways street directory. The journey that separated him from the ordinary man about whom Justice George Hampel spoke in the Supreme Court began alongside the Merri Creek. From the single-fronted weatherboard at 31 McLachlan Street, Northcote, he meandered back and forth across High Street and the Epping railway line, leaving his mark like a dog pissing on a tree. As coincidence would have it, Lorna Cleary had never been far away.

In August 1945, at age twelve, my mother waited under a marquee at Camp Pell for her POW father to re-enter civilian life. Fractured by the trauma of war and an absence of love in the eyes of his 27-year-old-wife, Gladys, he would soon descend into alcoholism. While the soporific plonk eased Ted's pain in a railway cutting south of the Brunswick Baths, a short distance away the one-time military camp swelled with the displaced homeless of the old working-class. Two years and six months after young Lorna left Camp Pell with her troubled father, Mildred Keogh gave birth to a son, Peter, in adjoining Carlton. One day that boy would tell an arresting copper he'd been born at Camp Pell.

Only six years before Peter Keogh entered the world, an American GI covered in yellow clay entered the toilet block of the 52nd Signal Battalion at Camp Pell. It was 8.30 pm on the night of 18 May 1942 when a fellow GI spotted the mud-spattered Private Eddie Leonski. Later he would describe him as being in a 'sort of daze'. Leonski had just murdered Gladys Hosking, the third and last of his Australian victims. Before he was executed, Leonski would describe that night.

> The next morning I awoke and saw the muddy clothes. I thought to myself, 'My God, where have I been? What have I done?' I then got up and washed the muddy clothes.

'What have I done?' One day Peter Keogh would utter a set of words identical to those used by the woman hater, Eddie Leonski. As we drove home from the Royal Melbourne Hospital after Vicki's murder we passed the very spot where, as a child, I heard my father say, 'That's where Leonski killed the woman. He was mad.' No one ever imagines a mad killer will find his way into their life.

The absence of a father, some said, made Keogh a killer. It only made our mother all the wiser. During the war, Mum and her mother would catch the tram into the city then board another tram for Richmond where Gladys' grandmother, Harriet Roberts, lived. Enveloped with smog and beset with misery, Richmond did its name, Struggletown, proud. A tight-knit community brought together by poverty and a labyrinth of thoroughfares so narrow that neighbours could carry on a conversation across the street without leaving the front fence, Richmond was a place to escape.

When ten-year-old Lorna rounded the corner and knocked on the door of the neat little terrace at the southern end of Bunting Street, she could never have imagined that Peter Keogh would one day put his stamp on a house only 100 metres north of her grandmother's home.

Marilyn Reeves and her sons had fled to 30 Bunting Street while her de facto was doing time for the kidnap and sexual assault of a neighbour's nine-year-old daughter. Upon his release on 6 September 1977, Keogh went in search of his recalcitrant ex. As always, parole officer, Margaret Hobbs, and a circle of female consultant psychiatrists had gathered around him. The cold harsh world would again be blamed for the rapist's struggle through life.

'Peter Keogh's now a supervisor with a local council. I've advised him to seek legal advice regarding supervised access to the children,' Dr Lillian Cameron would write on 6 June 1978.

Three weeks later she said he was managing well, seeing his son covertly and not drinking. Just as his father gilded the lily when he told his family he was an engineer, so his son lied when he told Cameron he was a supervisor. Dr Cameron's letter a few weeks later confirms how educated professionals fell for the deceitful Keogh's three-card trick.

Dear Mrs Hobbs

Mr Keogh is maintaining a good remission. He is not drinking. He sees his son Damien, seven years, at weekends. His wife has threatened the boys with absolute rejection if they see their father. The boys find it difficult to relate to the Turkish de facto husband of his wife so their desire to see Mr Keogh is understandable.

Unfortunately Mr Keogh has lost his job through an informer but seems confident that he will find another.

I am seeing him on a monthly basis at present.

He seems to be continuing to behave in a stable manner and is not unduly depressed.

Lillian Cameron

A Turk, an informer, and a callous ex-wife—all had brought pain to the poor convicted child rapist and Aussie pervert, Peter Keogh. The thought of the little racist there on the couch at Parliament Place at the taxpayer's expense, spinning Cameron a yarn, is nauseating. The truth, as Dr W C Canning saw it, was quite different. Canning had seen Keogh in September of 1977.

Dear Mrs Hobbs

Although he has marked guilt feelings about his past behaviour most of his problems, as I see them, are socially determined and at the present time I see little room for manoeuvre. He claims to have changed but time is the best measure of his ability to withstand the pressures of everyday life. There is little hope of reconciliation with his wife, if any and it would appear that the whole family have turned against him although I suspect that this is not a sudden decision on their part.

I think the most you can do is to support him and I have agreed to see him as and when is necessary, according to his mental state. I think at the present time there is very little risk of self-harm and indeed he seemed to be enjoying himself when I observed him at the racetrack on Saturday afternoon! I have not given him another appointment and I will rely upon your judgement as to when I should see him again.

Dr Canning

Keogh quickly realised that Canning was not some bloke to be run around the finger in the manner of parole officer Hobbs. She genuinely cared about rehabilitating Keogh, but had been wooed by his lies. Canning, by contrast, left no one in any doubt as to the source of Keogh's problems.

That Keogh's problems were 'socially determined', was as close as anyone came to fingering him. It was as simple as that. He was a nasty, cunning bloke with a nihilistic bent that knew no bounds. Keogh didn't continue to see Canning. He preferred the soothing words of Lillian Cameron.

While he sat in Lillian Cameron's rooms, relaying a tearful tale of life's hard knocks, Peter Keogh was at war with Marilyn Reeves. Until his parole period expired on 13 May 1978, the terror had to be discreet. Threats on the phone, covert stalking and intimidation were the favoured methods. Then, once the parole expired, the real terror came. When Reeves returned home to find a shotgun had been fired through her front door, her house trashed and her TV gone, she knew her worst fears had arrived.

'I need protection. He's violent and dangerous and has stolen my property,' she told the police. Not even a restraining order could stop him confronting Reeves outside her house and threatening mayhem. Listed to face unlawful assault and theft charges at Prahran Court on 18 September, Keogh received a reprieve. 'Can't pin anything on him, Mrs Reeves. He's saying someone has set him up. We've decided to drop the charges,' said the police.

The unconstrained Peter Keogh who ransacked Reeves' house was a far cry from the man who popped a few pills in a fake, sympathy grabbing suicide attempt while on bail for the kidnap of the little girl in Richmond. So, too, was he nothing like the bloke who had Hobbs nodding in approval in September 1978 when he said he'd avoided contact with his wife and family because of how they might feel about him.

Lunging at a copper with a knife was a noble act in the inner suburban working-class maelstrom. The abduction and sexual assault of a nine-year-old girl in the company of his own children set Keogh apart from the anti-authority larrikin. Keogh didn't build networks and acquire status in Pentridge. He was a protected prisoner. What had become of the ten-year-old-boy who rolled cigarettes for his invalid father at 31 McLachlan Street? his mother asked. Was he a product of a bullyboy father cast in the image of a rough, and tumble, union? Or was there, as Hobbs wrote, some dark family secrets that drove this man?

History shows that Keogh's antecedents were either non-committal or luckless where marriage was concerned. Keogh's Irish Catholic grandfather, John, and his own father, John Thomas, were both closing in on fifty when they remarried and had children. Neither would emerge as a substantial father figure in the home. On his mother's side, the patterns were similar

Shortly after Keogh's mother was born in September 1917, her Presbyterian father, Irving Saddington, departed for greener pastures leaving wife Lillian with two young daughters. By 1922, Lillian Saddington had tied the knot with a new man, to whom she immediately bore a daughter. In 1926, her former husband followed suit. Irving Saddington was thirty-five years of age when his twenty-year-old bride presented him with a baby boy. They'd been married seven months.

Whether the constant fracturing of relationships imbued Keogh's world with a lack of intimacy is a moot point. Did the 22-year-old Mildred really love the 47-year-old man she married in a Methodist parsonage in Hawthorn in February 1940, one month before the birth of her first child? Or did it aggravate an already deep neurosis? That Mildred Keogh frequently used sleeping tablets, and the rest of the family called her troublesome son 'it', suggests it wasn't smooth sailing in the house above the creek.

murder changes everything   95

Mildred's older sister, Dulcie, was less than enamoured of her sister's household. 'Jack Keogh was too old, and was more interested in politics than children. And as for Peter, well, he has no compunction about lying his way out of trouble, and will maintain a lie in the face of undeniable evidence to the contrary,' she would tell a parole officer when answers were sought for the shooting at Preston Station in 1963. They were prophetic words from the woman whose husband the wounded, drunken Keogh had named as the 'gunnie uncle' who'd fix up the coppers.

Jack Keogh had an eye for the girls. His first marriage, to Gertrude Griffiths, whom he'd married at St Patrick Cathedral in 1913, ended in divorce. He was living in a flat at 8 Bennett Street, Fitzroy when he happened upon Mildred Saddington. A boot machinist, Mildred lived around the corner from the smooth talking Keogh at 8 Rushall Crescent, Clifton Hill with her mother, stepfather Wallace Green, and two sisters.

As his Irish born father had done, Jack Keogh had managed to pluck a woman more than twenty years his junior. It's hard to believe he would have wanted marriage and more children. A sexual relationship with the young Millie would have been beguiling, but these were difficult economic times and Jack knew the pressures children brought to domestic life. When she fell pregnant, there was no rush to the altar. Maybe that tells a story.

Young and fertile, Mildred presented her husband with a succession of children. By the time he'd reached sixty, Jack Keogh had added six children to the four from his first marriage. Young Peter's arrival in 1948 was followed by difficult times for Jack and his Labor Party. In 1949, Chifley's party would fall to the Bob Menzies Liberal Party. In 1955 the DLP would split the party asunder and, by 1958, thrombosis had transformed a once-proud union man into a bedridden invalid. As the hard yakka of factory work and the pressure of domestic life began to take its toll, life was unravelling in his family.

Jack Keogh was a top tyre builder by the time 25-year-old Harvey Mynott took up a spot on the factory floor at Dunlop's Montague plant up the road from the Port Melbourne Football Ground. It was

February 1957 and the man he came to know as the best A25/15 tyre man in the plant was coming to the end of life. Jack knew the short cuts and was quick to show Mynott how to weave some magic on a spinning drum. Keogh had a vision beyond the hum of the tyre drum in the Number One mill, Montague. He was in the thick of political action when his namesake, Jack Kehoe, made a push for the treasurer-secretary position of the state branch against the popular Mick Kennedy in 1955. The distinguished-looking, grey-haired Keogh always took a union line but, never, said Mynott, did he display the brooding malcontent and aggression that would become a feature of his son's journey through life.

Although Mynott ranked the tyre builder a skilled man above the mob, Keogh never rose to be foreman or managed to escape the factory floor. So why did he list his occupation as engineer when he married the impressionable Mildred? And why did the family repeat the myth when he died? Was it but another illusion fashioned to camouflage the failed aspirations and inadequacies of life in the Keogh home?

Although politics had overshadowed Jack Keogh's love of children, comrades didn't rally around when thrombosis claimed him. Only three death notices, one from his sister and two from the family, appeared in the *Sun* after he died at home on 27 April 1960. So, if the plain-speaking older man in overalls that Mynott admired was no thug, why was his son so disturbed? And why was parole officer Margaret Hobbs moved to write that 'the presence of heavy drinking and aberrant behaviour in other siblings is evidence of a disturbed family life'?

When defence barrister John Champion sought answers for Justice George Hampel, he drew on Keogh's lack of education and the deprivation of his family life. Yet the minute Keogh had been reprieved of murder, it was the loss of a proud and respectable father that was blamed for a son's decline. Was it as simple as this?

'It was terrible. They sent me away while he was dying. When I got back, he was already buried. My mum done the wrong thing,' Peter Keogh would tell Lorna Cleary in the lounge at Beauchamp

Street, Preston in 1983. Although the bloke Vicki had chosen for a mate was thirteen years older and had the look of a loser, Lorna was touched by the sensitivity of the words. Lorna and Ron weren't snobs. It was what was in the heart that mattered. For now, Peter Keogh was welcome. As always in the Cleary household, generosity had again triumphed over petty bourgeois prejudice. I wished it hadn't.

When Keogh left Fitzroy High after his fourteenth birthday in February 1962, he told his mates he wasn't coming back. Most, including the principal, were glad to be rid of him. 'He treats me bad. Won't let me change school. Always on me back,' he'd told his probation officer, Mr Larkin. Larkin never recorded the principal's version of Keogh's early years. Although he should have been entering Form Four in 1962, he'd not yet passed Form I. Children's Court appearances in 1960 and 1961 had fractured his school appearances. At school, Keogh always had money for fags and wasn't much interested in girls. It was war that captured his imagination. War on the unsuspecting and vulnerable stirred his passion.

Not one of his teachers could find a kindly word about the boy with the swept-back hair and poor grasp of language. Fitzroy High was a colourful stage that captured the vicissitudes of a turbulent changing Australia. Here, Greeks and Italians jostled for status and a slice of the life that born-to-rule Aussie battlers claimed as their own. Chris, the sad face of alienated youth; the cool Greek, Jerry; the politically savvy Dennys Martin; Keogh's one-time mate, Ray Quick were all memorable actors in this suburban drama.

Chris was no saint and was to become well known to the police. Quick moved on and settled down, and Martin's ascendancy in the public service proved what could be done with a bit of education and discipline. But Keogh was different. Jackie Young, the teacher whose country-girl wisdom had seen danger in his eyes, knew tragedy waited for someone whose misfortune it was to fall into his trap. It could have been anyone. It happened to be my sister.

'Going nowhere, this bloke,' I thought when I laid eyes on him in Dad's butcher shop in Elizabeth Street, East Coburg in 1985.

'G'day,' I said as he slinked away to the back room where Dad was making sausages. There was no warmth between us and I knew he was wary of me. It was only the second time I'd seen him. Dad had given him some work boning meat. I wasn't happy about it.

'That's Vicki's boyfriend. Don't ask me why. I never picked her as some working-class girl infatuated with tattoos,' I remarked to a friend the moment I left the shop.

One lasting image remains of Peter Keogh. It was 1986 and I was playing-coach of Coburg at the time. As I walked through the social club, I spotted him alone at a table littered with empty glasses. Bleary-eyed, and the victim of an aggressive twitch, he was more than just a bad drunk. While Vicki captivated the crowd with her smile and love, he was a man of turbulent thoughts. I imagined how those empty glasses would have become missiles when his blood boiled. I'd seen blokes like this before. I sensed he was a man at war and knew he and I could never break bread. Privately, Vicki was telling Donna the relationship was over.

By the time the killer entered my life, I'd stepped beyond the geographic and cerebral constraints of that stratum of life in the northern suburbs. I could find nothing romantic about petty crims feasting on the hard-earned cash of other struggling denizens. Nor was the tattooed thug who wanted to punch the first bloke who looked sideways at his sheila, and who called one of Henry Bolte's prefabricated boxes in Reservoir home, my cuppa tea. Vicki had a sensitivity that Peter Keogh would never satisfy. A mixture of bad luck, innocence and insecurity had led her into a relationship with him. But I knew she'd move on.

None of us were aware of how much probation officer Margaret Hobbs knew about Keogh's life. Had she offered but a few words of it, Vicki would be alive today. If we'd known that behind the tats was a convicted sexual predator and a serial woman-hater, we'd never have left Vicki vulnerable to an attack. And had he tried, he'd have been dead long before the carbon monoxide sent him into gentle unconsciousness.

How these memories must have weighed on Hobbs' mind in 1992 when Robert Arthur Selby Lowe settled into the very chair Keogh had once occupied. As he drew salacious and manipulative scenarios about the 1991 rape and murder of Frankston schoolgirl, Sheree Beasley, Hobbs began to wonder about her client. As Keogh had done, Lowe opened his heart to Hobbs and expressed some dangerous thoughts. Neither was aware the walls had ears. Even before Hobbs told police of her fears, they'd bugged her office. On 31 March 1993, Lowe was charged with murder. Around 1998 he would write to me from his prison cell claiming he had nothing to do with the 1984 murder in Preston of schoolgirl, Kylie Maybury. DNA tests eventually cleared him. But did he write to me because he knew of my interest in Hobbs and Keogh? And was he sending me a coded message about Keogh? I thought so.

Unaware of the danger Peter Keogh posed for Vicki, we waited for the relationship to end. Relieved that Keogh's vasectomy in the mid '70s precluded the arrival of children that might tie Vicki to him forever, Ron and Lorna waited for the inevitable day when their daughter would say it was over. Dad wanted Keogh out of his daughter's life, but such was his love of Vicki, he couldn't bring himself to say anything that would upset her. And she so loved her dad, she hid from him the terror that followed the separation, for fear his blood pressure might bring him grief.

There were no such errors of judgment in Lorna Cleary's early life. A child of the Great Depression she was wedded to the belief that only through love and mutual respect could happiness be found. At eighteen years of age, Lorna married Ron and fled the cluttered and claustrophobic surrounds of Heller Street, Brunswick. She loved her mother, but it was not the life for her. With a traumatised father clinging to life in a pile of grey alcohol-sodden blankets in a dingy bungalow, and her young brother's rebelliousness leaving the nuns at St Ambrose bereft of solutions, Lorna saw marriage as her salvation. Better still she loved the butcher, Ronnie Cleary, and knew he'd never do her harm. The son of a wise old Fenian seafarer, he was a good man. Love would ensure that none of her children went the way of the Peter Keoghs of the world.

Although she was only twelve years of age when her father returned from the war, Lorna had already mapped out her path. Hearing him screaming as the imaginary bombs pierced the quiet of night and sent him scurrying alongside the bedroom wall like a frightened rat was abjectly unnerving. Afflicted by alcohol and unrequited love, the emaciated POW choked to death at the kitchen table a few months short of his fiftieth birthday. It was an inglorious end for a Digger who had once stood stoically before the camera on the hills of Austria, and survived heroic escapes from Stalag 18A. He'd failed as a father.

Lorna Cleary would never have blamed her father for anything she did. 'Fancy blaming the poor mother and father when they're dead and can't say anything,' she remarked as we left the Supreme Court at the conclusion of the trial. My mother had done it every bit as hard as Peter Keogh had. But she moved on while he always had an excuse for being stuck in a brooding state of war.

At 8.10 am on 25 August 1987, the man said to have been failed by his father and mother stepped from the cover of a driveway in Cameron Street, Coburg, traversed the ten metres to Vicki's car and struck. The ferocity and clinical nature of the attack was to shatter all who bore its consequences. Bernie Bell said he was never the same. From his car he saw the killer's march. Then, from the road, he witnessed the screams as the killer dragged the girl to the passenger side of the car and pushed her into the passenger seat. Next he saw the knife lifted above the killer's head and plunge towards the girl's face and body. He didn't speak a word. He couldn't. At the trial he tried to speak, but no one listened. 'I was stunned by the callous way he wiped the blade,' he told the committal hearing.

It was unfamiliar territory for Bell, but not for the man in the overalls with the peaked cap on his head. For the man who'd wielded a knife with the dexterity of a pen, slashing Vicki was as easy as carving dog meat. The killer who cried as he told about his brush with a boarder all those years ago showed no compassion for the mother who'd listened to his tale. When the news broke, our mother was left to ponder why.

There is only heartbreak in murder. Neither the apprehension nor punishment of the killer can soothe the pain. Compounding the misery are courtrooms inhabited by barristers who speak on behalf of the dead girl, and who can't understand the depth of agony wrought by killings of the intimate kind. As a matter of course, old scripts, tried and true, are resurrected and dead women transformed into provocateurs.

In the *Age* on 21 April 2001, fourteen years after Vicki's murder, Gary Tippet delivered one such script under the sexy title 'Murder is his Mistress'. As Tippet dragged us on the angst-ridden journey of criminal defence barrister John Smallwood, I flinched. For those of us who'd seen a daughter sacrificed on the altar of patriarchal justice, the emotional turmoil of the barrister was nothing more than self-indulgence. As with so many killings of a woman by a man in her life, the victim became an insignificant caricature. Drawing on the words of the accused, Tippet saw it this way:

> Dianne was a friend with a heroin habit. Gabriel Chang had been lending her money, but this time he said no more. She lost her temper and hit into him... he fended her off... remembers her falling back... Just why he hit her with the meat tenderiser he doesn't understand.

Just what caused Dianne Psaila to hit the floor or the couch with enough force to leave her dead, Tippet never explained. If Chang didn't mean it, then there was no murder, only an injustice. The problem is a woman was killed, and she's been implicated in her own death. Just as importantly, it was the compassionate barrister who became the focus for our sensibilities. In Tippet's world, barristers were 'angst-ridden, anxious people who cared enormously about what they did', and Smallwood was a man who 'put himself on trial' every time he defended a killer. Bullshit, I said. Who was he talking about? Was it the combative, confident Frank Galbally, the eloquent wordsmith, Bob Vernon, or the prostitute's enemy, Bob Kent?

Insensitive to the dead girl's family, Tippet proceeded with the orthodoxy. 'One member of the family had hissed "Yesss" as Chang's wife blanched and began to cry,' said Tippet. In contrast to the vulgar triumphalism of the victim's family, the compassionate Smallwood took the verdict like a 'jolt to the head'. Murder's no picnic for a dead girl's family. If only the apologists understood that.

Ten years before Vicki fell to Keogh's dagger, Suzanne Armstrong and Susan Bartlett saw the same thirst for violence in the eyes of a man. The identity of the monster that entered their house in Easey Street, Collingwood on 10 January 1977 and savagely stabbed both girls to death has never been established. The thoughts of one policeman as expressed in a memo in the early days of the investigation could hardly have produced a burst of empathy for the murdered girls: 'Suzanne Armstrong and Susan Bartlett visited Greek clubs seeking sex, not trying to sell it.'

How, I thought, could justice be done if women were pilloried when they were killed or raped. The implications for Armstrong and Bartlett were clear. By daring to engage in pre-marital sex, they were deemed less worthy than a married woman and that's why they died.

Had the man rejected by Susan Armstrong in her bedroom that night been charged over these murders, only insanity or provocation could have saved him. Whoever killed the girls bore the same traits of misogyny and obsession as Peter Keogh. Like Keogh at the kindergarten, he arrived with a knife at the ready and refused to take no for an answer. This man, however, slipped from the house undetected and needed no patriarchal defence. Had he arrived at John Smallwood's office, it would have been a different story. The killer would have told how Armstrong scoffed at his advances and ridiculed his sexuality. Had that killer been Peter Keogh he'd have probably sought a provocation defence and who knows, he might well have walked away with a manslaughter verdict.

Three-and-a-half years after the infamous Easey Street murders, it was Maria James' turn to experience the cold steel of unrequited love. The estranged wife of Fitzroy Town Clerk, John James, Maria most surely paid for her refusal to come to heel. Twenty years later, the killer is still at large. At the Junction Hotel a block away from where she died, they have always claimed to know who did it. So why wasn't he apprehended? You don't lag on a bloke who kills the missus. That was the rule of thumb for the blokes who came to manhood on the byways of Melways map 30. And, anyway, Maria James was sleeping around. It was no wonder some bloke necked her.

Without the expressed thoughts of Justice Hampel and the verdict of manslaughter in R v Keogh, I'd probably have only taken a passing interest in the 1984 Melbourne Cup Day murder of Preston girl, Kylie Maybury. The body of the six-year-old girl was found dumped around the corner from where Keogh lived with Vicki. Likewise, the gruesome Easey Street and Thornbury Bookshop murders would not have figured significantly in my thoughts. However, once I tasted the insensitive words of a middle-class judge, the journey acquired a life of its own. It was a painstaking journey. Bit by bit, I collected the facts, spoke to the people who knew Keogh and built a picture of his life.

Notwithstanding my anger with Justice George Hampel, without Judy McNulty's phone calls to my mother after the trial, I might have done no more than dissect the law of provocation and rail against judges who offered it to murderous men. McNulty's calls after the trial changed everything. At first I didn't believe any of what she told Mum, then suddenly something changed. When I discovered the real meaning of her coded messages, it all fell into place, and I knew Keogh's life had to be exposed. The demands of life and work meant I didn't get Detective Jack Jacobs on the phone until late 1995. When I finally did, it was worth it.

'G'day Jack, how are you?' I asked.

'Good, Phil. You want to know whether your man was interviewed over Maria James, do you?'

'Yes, I do, Jack.'

'Well, I've had a look, but I can't find anything in relation to him.'

'Really? Oh well, there you go. You know what it's like. He does one murder, so everyone assumes he's responsible for everything that's ever happened in the northern suburbs. Thanks anyway.'

'No problem, Phil.'

When I told Mum, she wasn't convinced. But Detective Jacobs had done time in the Preston area in the eighties and reckoned he knew his way around. For now though, the matter was closed.

The man Constable Bellesini could easily have blown away, Keogh had put his stamp on Map 30 well before he found his way into

Detective Jacobs' brief. In 1952, after a stint at 188 and 201 Clauscen Street, Jack Keogh put down a deposit on a single-fronted Victorian weatherboard in McLachlan Street. To the west was the Merri Creek and, to the east, the Northcote Football Ground. Keogh didn't take to football. The collective spirit of football was something missing from his life.

By the time he might have considered pulling on the boots for the local team, the once-mighty VFA Brickfielders struggled to attract young blokes to the green and gold. In the thirties the team was so tough and hungry for success only the very brave ventured there without deep trepidation. Smashing rock in the local quarry was perfect preparation for rearranging human flesh on the Northcote ground, up Westgarth Street from Peter Keogh's home. Bill Downie, a champion Brickfielder, was so averse to being stood over by his Japanese captors, an affronted officer of the Imperial Army took his life. They weren't all like Keogh in Northcote.

Twenty years after Downie died, sinewy blokes in Lee jeans and sleeveless shirts that exposed rows of tattoos cruised the streets in FJ Holdens and swarmed into the Peacock, the Croxton Park, the Commercial and the Council Club Hotel fuelling testosterone with amber fluid. Plod and his baton were never far away. When the clock struck 6 pm and the publican cried 'last drinks', the boys grabbed a flagon of plonk and a few bottles and headed for the creek. Later they'd emerge in search of a known whore or a girl who might be ready for the initiation. At the Planet Theatre and the Arcadia Dance Hall, they lingered in the hope that one such girl would emerge. Peter Keogh was among them.

Little has changed in this section of the street. A block north of the bookshop, as if lost in a time warp, the Junction Hotel, with its 1940s facade, straddles the lopsided intersection of High Street and Plenty Road. Across the road the once-stately Planet Theatre is now a bland, barn-like building, devoted to the sale of automobile parts. In its day it entertained swarms of children born during and after the war. South of the intersection little shops struggle to survive against the impact of globalisation and 24-hour shopping.

Troubled by Jack Jacobs' recall of events in this insignificant section of High Street and my mother's doubts as to his recollections, I decided to ring him again. This time he had a different story.

'Sorry about that, Phil, it seems your man was interviewed, but the alibi was watertight. He was with his girlfriend at the time,' he explained.

'Are you able to tell me who she was?'

'Look, haven't got that information with me, Phil.'

'No worries, thanks, anyway,' I'd replied, at least satisfied that my man wasn't the bloke they were looking for. Six years later, our paths would cross once more and the topic of conversation would be the same bloke, the bloke Homicide interviewed over the murder of Maria James.

It was cold and windy when Maria James took a phone call in her drab-looking second-hand bookshop in High Street, Thornbury, within sight of the Planet Theatre. A year older than the girl raped in the paddock behind Station Street in 1959, she was still young enough to experience the era of free love that was sweeping the west. Sex was not a sin. Or so she thought. On Tuesday 17 June 1980, Maria met the dark forces that drive some men.

'Hang on, there's someone in the shop,' she said, letting the phone drop before the words, 'Get it yourself', and a scream sent a bolt of panic through the man on the other end of the line. That man was her estranged husband. When he whistled into the phone and received no response, he sensed something was wrong. Maria and her husband had been separated for several months, and the sudden attention of men was something for which she was unprepared. 'I'm about to start a relationship with a man called Peter,' she'd told her doctor with a tinge of embarrassment.

Although no one identified the man who visited her shop in the dead of night, he was believed to be a suitor. Many a time I've imagined what confronted the 38-year-old James in the weeks and moments before her murder. I see a man who won't take 'No' for an answer. Words like 'No one stooges me' were stock in trade for this kind of Aussie bloke. When James told him she didn't want to see him, he first tried flowers. Carnations were popular out Preston way. He was the unidentified man who bought the carnations a few weeks earlier.

'Did you receive the flowers?'

'I did, but I don't want to see you any more. That's all there is to it.'

'Make me a coffee, will you.'

'Get it yourself.'

'Listen, no one takes me for a ride.'

'Fuckin' bitch, think you can give me the arse, do you,' he said, drawing a knife from the homemade scabbard attached to his shin and cracking her on the head. Strongly built from labouring and skilled with a knife, the killer was more than a match for the woman who'd shunned him.

'Scream and you're dead,' he growled, placing the knife at her throat and forcing her into the bedroom. Even when the raving man produced the nylon cord, the worst James expected was rape. The killer had other intentions.

Back at Fitzroy Town Hall, John James had gone into a panic. As he ploughed his car down High Street, he tried to tell himself there was nothing to worry about. 'Why didn't she answer? Surely not…,' he thought. In the ten minutes that transpired, the bedroom on the corner of Mansfield and High Street had been transformed into a torture chamber. One after the other, the knife wounds multiplied across the woman's body as she struggled to escape the monster's grip. She had no hope. After he'd inflicted more than 60 piercing stab wounds, only one remained. Grabbing James' head he slashed the knife across her throat. As he lifted himself from the floor, he noticed a photo of Elvis Presley. Elvis had seen everything.

'Not fuckin' bad, eh, Elvis?' he would have thought, as he stepped over the corpse of the woman whose mistake it was to say 'No'.

Then came the knock at the front door. 'Shit!' he muttered as he planned the next move. Gently sliding the curtain sideways, the killer spotted John James at the front door. When he heard the rear window being prised open a minutes later, he darted for the front door and burst onto High Street like the eternal Hollywood fugitive. Across the road was Hutton Street, which led to the railway line and St Georges Road. Desperate to reach Hutton Street, he scurried into the path of a car driven by Mrs Jeaneatte Hodson. At that precise moment, the killer's face appeared before her like a picture in a frame. And there it stayed.

As the man with the receding hair made his way across High Street, Hodson had no idea of her role in history or that of the man whose image had filled her windscreen. At the railway line he paused for only a second, then continued. The train to Merri Station was an option, but maybe the signalman saw me, he thought. Indeed he had. So too had Patrick Cashman at number 14 Hutton Street, just east of the crossing. Escape wasn't as quick and clean as the killer had hoped.

Cashman noticed how the man struggled to negotiate the boom gate, his weight or something in his make-up impeding his progress. Some time before 1 pm the killer opened his front door and began the clean-up operation. Nearby, High Street was buzzing.

'That'll teach the bitch,' he would have thought.

At flat 3/223 Westgarth Street, Northcote, a few blocks south of the murder scene, Peter Keogh was preparing for the 4 pm shift at Pampas Pastry in Oakover Road, Preston. For a bit of cash money, Keogh did some casual boning at various butcher shops in the area. At Terry Gannon's Newsagency, customers discussed the news and speculated on who would do such a thing. 'The Thornbury Bookshop' had entered the lexicon. By 3 pm even the bloke in the local milk bar up from his Westgarth Street flat was a full book.

'G'day, Pete, hear about the murder?'

'No, where's that?' he replied.

'That bookshop near where you do some butchering in High Street.'

'Really! I think I've seen that woman at the coffee shop where I buy me smokes,' Keogh added, the arrival of workmate Judy McNulty's car bringing the exchange to a halt.

It was a difficult time for McNulty. The 33-year-old mother of daughters, Terri and Allison, and son, Bill, she was experiencing intense pressure from Keogh to end her marriage to husband Ray. At the Pampas Pastry factory, he was like a love-struck puppy. Flattered by the attention, Judy suddenly felt important.

'He talks to me about things that matter,' she told her sister Dot. A glamorous, fine-boned woman with poise and strength of character, Dot couldn't believe her sister would talk about Keogh in this way. As with the rest of her siblings, she had no time for the man. Aware that her sister had a deep maternal streak that drew her to those in need, she wondered what would come of the relationship. Nothing Judy said could erase the sense of foreboding her sister felt.

Night shift meant Judy and her suitor could meet during the day. His arms a photographic jungle of ferocious animals and birds and the obligatory semi-naked girls, she thought there was something intriguing about the man. He'd been to some strange places, that much she did know. Like Judy before her, Vicki would be smitten by Keogh. 'He's too good to be true,' she remarked to workmate Janet Benstead after her first encounter with him. Keogh knew the lines off pat.

Judy's kindly warm face, sparking eyes and vivacious figure set her in stark contrast with the short, unremarkable man in her life. In his bone-coloured zip-up Crestknit cardigan and blue jeans, he was a throwback to another time. Clinging to a style and an era when women were at the beck and call of aggressive men, Peter Keogh was a bloke in danger of being left behind.

'When are ya gunna tell him?' Keogh barked at Judy, as they parted on the night before Maria James was murdered.

'Did you tell him?' he asked when she collected him the next day.

'Not yet,' she replied as they took off down Westgarth Street. Suddenly the mood changed. When the first news bulletin blared out the latest on the murder, he listened intently, then began switching stations in search of more news.

'What's up, Pete?' she asked

'Fuckin' murderers. Should be locked up for life or strung up. Women just can't trust anyone,' he replied. Judy McNulty never forgot those moments in the car when the news broke of the murder of the bookshop woman.

'He was very strange, Lorna,' she would tell my mum.

killings of the intimate kind

Although it was warm in Melbourne, inside the solid brick austere walls of the Supreme Court, the air was still and cool. Every step echoed through the corridors as men in white horsehair wigs strolled past, their self-importance unmistakable. Court Three was like any other. The bigwig, Justice George Hampel, was perched way above the actors in this Gothic drama, while a stream of witnesses waited outside for the call. We sat inside to the right occupying two rows of church-like pews. Directly opposite were the twelve men and women of the jury and, at the rear, watching intently, was the man himself, Peter Raymond Keogh. Graham Jones, the truck driver from Moreland Auctions, looked anything but pleased to be waiting for the call.

Jones' job involved carting goods to and from the Auction Rooms. A long rectangular building 200 metres south of Moreland Road, the Auction Rooms sit in a busy section of Melbourne's most congested thoroughfare, Sydney Road. Nearby is a collection of Turkish and Greek cafes. The poker-faced Jones knew the grubby-looking bloke at the back of the court quite well. Keogh often wandered into the Moreland Auction Rooms on the lookout for a bargain. He fancied himself a bit of a polisher and restorer of antiques.

The truth was he wasn't much good at all. It was Vicki who appreciated the beauty of a crystal cabinet or the history of an old washstand. Always the master of subterfuge, he used the pseudonym Peter Cleary when purchasing goods, usually with her money.

Keogh hadn't worked since receiving a dodgy $60 000 compensation at Pampas Pastry in 1982. At the trial his barrister told how he'd used the payout to purchase the house in Broadford. What John Champion didn't say was that despite supporting the killer during the four years they lived together, she didn't ask for a cent from the sale of that house. Although she was legally entitled to something, all she wanted was her freedom.

Graham Jones didn't notice anything unusual about Keogh when the killer arrived unannounced through the back door of the Auction Rooms at 8.22 am. Seven hundred metres north as the crow flies, Ivano Forte and Steven Moody had only just brought their ambulance to a halt alongside the Shirley Robertson Child Care Centre. In the gutter was a girl lying in a pool of blood. Unable to locate the source of the bleeding, Forte cut away her blouse. There he found four stab wounds.

'She's seriously ill,' Forte told them at the Royal Melbourne Hospital.

When the ambulance first appeared in Cameron Street, Peter Keogh stopped momentarily on the edge of the tram depot 200 metres south of Moreland Road, to watch the progress. As luck would have it, he'd disappeared into the laneway that led to the depot only seconds before a police van wheeled into Moreland Road. With the rear of the Auction Rooms only 100 metres away from his vantage point, he'd accomplished the first leg of the journey. From here he saw the first moments of the police operation.

According to Jones' evidence, he was oblivious to the bloodstains on the front of the left leg of Keogh's jeans, the bundle under his arm and telltale red spots on his white Dunlop runners and Nike top. If, as Keogh claimed, Jones had heard about trouble at the kinder, it was remarkable that Keogh's demeanour didn't send the bells tolling. An hour later Jones would tell another employee of Keogh's early morning visit. Remarkably, they either didn't hear about Vicki's murder or simply chose not to contact the police. These days, Jones lives in a former commission house on the edge of 'Little Chicago'. I did leave a message for him to ring me, but unfortunately he hasn't rung. So who said what after Keogh's arrival at the Auction Rooms that morning remains a mystery.

'G'day,' Keogh had said as he stepped under the roller door and made his way to the front of the shop.

'In a hurry,' thought Jones, as he watched Keogh scurry away. After depositing the box, the killer slipped into the toilet, gave himself a wipe down, then returned for small talk. Outside the kinder, the hysteria of ten minutes earlier had given way to urban pandemonium as the police van, then the ambulance captured the attention of a cluster of commuters. A few minutes later Sydney Road lit up as the ambulance carrying Vicki sped past, headed south for the Royal Melbourne Hospital. It was now 8.38 am. At the Royal Melbourne preparations were under way to receive another female victim of male vengeance.

Nowhere in Jones' statement or in any court transcript is there any record of him saying, as Keogh claimed, 'Something's going on near the kinder.' Petrified that the police or one of Vicki's brothers might suddenly appear, Keogh struggled to hide his panic. Jones noticed how his eyes darted back and forth around the rooms. Having been ensconced in the Auction rooms since around 7 am, Jones had absolutely no knowledge of what had transpired outside. Nor did he see the clothes Keogh claimed he left on the bench when he arrived. The truth is he had them in a box when he slipped in through the back door.

In his interview with Detective Jim Conomy at Homicide, Keogh made no specific reference to Jones having talked about the kindergarten. Instead he said, 'Some chap there said the police or an ambulance or something was going on at the kinder.' When he spoke with psychiatrist Dr Lester Walton in Pentridge on 28 September, it was definitely Jones he was talking about and the defence had been embellished:

I took off me coat and overalls and washed me hands, wrapped the clothes up and walked along the laneway. I ended up in the auction room where I expected to be later in the day. I was in a daze sitting in there. Police were going up and down Sydney Road. I left the clothes on a bench. A worker said 'Something's going on outside, they're looking for somebody, something near the kindergarten, it's all blocked off,' and I thought, 'Hang on, I was up at the kindergarten, police, blood all over me' and I grabbed the clothes, put them in an empty box and left with the box. I wandered around in a daze. Got on a bus and then got off and got on another bus. I got off again and walked along in Northcote somewhere. I took a taxi to Reservoir to find a friend. I was looking at the clothes, the blood... I tried to recall what had happened. At Reservoir I couldn't wake up me mate, so I rang his girlfriend. And she picked me up at the shops.

The story of Chamberlain being asleep was a lie concocted by Keogh to protect his mate. The problem was he'd forgotten he'd told a different story at the Homicide offices. Nor did Jones ever say in evidence that he knew of events outside the kinder. By putting the story about trouble at the kinder in Jones' mouth, the preparation for the lie that would save him from murder was under way. Jones became the link and the means by which to explain how it dawned on the 'dazed' Keogh that the blood on his overalls was due to a stabbing at the kindergarten. No one at the Auction Rooms ever suggested Keogh was in a daze. He hadn't sat there perplexed about what had happened. 'It's an impressive sale,' he told Jones, as he scouted around the auction items and calmed his nerves with a coffee. There was no time for confusion and sorrow.

In the celebrated stoush with Bellesini at Preston Railway Station all those years before, alcohol and amnesia had saved him. The killer remembered that victory as he spun Dr Walton a yarn. As always it was selective amnesia. Walton heard how Keogh remembered waiting in the driveway and seeing Vicki park between two cars. So also he recalled crossing Cameron Street, passing the kinder and opening the front door of Vicki's car. He even remembered the car moving back as

Vicki attempted to properly align it. Nor did he forget the tenor of the words uttered by Vicki: 'Get fucked' or 'Piss off', or 'I don't want to talk to you'. He was sure of that. As for how the knife took its course, well, that was a mystery. 'It's like a bad dream, Dr Walton,' said Keogh as they concluded their discussions in Pentridge.

'Oh and one other thing. Your contact with psychiatric services dates back to around 1961, but is there any alcoholism, criminality or psychiatric disorder in the family, Mr Keogh?'

'Definitely not, sir,' he replied.

Had Walton looked at Keogh's parole report of 1964 he'd have known this was totally untrue and that the family was a mess.

Keogh was a regular at the Auction Rooms. Wednesday was auction day and provided him with an excuse for being in the vicinity. 'It's where I expected to be later in the day,' he told the shrink. When owner Bob O'Brien arrived around 8.40 am, he found nothing unusual in the demeanour of the man who passed him at the front door. There was the same old twitch in the eyes, but he was very calm, O'Brien would tell me. 'May be back later,' was his calculated reply, when the owner asked if he'd see him at the auction. Although he knew he wouldn't be back, it was the right answer for the moment. Keogh always knew the right answer. Only a couple of weeks earlier he had called at the rooms and told them not to let Vicki near any of his goods.

As he jumped in the cab bound for his mate Chamberlain's house in Reservoir, he had more than a few trinkets on his mind.

Unbeknown to Keogh, as he filled Dr Walton's head with his defence against murder, Cole and Chamberlain had already recanted on their original stories. The appearance of the box of clothing in the garage left them vulnerable, and they knew it. A week after Cole claimed to have found Keogh by accident near the video store and Chamberlain omitted ever seeing him that morning, something closer to the real truth emerged. Now, Cole would tell police she'd agreed to collect Keogh after a phone call from Kevin Chamberlain. Chamberlain had no alternative but to admit that Keogh had been in the house. But did Keogh ring him as he claimed in the police interview? I've always wondered...

Despite Keogh, Cole and Chamberlain having either admitted lying or being shown to have lied about Keogh's arrival at their house, not once did prosecuting barrister Bruce Walmsley expose the lies or articulate what they meant for the credibility of the evidence. When Chamberlain did speak, he painted a picture of a killer desperate to survive. Frightened that Vicki's brothers might arrive and thwart his pursuit of a solicitor, Keogh was catatonic with fear, not overcome by sorrow at what he'd done to his former girlfriend. The bully had fucked up, and now he was shitting himself.

Although Chamberlain and Cole had met Keogh within minutes of each other, their respective accounts of his demeanour were tellingly different. Where Cole found a distraught, confused, 'zombie-like' man who 'loved the girl' he murdered, Chamberlain had greeted a sweating, nervous bloke obsessed with contacting a legal mouthpiece. Whatever the explanation for Cole's words, it was those words that would help save Keogh from a murder conviction. Yet a year earlier, the night my distraught sister arrived on her doorstep, it was a different story.

'He's an arsehole. You should leave him,' Cole had said when Vicki told how Keogh had threatened her, then spat in her face. Yet now, the man Cole previously labelled as overbearing, brooding and possessive, had become a victim of unrequited love.

Instead of ringing the police, as she was duty-bound, she took him to the solicitor. Then she lied about how she came to find him that morning. In the Supreme Court, Cole would become a principal witness for the defence. Never did she tell police, as she told me years later, that Keogh had told her the box with the knives and bloodied overalls was in the garage in Reservoir.

Neither Cole nor Chamberlain was asked what they knew about life at Freake's house in Highview Road in the weeks before the attack. The night before the murder, Freake had laughed and run his spindly fingers across the table when asked how the boys were bearing up. 'Girls, Pat, I just ring 'em,' he laughed. Keogh might have had trouble getting it up with the woman in his life, but with a 'pro', it was different. Cool, clinical and detached, not warm and intimate, was how he liked it.

Despite all she knew about Keogh, Pat Cole's first instinct was to explain away his violence. 'I know Peter still loved Vicki. He took the split exceptionally hard, and I think because Peter had to sell his antiques at the auction on the day Vicki was stabbed, this might have triggered him off,' she told police. 'The day Vicki was stabbed'—what an insult to my sister. How could she say that, I thought.

The next day she would drive Brian Watson to Pentridge to meet the killer. While they discussed what to do with Keogh's furniture and his dogs, we spent the day crying, ignorant of the conspiracy that had engulfed the girl being surveyed by Dr Collins in the morgue.

If it was appropriate for counsel for the defendant to ask Freake, Cole and Chamberlain about the relationship and about Keogh's state of mind after the separation, why was Cole not asked about what she knew? Why were Vicki's friends and relatives not asked what they knew about developments in the weeks prior to the murder? If Keogh could assert that Vicki was supposed to meet him on the Tuesday night, why wasn't our mother or our sister, Donna, asked whether Vicki had a view about the visit? Why was Keogh's driver, Brian Watson, never asked to take the stand? Why, when Keogh told police Vicki drove past going to work, didn't they ask how he came to be on the street at the time? Why didn't the prosecution identify Keogh's lies? There were so many unanswered questions. For whatever reason, there was only one narrative in the tale of how Peter Keogh killed a twenty-five-year-old girl. I imagined how it might have been had we been wealthy enough to hire our own solicitor to assemble Vicki's story for the prosecution.

Only an hour before Keogh's arrival at the Auction Rooms, Vicki Cleary had enjoyed a breakfast with her new boyfriend, Chris Wheeler. It was a beautiful day in Melbourne, and in leafy Montmorency the birds were in full voice. Two weeks later, Wheeler would offer police a sad tale of Vicki's last months and hours.

The last few months she would stay at my place for maybe four nights a week at the most. Vicki used to tell me about having hassles with Peter over the car. I remember saying to her once if he is causing so many troubles why don't you go for half of his house? She said no and said she didn't want the hassles. She told me about a fortnight ago that he had asked her to get married and he would have his operation reversed so he could have kids. She said no way.

Vicki mentioned to me that Peter had asked her to go to his place on Tuesday night. This was the night before she died. I told her not to go and said if he wanted anything that he could go to Broadford and pick the stuff up. Apparently there was a print or something at Broadford. She stayed with me Tuesday night and the next morning we got up at about 6.30 am, and I left for work at about 7.10 am.

I was backing out the drive and I looked at her and she was waving at me from the window. She had never done that before. She was worried about taking her car to work because Peter would know she was at work. At one stage she would park in The Grove in Coburg and on other occasions she would park near my bus depot and catch the bus to work.

Because that Wednesday she needed the car to go to a kitchen tea that night she drove to work. That morning she would have got to work on time, usually she was a few minutes late. I didn't see her after leaving the driveway of the house.

Chris Wheeler was never asked to give evidence.

No one at the trial ever mentioned the vasectomy Keogh told Vicki he'd had after his son Damien was born in 1971. Yet when he appeared in the County Court in 1976, charged with the sexual assault of a neighbour's daughter, the court was told Marilyn Reeves had suffered a miscarriage because of the trauma.

Vicki had never bothered with contraception and never became pregnant. So how did Reeves and the mysterious 'other woman' named at the Commercial Hotel get pregnant? And why didn't Vicki get pregnant? It was a mystery until I met Julie McAllister.

'He had a vasectomy in 1998, saw the stitches myself,' Julie would tell me after the suicide. Suddenly it all began to make sense. In the seventies, the contraceptive pill freed women from the inevitability of the pregnancies that confined Mildred Keogh in the 1940s. Although the responsibility for contraception fell solely on women, Keogh was frightened by its capacity to give them the freedom men had always enjoyed. But without contraception, Vicki would need to be very careful if she strayed. And if she did, he'd know. The vasectomy was nothing but another cunning lie. Keogh was a man of a different world. Trapped in the patriarchal vortex of his father, Peter Keogh was terrified that Vicki might discover someone better than him. Whenever she returned from a shopping trip to Ojas in Clifton Hill with Freake's friend, Pam Duggan, Keogh's response was the same. 'Meet some blokes, did ya?' he'd snarl. A paranoid prick, that's what he was. Instead of gathering some humanity, he sank further into brooding contempt and manipulation. He'd lied about the vasectomy in a pathetic attempt to clip the wings of a girl who could no more cheat on her partner than harm a child. Now as his rage grew, he was forced to erase one lie with another.

'He's done some things to me I could never tell you,' she told our sister after the separation. Somewhere in those words lies an explanation for the absence of a child. 'You don't need to talk to him. He won't hurt me. There's nothing to worry about.' That's what she told me when I asked if all was well. Standing there in the kitchen in West Brunswick, listening to her words bounce down the phone line, I had no idea of the danger she faced. It was Tuesday 9 June 1987 and she'd been separated from him for nearly a month.

As Wheeler navigated his car down the driveway at Montmorency on that fateful morning, he unwittingly sensed the danger that lay ahead. For a fleeting moment he wondered why she was so serene. A couple of miles from Cameron Street, I was boiling the kettle and reflecting on the upcoming VFA football semi-final at the Junction Oval. A month before the finals, I'd hit the turf at Frankston with a nerve shattering thud. I knew I was in trouble. As the trainer ran the towel across my face, a Shroud of Turin outline appeared on it. Another couple of wipes and I soon realised my three front teeth were loose and blood was trickling from the side of my mouth. It was my last game as playing coach of the Coburg Football Club.

Two-and-a-half months before her murder, Vicki had stood on the terraces at Coburg and savoured the euphoria of my 200th game.

Not only had we crushed the VFA ladder leader, Frankston, but at 34 I'd turned on one of my best games for the year. There's life in the old dog yet, I thought, as the players carried me from the ground. On the terrace beneath the grandstand, I spotted Vicki, a beacon in the Cleary clan. After the match she larked for a couple of blokes with a movie camera and bestowed joy like confetti on the rollicking crowd in the smoke-drenched Coburg Social Club. There and then I was offered a rare insight into the soul of the sister I was just coming to know.

With the nine-year age difference between us now losing its significance and Keogh's mob expunged from her world, we were about to become the greatest of friends. Whether the collision at Frankston was an omen, I'll never know. Whether some God, or fate was at work, the euphoria of 7 June was to dissipate with telling consequences. For the first two weeks of August, I was in and out of the dentist's chair then watched forlornly from the coach's box as we lost crucial games to Springvale and Port Melbourne and dropped from the finals race.

The last match was on Sunday 24 August, at Coburg against the local enemy, Brunswick. It was a still mild night on the Thursday before the game. Standing in the goal-square I had a moment to reflect on what might have been had I not gone after that swirling ball at Frankston, or at least seen team-mate Steve Gumley's shoulder steaming towards my jaw that day. All around, ageing red-and-tarnished-white Sherrins whizzed through the twilight. Spring was in the air, yet I wore a peculiar sense of ambivalence. Beyond football and the state of my teeth, something else troubled me. Problem was I couldn't pinpoint it.

Only two hours before I'd thrown the jeans and T-shirt in the locker and donned the tracksuits and the red boots, Vicki had appeared from nowhere in the carpark outside the ground.

'How are you, girls?' she said bending down and running her hands across the face and arms of my daughters. I'd separated from my wife Kate in April 1985 and was working part-time and looking after my daughters, Sarah, seven and a half, and Beth, going on six, during the day. They've never forgotten that afternoon in the carpark with their aunty.

'Where did you come from?' I asked.

'I saw you from the tram and jumped off at the market,' she said a smile lighting up her face as placed her hands on her hips.

'Yes, last training night for the year,' I explained.

The next time I saw her she was laid out in a rosewood coffin at Mulqueen's Funeral Parlour in Sydney Road, across from her old school. 'She looks so beautiful,' said Mum, delicately placing a strand of hair where her daughter would have preferred it. My eyes were drawn to the deep but now cosmetically camouflaged cut on her bottom lip. How could we let this happen, I asked myself? Why didn't you tell me? What's the use of brothers if they can't deal with some arsehole like Keogh? I wanted to ask her. He's dudded us, that's what he's done, I thought.

At 8.20 am on Wednesday 26 August, I flicked open the door of my 1975 green soft-top 4-wheel drive Suzuki, turned the key and began the twenty-minute drive to Avondale High School where I was a teacher. As always it was quiet in Hoffman Street, Brunswick. I didn't have a car radio, so I was totally oblivious to the machinations of the outside world or to the fact that two stops north up the Upfield line police were combing the 8.17 am train to the City in search of the man who'd just stabbed my sister. As my old car bumped its way over the bluestone bricks in the lane that led to Puckle Street, violence was on my mind. 'Guns, men and violence'—that was the topic for the morning's class.

I could never have imagined that only ten minutes earlier, Keogh's thick hands had prised open the door of Vicki's Ford Sedan, grabbed the keys from the ignition then swept around and cornered her. The thought that I could have been so close yet a million miles away still haunts me. If only my sister's words had made their way to me in a dream.

'I think I'll drive rather than take the train. I'll park outside the kinder. It'll be safe there. He won't come to the kinder again,' she'd told Chris Wheeler that morning. If only he'd picked up the phone at 7 am and said, 'I'm worried about Vicki.'

On Tuesday afternoon, Vicki had told our sister Donna by phone

killings of the intimate kind   121

of Keogh's dangerous demands. 'He said if I don't meet him at Brian Freake's tonight there will be trouble,' she said in tones that revealed an escalation of Keogh's campaign of terror. Donna was now 23 years of age. She'd first lived with Vicki and Keogh when she was only nineteen. Compared to where Keogh had been and what he'd done, my sisters were babes in the woods. Donna was worried enough to ring her mother and tell her what she'd heard.

'Don't you go near him,' Lorna Cleary told her daughter. Worried about Keogh's state of mind and what he'd said to Vicki, Lorna decided to ring Freake's house. It was around 7.30 pm when she phoned, but there was no answer. Keogh had gone to find Vicki. At Montmorency, he saw her car in the driveway. He'd decided what had to be done. Tomorrow was auction day. This gave him a reason to be in the vicinity of the kinder. As Watson drove him back towards Preston, Keogh began to picture what the next day would look like.

'Fuckin' bitch! Thinks she can stooge me. We'll see about that,' he told his driver. Later that night Freake would hear the same story.

While the phone rang out, Freake, Cole and Chamberlain made small talk at one of their favourite sites, Cramers Hotel. A barn-like pub next to the Preston Football Ground it was no debonair establishment. I'd never been inside. Nor had I tasted a beer in the Croxton Park, the Commercial, the Peacock and any of the string of watering holes in and around High Street. Preston had produced some great football teams, but its pubs were roughhouse and housed the likes of Peter Keogh. It was an aspect of working-class life I could neither romanticise nor enjoy. In my father's animated and exaggerated stories, the hard men who walked in the shadows of the northern suburbs were funny and heroic. The reality was something different.

When Cole and Chamberlain returned from the pub around 9.30 pm, Keogh was seated in the lounge room with a coffee and a pizza. At the trial, he and his barrister would claim he'd been drinking most of the day and into the evening. It was uncorroborated bullshit. 'He was fairly quiet,' Cole would tell the court. Underneath he was fuming. Like the women before her, Vicki had flouted his demands. Margaret

Hobbs, his former parole officer, had seen him in this state before. 'He's a woman-hater,' she had told colleague Jim Goulding in July 1980. For some inexplicable reason, it was a view she refrained from until it was too late.

Tall and in his prime an agreeable looking man to his own kind, Brian Freake was beginning to show the strains of alcohol and drugs when it came time for him to make his way to the Supreme Court. A cancerous growth on his face had swelled in his nose, giving him the look and facial colour of a seasoned drinker. And although Kevin Chamberlain told him his hands were easily fast enough to deal with Keogh, he chose not to test them. Freake, it seemed, was either awestruck by his mate's record, or genuinely liked him. Any bloke who survived being gunned down by a copper was always going to carry some status in the north. Better still, as with Freake, Keogh was sexually excited by the prospect of plying a young girl with drugs and having his way with her. At Highview Road, anything went.

The quiet of my California bungalow in West Brunswick was in stark contrast with the pandemonium that had beset number 5 Highview Road that morning. 'Going after the bitch,' Keogh told his mate when they passed in the kitchen. Freake knew he meant business. In his hand was the knife they used to cut the dog meat and in the pockets of his yellow overalls was a roll of packing tape, wire cutters, pliers and a Stanley knife. To round out the battle fatigues, he'd plonked a black cap on his head. The Peter Raymond Keogh who slipped into a taxi at 6.40 am knew the resistance would not be enough to thwart his intentions. Our sister had no hope.

The moment the weatherman announced that the people of Melbourne were in for a glorious day, Vicki Rogers picked up her bag, closed the door on her house at 7 Audley Street, crossed the railway line and headed south for Moreland Station. The time was 7.13 am. As she passed the Child Care Centre, she noticed a man in yellow overalls ambling northwards along Cameron Street. He wasn't a regular. It was now 7.16 am. 'He wasn't walking with a purpose,' she told prosecutor Bruce Walmsley. Well-rested after hitting the sack around 9.40 pm Keogh had almost an hour to kill before Vicki arrived.

124 just another little murder

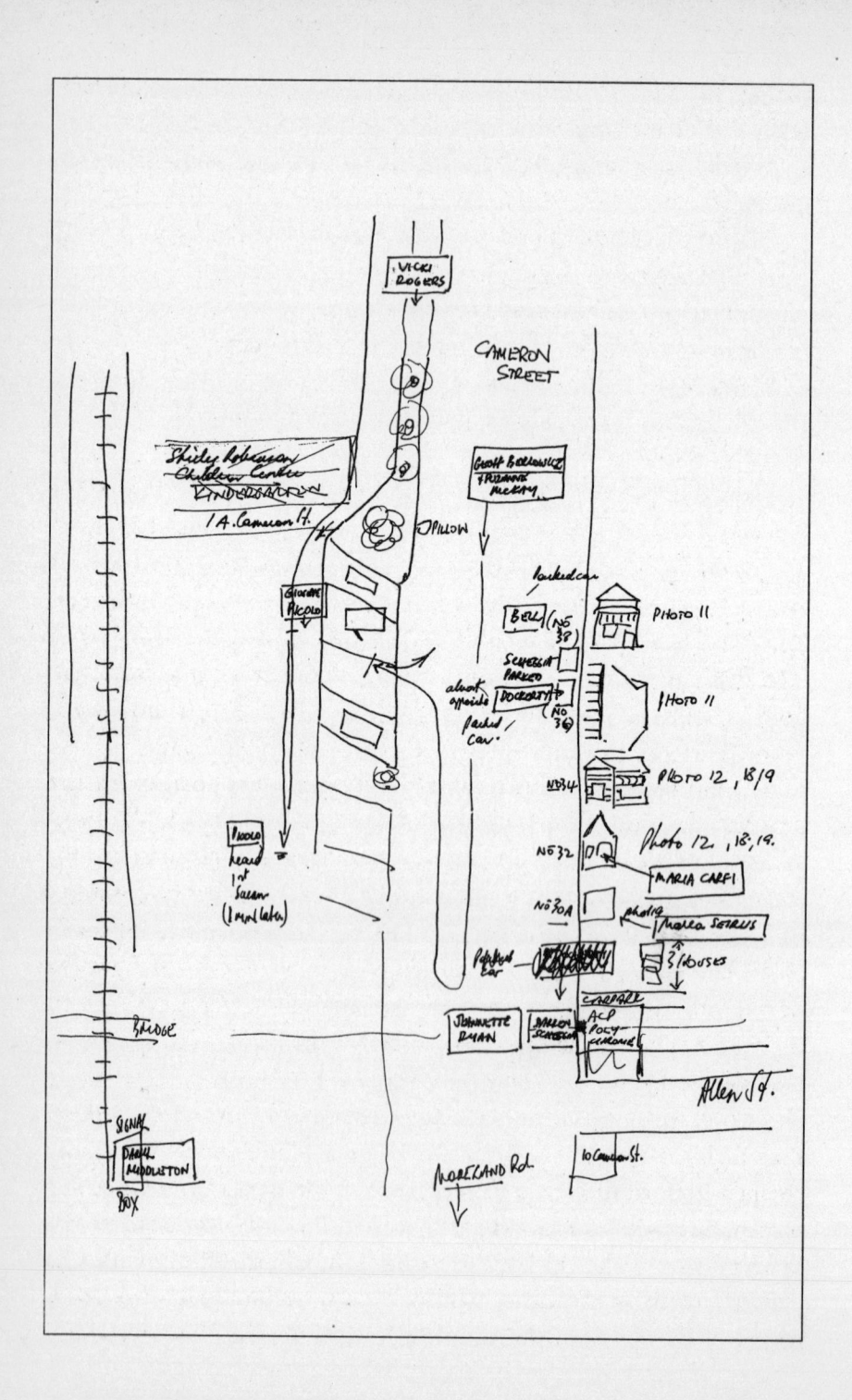

During the interview with Detective Jim Conomy at Homicide later in the day, he told a different story.

'Right, so what happened after the taxi dropped you off?' asked the Detective.

'I told you. It was about a quarter to eight or ten to eight.'

'What time does the kinder open?'

'Seven, or half-past seven or something.'

'When you walked past the first time, was it open?'

'I don't know, I'm not sure.'

'Well, were there children going in there?'

'No, no.'

Four hours after the attack, Keogh had the script down pat. He lied about when he had arrived in order to enhance his chances of defending the claim that he'd suddenly lost control. Vicki hadn't arrived within minutes of Keogh's appearance in Cameron Street. Keogh had been waiting for nearly an hour. Prosecutor Bruce Walmsley identified the discrepancy in his notes, but I believe more should have been made of it. Keogh had deliberately lied in order to run a provocation defence. Yet again, the murderer was let off the hook.

At Homicide, Keogh claimed to have taken a position in the driveway at number 40 Cameron Street, directly opposite the front gate to the kindergarten. Minutes before, he was seen soothing his parched throat with water from Mrs Carfi's tap, next door at number 38. From here he would have had a full view of the parking bay south of the kinder and the route Vicki would take by foot or car from the north. But was he really here or was he hiding somewhere else? When the figure of Giuseppe Piccolo appeared to the north of the kinder at 8.07 am, Keogh was nowhere to be seen.

As Piccolo closed in on the kindergarten entrance, Keogh saw Vicki's car enter Cameron Street from The Avenue. The killer stepped back from view and prepared for the next move. Once she passed, he made his move. If he'd been in the driveway opposite the kinder Piccolo should have seen him, and Bernie Bell, who was driving north at the time, would have seen him cross the road. Although the defence made much of Keogh choosing a so-called busy street to kill Vicki, Piccolo walked right past the nose of Vicki's car, yet testified that he never saw him. So it was for Bell, who claimed to have caught only a fleeting glimpse of the killer as he made his way towards Vicki. Keogh was hiding. There's no doubt about that.

For accounts clerk Bernie Bell, it was just another trip from Rosanna and another day in sleepy Cameron Street. Little did he know that as he wound his way out of Rosemar Circuit, that a girl in a Ford Falcon was passing by headed for a parking spot only metres away from his destination in Coburg. For the next 35 minutes they'd never be more than a few hundred yards apart. As Bell turned into Cameron Street from the south just after 8 am Vicki emerged from The Avenue, just north of the kinder. As Bell approached the kinder, Vicki's Ford appeared before him and he slowed to let her turn into the right angle parking bay on the western side of the street. With his turning space taken, Bell continued north and U-turned at The Avenue, 150 metres away.

Years later Bell would tell me he saw Keogh 'loitering near the kinder' as he drove past. What he saw was Keogh on his way to Vicki's car. By the time Bell had brought his car to a halt outside number 38 Cameron Street, Keogh was at Vicki's front car door. It was now 8.10 am. Twenty minutes later, Keogh, with the overalls, jacket and knife tucked away, was sharing a coffee with Moreland Auction Rooms employee, Graham Jones.

'Jesus, he's stormed out and says he's going after Vicki,' Freake had told his ex-girlfriend, Pam Duggan, the moment Keogh disappeared out the door that morning.

'Well, ring her up or something. You have to do something,' said Duggan.

'Leave it with me,' replied Freake as he lit a fag and pumped a shaft of nicotine through the veins. Scared of getting involved, Freake chose to shut up and wait. It had been a different story a few days earlier.

'Vicki, ring Brian Cooper. Urgent,' read the note from the kinder I found among her possessions. Cooper was Freake's alias. When Vicki did ring, it was the killer who was by the phone. And when she took a call from Freake at the kinder two days before her death it was Keogh's voice that confronted her.

As with so much I was to discover in my pursuit of Keogh, the revelation that Freake preyed on street kids came as a complete surprise. So too was the story that Keogh's drugs came courtesy of a doctor accused of trading speed and Rohypnol in exchange for fake Medicare accounts. Local detective, Bernie Gaffney, had heard all the stories. He had a good eye for the machinations of the stratum of low life that peeped out from behind tinted pub windows and traded in amphetamines in corners once the domain of the local SP bookmaker.

Gaffney had been on the scene when Bonny Clarke was found dead in her Northcote home, on 21 December 1982. The six-year-old had been sexually interfered with, and her vagina pierced during her ordeal. Gaffney had laid the sexual assault charges that led to Keogh receiving a gaol sentence a month before Bonny's murder. As coincidence would have it, she had been at St Joseph's Primary school with Allison McNulty, daughter of Keogh's girlfriend, Judy. It wasn't the only coincidence. Bonny lived in Westbourne Grove, only a short distance from the Commercial Hotel, Keogh's then watering hole. Twenty years later, DNA testing resulted in Detective Ron Iddles finally charging a man with the murder. Although it removed the nagging doubt that Keogh might have been the man, it seemed scandalous that it had taken so long. And still we waited for word on whether Keogh had killed Maria James.

There were no drugs and not a semblance of the demon drink in Keogh's blood when he threw on the jeans and track suit top and slipped into the boiler suit at 6.30 am on Wednesday 26 August. Throughout the killer's life, the men of the bench had concluded that he and the foxy devil could not peacefully share each other's company. Before globalisation tore the heart out of manufacturing in the northern suburbs, most working-class kids had come to taste the claustrophobic air of a factory and the soothing swill of beer. From the multinational Yankee Kodak in Coburg to the tiny shoe and clothing sweatshops of Fairfield, local and overseas capital had an endless stream of cheap labour. At shift's end, grubby-looking factory hands clambered over each other in the legendary six o'clock swill, then decamped for a bit of action. It was no place for a woman, they said.

Peter Keogh was the embodiment of an underclass within the generation and the milieu. By the end of 1964, he was still a year-and-a-bit shy of the legal drinking age. With a threatening countenance that belied his years, and a torso covered in tats, he had no problem at the bar. The Koala Shoes plant in Chingford Street, Fairfield was only a stone's throw from the Grandview Hotel.

On the afternoon of 10 November 1964, Keogh and a mate grabbed a couple and headed back to the factory for a rendezvous with the foreman. The ambush was swift and savage, and the assault charge a mere formality. In the Magistrate's Court Keogh was ordered off alcohol, but the local constable merely shook his head. 'He'll act in contempt, Your Honour,' the Constable had pleaded. Keogh was unmoved. Only five months earlier he had scurried from the Supreme Court, his mother beside him. The fall person in his descent into crime, Mildred Dorothea Keogh, was a mother under siege.

Connie Valente had moved into 33 McLachlan Street only a year before Keogh fell at the hands of Frank Bellesini. She and her husband bore all the anxieties of post-war European immigrants in white Anglo Australia. At Fitzroy High many Anglos had learnt to hate their Italian neighbours. 'Nothin' better than firing bullets at spags,' one bloke boasted in tones designed to infiltrate the hearing of 24-year-old Peter Stapleton. A progressive left-wing teacher, Stapleton had many fond memories of the school. But he'd seen the bleak side of the working-class and understood what those of Peter Keogh's stratum thought about the world.

Whereas the teacher Stapleton could leave Keogh behind at the end of the day, Valente had no such escape route. The constant appearances of the police next door throughout the 1960s and the disdain Keogh showed for her family was a constant reminder of the vagaries of life for immigrants in post war Australia. In Keogh's world the neighbours were uninvited 'spags' who should have been put on the first boat home. 'They were a bad family,' she would tell insurance investigator Jack Jacobs when he called seeking information that might be of relevance to the arson attack on Julie McAllister's house. In less-than-perfect English, Connie told Jacobs she remembered someone dying in the bungalow next door not long after they moved into 33 McLachlan Street. Was the dead man the boarder about whom the Keogh boys told stories? Was this the 'traumatic experience' about which Hobbs spoke?

After searching everywhere for someone who might offer me a glimpse of life in the Keogh house, the phone in April 2002 was a bolt from the blue. Israel and Klara Rochwerger had moved into number 33 McLachlan Street, Westgarth, after the war. I found their name in a Sands and McDougall directory, and left a message on an answering machine at an address in Caulfield. When their son, Isaac Rochwerger, rang back and told me he'd gone to Merri Creek Primary with Keogh and had lived next door, I was almost speechless.

Isaac is a pharmacist these days. His father's family were murdered by the Nazis in Auschwitz, and his parents met in a displaced persons camp in Europe. Nothing that beset the Keoghs could ever compare with the memories carried by the Rochwergers. Yet it was the Keoghs who seemed to carry the scars of malcontent, anguish and chronic anger. Growing up in a family that didn't drink alcohol only made young Isaac more conscious of the alcohol-induced turbulence that engulfed number 31. The verbal obscenities and the screaming that fractured the quietude of an otherwise friendly neighbourhood are indelible in his memory. So too is the picture of the beer bottles that littered the Keogh backyard.

Isaac Rochwerger's first brush with cigarettes had come courtesy of Peter Keogh. Such was Jack Keogh's frailty, the young Keogh had no problem pinching them in abundance and supplying them to the local kids. Although acts of generosity weren't the rule from the Keogh boys, when young Peter wasn't at war he was happy to share a fag with his neighbour. And although the quiet Jewish boy received his first taste of Aussie street law from the fists of Keogh's big brother, Barry, he had no trouble holding his own with the emerging thug, Peter.

On Friday 1 July 1960, Israel Rochwerger opened the *Sun* newspaper at page sixteen and asked his son to take a look. Beneath the headline, 'Three Guilty of Attack on Girl', Isaac found a remarkable story about a boy from McLachlan Street. Although 'guilty of forcible abduction and rape' needed no translation in the Keogh household, for eleven-year-old Isaac it was foreign territory. Eventually however, his father found the words to explain what it was that Keogh's mates had done to the girl. Isaac had seen the convicted boy in action, but it was the last time he read or heard about him. Isaac's family had moved by the time Keogh's mate came home from gaol.

All the hazy memories aside, there is one fact about which Isaac is unequivocal. The man who lived in the bungalow was a bad man. The Keogh boys called him 'uncle', and Isaac has a recollection that he might have been friendly with Mrs Keogh. In his child's eye is a picture of a small, skinny, nasty man, afflicted by drink. It matches perfectly the man Keogh claimed to have killed one night in the early sixties.

The man of the house, Jack Keogh, was a grumpy, shell of man when Isaac Rochwerger knew him. Bedridden, with failing vision and a debilitating lack of blood circulation, he was literally on his last legs. Although his co-workers remembered an energetic man who worshipped at the altar of the Australian Labor Party and the Rubber Workers Union, John Thomas Keogh was totally incapacitated by the time his son's gang was cutting its teeth. Whether because of illness or psychological disposition, there was little intimacy or devotion in the Keogh home. All the talk about standing shoulder to shoulder on the picket line against the capitalist boss was no substitute for love.

Justice Monahan clearly believed the young Peter Keogh before him in the dock in 1964 came from a bad family. Like Justice George Hampel 25 years later, the judge spoke as if Keogh had a cross to bear. Although John Monahan came from the same tribe as Keogh, the judge's education at the prestigious St Pat's College, Ballarat, meant the only place the two descendants of Eire were likely to meet was in a bourgeois court. On 17 June 1964, nine months after Keogh fell wounded at Preston Railway Station, Judge Monahan dug deep into his reservoir of kindness:

Let me say at once that I regard the findings of the jury in your case as, in all the circumstances of the case, just and proper findings and I agree entirely with them (and) I hold firmly to the view that a state of automatism, even that which has been brought about by drunkenness, precludes the forming of the guilty intent which is the fundamental concept in criminal wrong-doing.

The skolling of a bottle of wine had saved Keogh from attempted murder. It was a recurring theme in the story of the petty criminal from Westgarth. Lost in the drama of the gun battle and the legal high jinx had been that one prophetic act. Why did the wild-eyed Keogh demand that a young girl on the station take off her clothes? At fifteen years and seven months, his predilection for sexual violence was already being paraded for all to see. The problem was, neither the police nor the judiciary were looking. All the police would say in their pre-trial brief was that the young girl could not be found.

Twenty-four years later, he'd not changed a bit. Gone were the boyish looks and crest of hair featured in the old photos. But the modus operandi and the language were the same. Ten years after Keogh put his stamp on Cameron Street and the Shirley Robertson Kindergarten, I walked the street and stood beneath a wise old oak that had seen it all. 'Very bad, very bad,' Mrs Carfi said when her son introduced me as the brother of the girl killed across the road all those years ago. From the quiet of the shadows, I imagined what had happened.

'Wanna talk to you. Told ya you wouldn't see me comin',' said Keogh, slapping the gear lever in park and dragging the keys from the ignition.

'Give them back, Peter. I don't want to talk. There's nothing more to say,' she pleaded. As the moments elapsed, Giuseppe Piccolo moved further away so that by the time Vicki had stepped from the car in search of her keys, he was one hundred metres away.

'Where the fuck were ya last night, ya fuckin' bitch? Think ya can stooge me, do ya?'

'Just give me the keys, will you,' said Vicki, now cornered in the narrow space between the cars.

killings of the intimate kind   131

'Get your arse in the fuckin' car. Get in the fuckin' car. I've got a knife,' he growled.

Realising the danger she made a run for the kinder. With his hand gripping her face, she tried to find the words that might alert the men across the road to her plight.

'Help!' she screamed. Suddenly the ten metres between her and the safety of the kinder seemed a million miles. 'Can I make it?' she would have thought, as she saw the knife unleashed from the cardboard scabbard he'd fashioned en route to the murder. 'Help, someone help!' she cried, as Keogh began to drag her to the passenger side door. In an instant the stories and the blood-soaked images flooded back.

On her final journey from Montmorency, Vicki had passed through the territory so inextricably linked to her young life. Pentridge Prison must have brought back memories—in October 1983, she had visited her new boyfriend, Peter Raymond Keogh, after he'd been convicted for drink-driving,

'Why did I ever believe him?' she must have thought. As she spotted the old grandstand at Coburg, I'm sure she remembered the celebrations and that joyful moment in the carpark only a week before. 'If there's a problem, I'll go and see him.' I can't believe she didn't remember those words of support I gave her after that game. 'I wanted to tell you, Phil. I wanted to tell you but I felt ashamed and I didn't want you to get involved. It would have been bad.' That's what I think my sister thought as her car drifted along Sydney Road.

I'm certain that as she passed The Grove, one of Coburg's oldest and most elegant residential streets, Vicki would have felt a twinge. I just know it. 'Fuckin' sheila didn't know what happened. Silly fucking magistrate sent me away with a $35.00 fine.' I'll bet that's what Keogh said after the relationship finally collapsed. In the dying days of the relationship and the weeks leading up to the final solution, Keogh spat out his priors like medals of honour.

Cheryl was one of them. Flat 8, 46 The Grove is a mere two kilometres from the kinder. When the woman who lived there opened the door of her first floor flat around 11.45 am on the 3 September 1970, she was instinctively apprehensive about the man on the balcony. If the darting eyes, the tats and the abrasive manner were a clue, she fancied he was no messenger of seventies peace and love. Under the guise of purchasing her car, Keogh had hatched a cunning plan.

It was only a short trip to Sydney Road, but the test drive couldn't end soon enough for the girl. Keogh had that effect on people. The distinctive lack of warmth and the edginess of her passenger were disconcerting. She was glad to be back in the parking bay of the flats and thought that would be the end of the visit. Then came the sting. At 4 pm Keogh arrived at the door and, after a quick discussion about the car, asked the girl whether she'd fancy a night out. Within a few minutes of getting him out of the flat, the door exploded under the weight of his shoulder and boots.

Once inside, Keogh treated Cheryl to the man who lurked beneath the tattoos. Tied up, bashed, and undressed, she was another female lamb to Keogh's misogynistic slaughter. Had her boyfriend not arrived, she'd have certainly been raped. And who knows? Murder was never out of the question. Although the words 'He's violent and cunning' were scratched on the police sheet, it counted for nothing. Again Keogh was treated with kid gloves. Like the hunter killer, Ivan Milat, he was only ever one step away from murder.

Sadly, there was no one to shield Vicki when the man with the knife arrived that morning. And when the chance arose to tell, like Saint Peter in the garden, one after another witness could not or would not speak of what they'd seen. Just what Bernie Bell saw has been lost in time and the deep recesses of collective guilt. Reserved and gently spoken, Bell was the one person to see what really happened. Although he saw so much, he was left to tell it all in a one-and-a-half page statement tended to Senior Constable Gallagher in a backroom at the kinder two hours after the attack.

Nowhere on the sheet did the word 'loitering' appear. Nowhere was Bell asked to detail how he'd seen Keogh at the driver's door, where he'd come from, or how the killer had dragged my sister to the passenger side of the car in an act that defied the legal principles of provocation. Glancing through the driver's side window of his grey Celica, Bell had a clear view of Keogh near the front of the kinder. On Tuesday 7 February 1989, the second day of the trial, Bell gave Prosecutor Bruce Walmsley the bare bones of shocking murder:

> The female was driving the vehicle and the man had come from the vicinity of the kindergarten. They were in the space created by the driver's side door being open. They were on the driver's side when I heard the first set of screaming. Then when I looked again the passenger door was open and they were struggling in the car, then the male pulled the female out of the car and I was stunned by the amount of blood on the girl and his overalls.

Just how Vicki came to be on the passenger side, Bell can't or won't remember. At the Committal Hearing on 16 June 1988, he offered us all a far more chilling portrayal of Keogh's actions that morning.

> The time was 8.10 am. As the grey Ford pulled into the parking spot I saw a male person approach the grey Ford. I then heard a woman scream. I was still in my car so I looked around and saw the passenger door was open and the male person, who had approached the Ford earlier, was holding a female. The male had his arms around the female's body and they appeared to be struggling. The female was still screaming and yelling out for help. The female appeared to have nearly broken the male's hold on her and she tried to move around to the front of the car, but the male pulled her back to beside the car. I looked away for a few seconds and then when I looked again I saw both people lying across the front seat.

With the spectre of a provocation defence rising above the terrible events of that morning, Bell's evidence could have been profound for the prosecution. He should have been asked to detail what, even to the casual eye, had all the elements of an attempted kidnap or a clear intention by Keogh to kill Vicki out of sight, well after the initial confrontation at the driver's side door. Why wasn't he? That's what I've always wanted to know. Is it because, as members of the legal

Born on 21 November 1961, Vicki Maree Cleary was Mum's first girl after four boys.

Vicki with me and Paul on a family holiday to Swan Hill in 1964.

Vicki prepares for her first day at school and I'm there to send her off.

Vicki at Mercy Convent while down the road at Pentridge, Keogh was doing time.

Emboldened by a spirit and an empathy that was unconstrained in its love.

Her job at the Shirley Robertson Kindergarten had been Vicki's dream.

Peter Keogh (centre) could never be like Vicki. Instead he milked her for the warmth the gods had bequeathed. Brian Freake is on the far left.

Keogh looked anything but Vicki's partner.

> Dear Chris,
> Thank-you for a great couple of weeks. I'll miss you something terrible but I'll be with you in spirit".
> I hope that you work everything out in New Zealand and that it's not going to be too hard for you over there. — Have a great time anyway
> Enjoy yourself on Saturday night. Don't be too cruel to poor Ross! I hope the night is a real success anyway.
> Have a good flight over to N.Z. and make the most of the break from work.
> I can't tell you enough how happy I've been. It's a great feeling. I'll miss you but I'll keep in touch. "All my love" Nicki xx

A bundle of words that spoke of redemption and love, this letter to her new boyfriend offered a snap shot of where she had been and was now going.

The relief of winning the VFA grand final was indescribable. We could feel Vicki's presence. Mum and my daughter Sarah were there.

Vicki posed for one last photo on the rail that bordered the decking outside the back door at Broadford.

The young Keogh (right), sleeves rolled up to expose the biceps that would be his badge of honour (with his mother and brother).

Keogh's view of life found its expression in the garish tattoos traversing his body.

Eyes downcast, his head framed by the shadow from the flash and his thick hands a patchwork of freckles branded with scars from the removal of tattoos, Keogh looked a pitiful figure. This photo was taken on the day he killed my sister.

The passenger-side door of Vicki's car where the knife attack began.

Wednesday 26 August 1987. An ordinary suburban street becomes an official murder site.

Julie McAllister. Too good for Keogh. (Nicole Garmston, Newspix.com.au)

Moe Court, 2000. Keogh lifts his head, and the photographer frames his angry countenance. (Nicole Garmston, Newspix.com.au)

Today I still visit Cameron Street and speculate about what happened when that door was ripped open. (Craig Sillitoe, courtesy of the *Age*)

fraternity claim, prosecuting murder cases isn't sexy? Is that why so much detail was left buried beneath the prosecuting team's notes? Keogh's defence should have been laughed out of court. Instead the farce became justice.

When the pictures provided by onlookers Stephen Docherty, and Suzanne McKay, a passenger in a passing car, were added to Bell's story, the sequence of events was unmistakable and damning for the defence. Vicki had been dragged from the driver's door past the front of the car then pushed into the passenger seat. Only then, and after he'd dragged her from the passenger seat, was Vicki stabbed. 'The man was trying to get her into the car when we drove past,' McKay had told the inquest. For some reason she was scrubbed from the witness list. From the passenger seat of Geoff Berlowitz's car, McKay saw the most compelling evidence of murder. She saw a man dragging a woman to the car, where he would begin stabbing her well after she allegedly swore at him. That she wasn't called to give evidence at the Supreme Court is inexcusable. Instead, her story would be subsumed within the somewhat confused account of the driver of the car. She, of course, was only a woman.

Throughout his criminal life, Keogh was labelled a lucky man. On many an occasion I'd asked whether someone wasn't protecting him. Was that why a local copper was reprimanded after Keogh's convictions for sexual assault were quashed in 1983? On 14 November 1983, two days after the conviction was set aside, a bizarre declaration appeared in the public notice section of the *Sun*:

Well Peter you got off again.
Little children beware.

What prompted someone to do this? And who was it? There's little doubt a member of the police force was responsible. When Keogh took action against a local cop for harassment the bloke was severely reprimanded. Freake was an informer and a drug dealer, who, local crims reckoned, beat a path to the Preston police station. But what was Keogh? 'Just lucky,' they said.

It was like that on the morning of 26 August. Giuseppe Piccolo stands about six feet tall and is a strongly built, handsome, dark-haired man with a warm and engaging manner. In 1987 he was 30 years of age and more than a physical match for the killer. Had he been forty seconds later, he'd have been at Vicki's car, rather than 60 metres south at the Children's Playground, when Keogh struck. Instead of being able to ask Keogh what he was up to, Piccolo was relegated to a passive role:

> I heard further screams and walked to the grass area and saw a male in yellow overalls between the silver Ford and another car and they moved towards the path then I saw the male walking across to the opposite footpath.

Although Piccolo only caught the final stages of the attack, the screams that shook the tranquillity of that innocuous August morning left Bernie Bell numb as he parked his car only ten metres from the rear of Vicki's car. While Bell grappled with his shock, Piccolo struggled to sweep the cobwebs of social prejudice from his mind. Wasn't it just a couple of lovers having a blue, he thought? While he looked for a better spot to take a squizz, Bell decided to act. When he did, a cantankerous seatbelt gripped his neck as if to warn him of the consequences. By now the knife was glistening in the morning sunlight, and blood was spraying through the air.

As for Vicki's provocative 'fuck off' to the man with the knife, words the killer dined out on in Justice George Hampel's court, no one could verify them.

'I didn't hear an argument or loud talking or in fact any talking as I walked along between the silver Ford and when I first heard the screams,' Piccolo told the Inquest. Hidden away on page 29 of Keogh's record of interview and in prosecutor Bruce Walmsley's notes is a set of words that throws some light on what really happened. Detective Jim Conomy was firing the questions it was hoped would bury Keogh. The direction Keogh had taken that morning. The reason he was wearing overalls and carried knives. How much he'd drunk the day before. All that was as clear as a bell in the liar's mind. Then came the difficult part of the story.

'So what happened then, Mr Keogh?'

'Well, I opened the driver's door and I said I wanted to talk to her and anyway she said "piss off" or "get fucked" or something about "I don't want to talk to you" and then I don't fuckin' know, I don't know.'

So what was it she said, I thought?

Yet, not once when prosecutor Bruce Walmsley addressed the jury did he explore the possibility that Vicki might only have said 'I don't want to talk to you'. A dead girl whose space had been invaded by an armed man with a record of violence had been asked to explain why her allegedly provocative words should not mitigate the crime perpetrated on her. Words heard by no one and unable to be described with certainty by even the killer had become her crime. Keogh couldn't describe the words precisely because he knew they were totally irrelevant in the context of him dragging her to the passenger side of the car. In the interview with Detective Conomy that afternoon, they read like an afterthought. Just as importantly, if amnesia and automatism were going to save him as it had in 1964, he couldn't afford too much clarity.

Once this barbaric proposition was set in motion the prosecution should have swept it aside. Why didn't the prosecution remind the jury that Keogh equivocated as to whether Vicki swore and what swearwords she used, and that all she might have said was, 'I don't want to talk to you'. I wish I'd been prosecuting.

As my courageous mother said, 'The poor girl didn't have a chance.' Deserted in Cameron Street, Coburg, near where she'd been born, and failed in court up the road from where she died—it was a tragic way for her to have ended her life.

While most of the witnesses were so destabilised by Keogh's attack as to be incapable of an act of valour, Geoff Berlowitz very nearly emerged a hero. He and his passenger, Suzanne McKay, had been driving south down Cameron Street when they heard the screaming and spotted Keogh on the path, dragging Vicki towards the passenger door. Berlowitz then U-turned about 100 metres south of the fatal struggle and drove his car alongside Vicki's Ford. This had been Vicki's one real window of opportunity. Having failed to subdue her in the first advance, the killer's options were severely limited. As the kidnapping option dissipated and the chaos took hold, Vicki's only chance of survival lay with Berlowitz.

While Berlowitz drove south to Allen Street in preparation for a U-turn, Piccolo stepped off the pathway to observe the struggle. Simultaneously, from a matter of metres, Bell and Docherty began to grasp the nature of the event. By the time Berlowitz steered his car alongside the rear of Vicki's Ford, it was too late.

'He's got a knife!' screamed McKay as Berlowitz prepared to jump from the car. By now Keogh had pulled Vicki from the front seat, where the knife was less able to find its way into her body.

Covered in blood from the deep cuts to her hands, the madman was about to inflict the final wounds. Smitten by fear and confusion, no one found the equivalent madness to rush Keogh. Now they watched helplessly as he tightened his grip around Vicki's neck and delivered the final blows on the footpath, alongside the passenger side of the car.

Again Berlowitz drove off, this time to the north. By the time he and his passenger arrived back at the murder scene Vicki was lying motionless in the gutter with only two hours of life left in her courageous body. Berlowitz was no real stranger to the girl he might have saved. His grandmother had been a customer at Dad's butcher shop in East Coburg. As a boy, I'd seen the name among a list of deliveries neatly set out on white butcher's paper on the shop wall. Now it would have a different meaning. While Geoff Berlowitz grappled with greatness and almost saved the butcher's daughter, across the road in 30A Cameron Street Mrs Maria Seirlis entered the fray.

Maria Seirlis doesn't like to talk about what happened that day. When I tried to gather the minutiae of that morning she was so aggrieved I had to prematurely end the conversation. People are funny about murder. Some think they're doing you a favour if they tell you what they saw. She was a 31-year-old process worker at the time of the murder. She'd risen at 6 am on that Wednesday. After driving her husband to West Heidelberg, she parked in Cameron Street at 7.15 am and set about organising her children for another day. Such was the pitch and force of Vicki's screams, Seirlis and her son were swept to the bay window that framed the turmoil across the road. Here she was transfixed by what she saw.

'I saw a man holding a woman. She had her back to the front passenger door and he hit her and she fell into the front passenger seat. Then he pulled her out and started stabbing her. That's when I saw the blood,' she would tell the court.

Remarkably, Bernie Bell still hadn't grasped what Keogh was doing to Vicki. He would tell police he lost sight of Keogh and when he next looked, the killer was on top of Vicki in the car, with his arm thundering down towards her. How Stephen Docherty, who was parked in front of Bell, heard the cry of help and saw Vicki pushed into the car, yet Bell didn't, continues to baffle me. Amidst the mayhem Maria Seirlis dialled 000, locked all the doors and waited for the police. At the trial she would offer some gripping and courageous insights into what had happened.

'I own a big dog and my dog is a very good watchdog. If my dog wanted to bite someone, he will bite them, but my dog is not sick or crazy, that is why I was referring to him like an animal. When an animal wants to do something he does it. He was out there to do a job and he wanted it done,' she said.

'Seems to suggest that the dog may be out of control?' suggested Prosecution barrister, Mr Walmsley.

'I don't think so. I've had dogs all my life; I raise them. To me a crazy person or a crazy animal jumps all over the place,' she replied.

Yet nothing she said about Keogh's actions resembling a killer dog influenced the judge. Whereas the questionable and speculative opinions of the psychiatrists for the defence were treated almost reverentially, Seirlis' evidence was considered incredible, if not plain stupid, by the judge:

> I would be very careful about assessing Mrs Seirlis' opinions ... you remember she talked about dogs and dogs grabbing things and so on. I think you would be venturing into a very strange area if you are going to draw an inference from that sort of evidence ... my advice to you, and this is the only piece of factual comment that I will make, put that

to one side, because it is really quite extraordinary that anyone can compare the behaviour of some watch-dogs with a person and draw anything useful out of it.

'As extraordinary as saying the bastard was out of control when he pulled the knife from his scabbard,' I remarked to my sister. The learned judge obviously didn't care too much for Russian physiologist and 1904 Nobel Prize winner, Ivan Petrovich Pavlov, who drew conclusions about human behaviour from the study of dogs. Scientific or not, Seirlis' observations put the psychiatric evidence and the verdict to shame.

On Thursday 27 August 1987, at 14.45 hours, in the Coroner's Court, Melbourne, pathologist Richard Byron Collins began work on case number 3732/87CR, the body of a woman he believed to be Vicki Maree Cleary, aged 25, height 5 feet 2 inches, weight 118 lbs. The only thing that differentiated her from every other corpse was that the post-mortem was carried out as a Homicide Investigation. Collins found that:

> The body was that of a normally nourished wavy dark hair (with occasional grey strands) young adult female. The pupils were equal and half dilated. The eyes were blue in colour and the teeth were natural. There was moderate post-mortem lividity of the back ... Thin blood-stained fluid oozed from the mouth ... Remnants of pinkish purple iridescent polish was identified on the finger nails ... three areas of brown skin discolouration ranging in diameter from 1 to 1.5 cms. in size were present on the anterior aspect of the middle third of the right thigh. The following recent shallow abrasions were noted: left lower leg antero-medial aspect middle third 2 cms. in diameter, dorsum of right hand between 1st and 2nd metacarpo-phalangeal joints .5 cm. in diameter. A recent sutured curvilinear surgical incision 38 cms. in length was present on the right side of the trunk ... Recent well-defined incised wounds were seen as listed: (1) midline of lower lip extending obliquely downwards to left angle of mandible 5 cms. in length and up to 1 cm. in depth, (2) right anterior aspect of chin oblique 2 cms. in length partial thickness, (3) two very fine right lower anterior neck and

midline of neck .5 and 1 cm. in length, (4) right hand dorsal aspect oblique over 4th and 5th metacarpal bones, (5) right fingers ventral aspects multiple ranging in length from 1 to 5 cms. (6) left fingers ventral aspects multiple ranging in length from 1 to 1.5 cms.

Recent stab wounds were seen as follows:

(1) anterior aspect of left side of chest below breast... approximately 3.5 cms. in width... (2) ragged somewhat S-shaped (had been sutured) anterior aspect of chest in xiphi-sternal region with extension to the left to involve the medial aspect of the left breast... then into the left lobe of the liver... (3) right side of chest anterior aspect 3 ft. 6 ins. from right heel and 3 cms. to the right of the midline. This lesion was somewhat triangular in shape... right side of chest anterior aspect... The wound track passed between the 2nd and 3rd ribs into... the right upper lobe.

The mediastinal tissues were heavily suffused with dark red blood... The coronary arteries and aorta showed minimal atherosclerosis for age and no embolization was seen in the pulmonary artery... the right upper lobe was collapsed and showed a stab wound on its antero-lateral aspect approximately 5 cms. in depth. Frothy pink fluid exuded from the cut surfaces of both lungs on compression, which also showed scattered intra-alveolar haemorrhages...

The stab wound in the superior aspect of the right lobe was identified, this measuring 3 cms. in width and 6 cms. in depth and the stab wound in the left lobe superior aspect adjacent to the falciform ligament was also identified. The liver in the region of these two stab wounds had been surgically opened over a length of 12 cms. and the oversewn hepatic veins and inferior vena cava were identified. The remainder of the liver substance was dark brown and firm. The gallbladder was thin-walled, mucosa normal, no ulceration, no calculi.

Stripped of the scientifico-medical language was a picture of a fearful fight. It was a fight about which we knew so little. There was no Bernie Bell or Stephen Docherty at my home on Wednesday afternoon to tell the Cleary family what they'd seen. My brother Paul's wife had seen Vicki's body at the morgue, but she didn't or couldn't speak about it. That night we tried to sleep, but it was impossible.

I could hear Mum and Dad talking, interspersed with tears, most of the night. It was literally a nightmare.

Every time I woke, I imagined for a split second that it was a dream and that Vicki would walk trough the door any moment. Even then we had no idea of the appalling struggle against Keogh's violence that had unfolded that morning. No one told how she'd been dragged to the passenger side of the car, or how four people had seen most of the attempted abduction and attack. The police never mentioned it. Nor did they tell me Keogh had a roll of masking tape in his overalls. Not once was that mentioned in the trial.

When we stared at Vicki for the last time in the open coffin at the Mulqueen Funeral Parlour, it was the wound that ran across her lip and down towards the left side of her chin that drew my gaze. Deep into her lip, it was a cut that spoke of purpose and power. The four savage and fatal wounds to her chest and the crude stitching down her torso were hidden beneath the gown, but her lip was there for all to see. At the Hospital it was this cut that had become my focus. Somehow everyone knew about the cut to her lip. I never for a moment thought she was going to die. And that being the case I was horrified at the prospect that the bastard's conquest of her space and his attack on her beauty would remain after he was gone.

This and the cuts to her neck and hands were inflicted in the early stages of the struggle. Dragged to the passenger door and bundled into the front passenger seat she'd raised her hands again and again as the knife cut deep into her fingers. Once he'd pinned her right thigh with the very knees Bellesini had shattered twenty-four years earlier and grabbed her hair with his left hand, Keogh was able to strike at her face and neck. Through the prism of Vicki's rear window, Bernie Bell and Stephen Docherty watched as Keogh's arm surged through the air a dozen times.

Although the knife was now red with Vicki's blood, Keogh still couldn't deliver the fatal blows. 'The little thing really fought,' my mum would later say with benign pride. Bell, Berlowitz, Seirlis, McKay and Docherty watched in disbelief from less than a few paces as Keogh pulled her from the car, drew hold of her clothing, thrust his left arm around her face and throat and prepared to deliver the final four blows.

'Why don't they come? Why won't they help?' she must have thought as she fought for her life. Already her face and his overalls were smeared with blood. Then came the four fatal blows to the left and right side of her chest, the blade slicing a path between her ribs and deep into her right lung and her liver. Although anaesthetist Dr Doug Wells was never called to give evidence, when I spoke with him fourteen years later, he had a definite view about how the wounds were inflicted. 'If the man was right-handed, the wounds to her right lung and the liver were more likely to have been made outside the car,' he told me. That's why Keogh dragged her from the car. I'd always thought that to be the case.

As Dr Collins' autopsy revealed, separation from Peter Keogh had only enhanced Vicki's life. That morning she'd eaten breakfast, brushed her wavy luxuriant hair, polished her fingernails and imagined the opportunities that lay ahead if only Keogh would leave her alone. Free of his obsessive unhappy moods and sexual incompetence, she had begun to discover her own sexuality. Suddenly sex emerged, she told others, as an experience capable of generating intimacy and human warmth. She wanted so much to live.

Janet Benstead's camera captured Vicki's despair in the last months of the relationship. Cocky yet blind to her unhappiness, Keogh, with the cigarette in one hand and the can of Victoria Bitter in the other, looks anything but her partner. The sad looking girl alongside the tracksuit-clad man was nothing like the girl I knew after the separation. As I studied the photos, I was taken by how little they reflected my sister's spirit. She was so desperately unhappy. Brazen and smart-arsed, he was a man crying out for a bit of roughhouse treatment. This dangerous man's threatening words on the Monday left Vicki in no doubt as to his state of mind. That morning she experienced some gloomy thoughts. 'He's a violent and disturbed man. He tried to take the car but it's mine. I paid for it,' she'd told co-worker Tina Trajanovski.

'The only place you'll be safe is if ya get ya arse to Broadford. I've had you followed by Brian Watson,' Keogh had snarled from the safety of the pub during the phone call on Monday. Of course, legal rule conspired against these words ever entering the court. As Vicki turned the ignition she must have remembered the threats about which no one would dare speak in the Supreme Court. In her heart she knew that her refusal to visit Keogh the night before would have him seething. Armed only with hope, she backed out the driveway and headed for Coburg. She knew she'd not heard the last of him. Vicki Cleary was in grave danger. What she didn't know was that on Monday night Keogh had pointed to the knife on the hall stand and delivered his ultimatum. 'That's for her if she don't turn up,' he told Brian Freake. In the morning he was more forthright about what he was going to do to Vicki.

I first laid eyes on Patricia Helen Cole at the Supreme Court in 1989. 'The shifty Pom,' Keogh had sniggered behind her back. The feeling, she told me, was mutual. A tallish woman with a gushy manner, she seemed older than the 30-year-old I saw in the Supreme Court. I knew nothing about her or about her relationship with Freake and Chamberlain when she made her way to the witness box. Within a few minutes that all changed.

Cole earned her bread looking after what the welfare system called 'wards of the state'. That morning in Reservoir, Keogh was her displaced child. Every time she recited the words, 'He was like a three-year-old zombie and he kept saying, "What have I done? I love you Vicki",' my heart sank. With not a moment's reflection she began a tale that would transform Keogh into a man whose act of terror could be traced to unqualified and unrequited love for the woman he murdered. The alienated and disgruntled working-class was her cup of tea. That day in court, she swept one of the great working-class sinners into her apron.

Not content with saving him from murder she hoped to save him from whatever god was looking on. 'When we passed the hospital, he crossed himself,' she added. Peter Keogh had repented. In the operating theatre, the girl for whom the murderous coward from Northcote had saved his Christian blessing was taking her last breath. What hope do women have, I thought, as I sat in the narrow pew,

Mum alongside me, listening to Cole's lumpenproletarian orthodoxy fill the courtroom?

Brian Freake was the first witness in the box on day one, Monday 6 February. He was a type. Such was our state of shock we never imagined what the angular sneaky looking Freake really knew about Vicki's death. 'You'll get yours,' he'd said to Vicki in the maelstrom of the separation. Freake was Keogh's willing ally. After he was murdered, a cop had innocently told me that Freake had had his throat cut. When I wrote this in *Cleary Independent* a member of the Homicide squad rang to tell me Freake's parents were distressed by the as yet unreleased fact. 'They even had a pot plant belonging to Vicki,' he added.'Do you know what part he played in my sister's murder?' I asked the cop. Not surprisingly he wasn't on top of the events or Freake's history. My mother lost a daughter to these gutless men and he wanted to tell me Freake's parents liked Vicki. Freake was as guilty as sin. He'd covered for the murderer, visited him in remand the day after the murder, and lied to me about what he knew. When a friend of mine, Brian Sanaghan, spotted him in High Street, Freake was so scared he crossed the road to avoid him. When Sanaghan took off after him, Freake squealed like a stuck pig. And when Freake was murdered, the killer copped fifteen years. It almost made me vomit with anger.

Behind the veil drawn by confidants such as Freake was a boy whose misogyny had never been truly confronted. There was always someone excusing Keogh's violence. On Wednesday 26 August, Pat Cole explained it away.

Lorna Cleary didn't want to be a victim. She only wanted justice and truth. No tears and fake hugs were going to resolve her pain. 'Don't bother. That evidence you gave was terrible. Fancy saying he cried, as if he really cared. You know what he was like. Just leave me alone,' Mum had said when Cole sought to engage her with sentimentality as we left the court. Before long, Cole would be living in the bungalow of Keogh's mate, Brian Freake. It offered her safety from a violent ex-boyfriend, she told me.

'Brian Freake offered safety?' I asked. I'm not sure she understood the irony.

Pat Cole shouldn't have been surprised when her de facto, Kevin Chamberlain, rang and said 'Christ, Keogh's stabbed Vicki at the kinder.' Nor would she have been surprised to know Chamberlain went back to bed when he heard about Vicki's perilous state. Cole had heard a raft of stories about the bloke they called Pete. She'd seen the way he treated Vicki. The aggression and the psychotic approach to the slightest glimmer of independence from Vicki were well known to her. Then there were stories brought home by Chamberlain from the pub. The story about a woman calling Keogh a 'child molester' at the Curry Family Hotel wasn't the only thing discussed on the pillow in Reservoir.

The murderer left nothing to chance that morning. He'd arrived bright and early dressed in the garb of a railway man and had her path to the kinder covered. With some of his goods due for auction around the corner, Wednesday 26 August was the perfect day to bring her to heel and wreak revenge for her assertion of independence. Why not kill two birds with one stone? The wire cutters and Stanley knife in his overalls confirmed his intention to only damage her car—the car he said was taking her away from him. How ironic that it was Vicki who'd taken out the loan and was meeting the payments! Unfortunately for Vicki, any thought of damaging the car dissipated the moment she appeared in Cameron Street and nosed her Ford into the kerb.

By the time Cole opened her car door in Reservoir, Keogh knew he was in deep strife. 'Get in,' she barked at the dishevelled and sweating figure standing by the roadside. Having been consumed by a desire for violent revenge, he now had to face the music. This was murder, and he knew it. As with the shrinks and the judges who fell for his hard luck stories and saw him as a tragic figure of no danger to the fabric of their life, Cole would now be milked for all she was worth.

The man she now protected had not missed a beat since he drove the knife into Vicki's liver, eyed Bell, Docherty and Berlowitz, brushed the dying girl aside, wiped her blood from his blade and casually crossed the road. No one asked why he chose to cross from the western to the eastern side of Cameron Street. It was simple really. Vicki's car was parked alongside an open park that bordered a railway line. Had

Keogh chosen this route he'd have been fully exposed as he negotiated the 250 metres that separated him from busy Moreland Road and his escape route. Although this was the shortest route to the back of the Auction Rooms, it involved passing Moreland Station and a stream of passengers making their way to the 8.17 to Flinders Street. Worse still, it left him in full vision until such time as he veered left for the refuge of the Moreland Auctions 500 metres away. He had a better idea.

As Keogh scurried across Cameron Street in a diagonal line towards Maria Seirlis' bay window, Bell and Docherty sought protection behind their cars. They had nothing to fear from the man in overalls with the peaked cap on his head. Keogh wasn't out of control. He was as cool as the famed assassin the Jackal. Busily dialling 000 and battening down the hatches, Maria Seirlis was denied one last sighting of the man whose violence she said brought her nothing but grief. As he left her house behind, he awkwardly wiped the blood from his hands, rearranged his clothing and under the cover of the houses lining the eastern flank of the street, made his escape. At Moreland Road he turned left, darted between the traffic, and slipped into the lane that headed south towards his next stop.

As the killer made his escape, he had no sense of the sacredness of the territory he traversed. At Moreland Road he glanced right to avoid being collected by the stream of cars making for Sydney Road. In the distance was the dying girl's birthplace, the Sacred Heart Hospital, where a month before the Christmas of 1961 the girl had arrived in a hurry. Twenty-five years later she would stumble fatally wounded into a gutter only a block away from that austere grey brick edifice. And while she lay there, dying, her killer would dart across Moreland Road, skip behind a parked truck and scamper into a lane alongside St Elmo's Hospital where the second of Lorna's three daughters had entered the world.

None of this mattered to Keogh as he escaped up the lane. A collection of hapless bystanders eyed his path, then returned to the business at hand. Work was calling and there was no time to devote to the antics of the man in the overalls. It was a desperate time for the killer. Capture would have exposed him to cross examination and the prospect of a confession or a narrative that omitted the girl's words. As the sirens whirled, he felt the perspiration gathering on his forehead and neck.

The moment he spotted the cardboard box he'd carefully positioned at the end of the lane, he breathed a sigh of relief, quickly unbuttoned his overalls and thrust them, the cap and the knife inside. With the box under his arm, he stepped right into Curzon Street, then left into the desolate extension of Cameron Street.

When the police rounded Moreland Road, an outstretched hand advised them that the man they wanted had gone into Moreland Road. By now he'd slipped the net. Darryl Middleton, a casual observer from the safety of the Moreland Signal box, knew they were on the wrong track. He told the court he'd seen Keogh disappear into the lane that led towards the Auction Rooms, but on the day, he didn't tell anyone what he knew. By the time Constables Tim Highett and Lorenzo Fernandez had skirted Moreland Road and brought their van to a screaming halt alongside the distraught girl, Keogh was throwing his head under the roller door at the Moreland Auctions.

Not far away, the man who'd once threatened to go and see Keogh after Vicki arrived crying at his Coburg house in 1986 was driving to work. When a news flash announced that a girl had been stabbed outside a Coburg kindergarten, Perry Cleary knew it was our sister.

'Oh, no! I should have fixed that bastard up,' he thought as he put the foot down. In Cameron Street there was no sign of Vicki. Outside the kinder, a police car barricaded entry to the murder zone and a line of yellow tape extended from Fabian Gatt's house across the road and past Vicki's car to the next tree, and from there to Mrs Carfi's front fence. It was here the killer took a drink as he waited to strike. A few metres north of Vicki's car, a pillow lay in the gutter and a windcheater sat in the dirt on the nature strip. Cameron Street was about to become an official murder site.

'Look, I suggest you forget about Keogh and get to the hospital. She's in a serious state,' my brother Perry was told when he asked where Keogh had gone. As the ambulance sped down Sydney Road, dark thoughts rose and fell in Vicki's swirling mind. As she grappled with consciousness, one thought dominated all others. She wanted to live. Free at last, she'd have dreamed of having children, broadening her knowledge and assembling fine furniture in a place she called home. She thought of how the killer had grabbed at her face and hair and how he'd been true to his words. 'You won't see me when I come for ya,' he'd told her on Monday. Occupied in trying to rectify the acute angle of her park, she had been oblivious to his arrival. From the cover of two trees outside the kinder, his descent on the car was undetected. Suddenly she spotted him in the rear vision mirror. The yellow overalls, the jacket and the cap were a sign he meant business.

If only the macho myths had been reality just this once. If only someone to rival one of the heroes who jumped across the television screen at 26 Shore Grove, North Coburg, had emerged that morning. But when a girl really needed someone, there was no swashbuckling Errol Flynn or gun-toting Allan Ladd to shout, 'Leave the girl alone, you bully!' Radical feminists might have said a woman couldn't depend on a bloke for her safety and that chivalry was only an excuse for control by the man in a woman's life. Was it as simple as that?

In some ways it was true that the weight of cultural assumption had been beyond anyone's capacity to cast adrift. 'We've got a domestic.' That's how they talked about the case at the Royal Melbourne. But the men in the street were no match for Keogh. Shocked and stunned by his callous disregard for human life, they knew not what to do. And by the time they grasped the extent of the barbarism, Keogh was on his way.

As Vicki stumbled past the rear of her car and collapsed only three steps from the kindergarten gate, the pain convinced her she was in trouble. 'I'm not going to make it,' she said as a kindly face appeared and a windcheater was placed across her. Not until the killer was well gone and the girl had lurched forward then crumpled in the gutter did the faces appear.

As Maree Matthews-Jessop, director of the kindergarten, drove past the kinder she wondered what had brought this unusual cluster of people together. At first the director thought the bundle in the gutter to be a bag of rubbish. Then, as she reached Vicki's car, a different picture emerged. On the duco of the car, in the gutter alongside the car, all over the passenger seat and in a trail from the gutter across Cameron Street, everywhere she looked there was blood. Soon she would realise that what she'd mistaken for garbage was a person she knew. From Vicki's chest, blood poured over her jumper and into the gutter.

'Oh, Vicki, who did this?' she asked. The director didn't really need to ask. Over the past months she'd lived with Vicki's terror. Now she grasped what Vicki's co-worker Pam O'Grady and close friend Fabian Gatt had always known: the girl was in danger.

Wednesday 26 August was Pam O'Grady's day off. Waiting on the back of an envelope in Vicki's pigeonhole was the message: 'Vicky (sic) Pam rang. Can you call her after the session.' Pam was so troubled by the tales of Keogh's harassment in the final weeks, she decided to break the impasse. 'Vicki, you have to do something' she had said, when she saw her crying at the sink after a phone call from Freake. Unfortunately, Keogh struck before Vicki had the conversation that might have changed everything. 'Why doesn't Phil Cleary do something?' Pam had wondered as she placed her arm around the distraught girl. The kinder administration just wished it would all go away. On Wednesday all the premonitions came to fruition and everyone realised how wrong those who used the words 'drama queen' to account for the tears had been.

With Vicki fading fast, the director picked up the phone and dialled the number of Vicki's parents in Broadford, 40 miles north of Coburg. As the phone rang, she assembled the words for a dying girl's mother. Conscious of the need to not frighten Lorna, Maree was brief and to the point. 'I thought I better ring you. Vicki's been stabbed. She said it was Peter Keogh. You better get to the hospital, I know Vicki would want you there,' said Maree.

In a dream during a fitful night in which the dogs barked and howled as if a stranger was in their midst, Lorna had struggled to identify the face of the daughter in a rosewood coffin. Now she knew which daughter she'd lost. As she prepared to head up the paddock to tell her son what she'd heard, Ivano Forte listened to her daughter's final plea.

Forte knew she was in a bad state but he thought she'd make it. As a trained ambulance officer, he'd come face to face with so much pain, yet each time it was as gruelling as the last. And this was no different except that Vicki pleaded that he not let her die. What Forte didn't know was that Vicki's liver was bleeding profusely from a deep wound and that she had only two hours to live.

At 8.47 am, 32 minutes after Keogh scurried down Cameron Street, anaesthetist Dr Douglas Wells had found a pale agitated girl with a blood pressure of 120/70. Coughing blood from the wounds to her lungs, she was clearly in trouble.

'Don't let me die,' she implored the 34-year-old doctor as he prepared her for the operation.

'Don't worry, I'll look after you,' he'd reassured her. The truth was he knew she had no hope. By the time the bells began ringing to summon me to class, the medical team was ten minutes into an emergency thoracotomy that would determine the extent of the lacerations to Vicki's chest and stomach. 'Oh shit,' someone had remarked when the source and full extent of the bleeding was unearthed. So profuse was the haemorrhaging from the liver that not even eleven units of blood could stem the hypertension.

By the time I was five minutes into period one with 10A, Vicki had been on the operating table at the Royal Melbourne Hospital for a full fifteen minutes. The topic for discussion that morning at Avondale High School was 'violence and society', and the young Aussie bloke in the front row had rather strong feelings about the massacre in Hoddle Street. 'Guns, Sir. It's all because of guns.' Nearby, Suzie, a girl with probing dark eyes and a pristine European face had a more thoughtful response. 'It's men, Sir. Girls don't use violence like men. It's men. That's the problem.' As I nodded my approval, I had no idea how profound were those words.

Oblivious to my sister's fight for life, I ploughed on in search of explanations for the carnage of Hoddle Street, Collingwood. The staggering events of Sunday 9 August when a skinny former cadet ran amok with an automatic rifle and slaughtered seven people and wounded another nineteen had paralysed Melbourne in the weeks preceding Vicki's death. A woman could kill her own child, but she just couldn't or didn't need to do what this bloke had done. Far beyond what George Hampel said about the capacity of social background to stir a man's primal tendencies lay something that defied even blokes themselves.

Julian Knight in his fatigues brought back memories of my visits to Pentridge with a bunch of sporting heroes in 1985. Beneath those savage colonial walls, I'd shaken hands with the famous murderer, Peter Lawless, made small talk with the kidnapper Edward Eastwood and met a stream of misfits. I didn't know Keogh had once been among them. Paul Mallender, a deluded man in fatigues, was sadly typical. He said he'd been training for months. It had done him little good. 'Couldn't run out of sight on a foggy night,' was one of those mildly derisive expressions I'd learnt from my dad. As I watched Mallender collapse after a couple of laps around the makeshift running track I remembered Dad's words.

'He's the one who shot the prostitute,' said Lawless when he noticed my wry smile. 'Jesus, and there's me shaking his hand like he's some fucking working-class victim of capitalist injustice,' I'd thought. Prostitute Kay Nesbitt had shown the temerity to tell him he should leave her girlfriend and flatmate alone and that she didn't want to see him any more. He'd responded by firing his rifle through her front door, sending glass and gunshot into her face. She was left horribly disfigured. Here in the claustrophobia of Her Majesty's Prison no one seemed to care about what he'd done to somebody's daughter. That's murder!

Like every aspiring socialist, I proceeded on the assumption that these were potentially honourable men struck down by capitalist property laws that protected the rich and forced the poor to subjugate themselves to the grind of the factory or illegally appropriate surplus labour. Marx called this surplus labour profit, and said it belonged to the worker. I understood and agreed with the logic. The problem was, Lawless' mob were a sullen, taciturn lot. I couldn't imagine them acting collectively unless there was an easy earn in it or the prize was the local 'bike' or a kidnapped woman. The way they hung around in aimless clusters and refused to smile was plain disconcerting. They and Keogh were so alike.

Lawless was different. In the land of the blind, the one-eyed man was king. 'Didn't do it. I was framed,' he said with such conviction I almost believed him. Yet somewhere a mother and a father grieved at the loss of a son, shot dead, said the police and the court, by Peter Lawless. And how they must have cringed as I sent that cheerio down the barrel of the television camera 'to the boys in Pentridge' before the 1985 VFA preliminary final. And how, when I tasted murder, I regretted that gesture of kindness. Murder always seems like someone else's business until it strikes you. The judge, the bystanders and the members of the jury never expect it to happen to them. Nor did I, until that phone call.

'A phone call from my brother? That's odd, he's never rung me here,' I thought as I took my leave from the class. There was hardly a soul in the staff room at 9.10 that morning.

'It's Paul, your brother Paul,' were the first words to come my way. After a collection of jumbled and disjointed sentences that included the words, 'Vicki ... hospital ... the bastard's stabbed her,' had passed between us, I thought I understood what had happened, but I didn't. Somehow the word 'accident' dominated all others.

'A car accident?'

'No. Keogh.'

'He's what? Where?'

'At the kinder.'

'Is she all right?'

'Don't know. She's at the Royal Melbourne.'

'A fight that led to an accidental stabbing. You silly bastard, Keogh.' These were the thoughts that led my thinking as I prayed her young face would be left untarnished by the surgeon's stitches.

As Paul and I spoke, a doctor's scalpel was tracing a 38 cm line from under Vicki's right breast to the umbilical cord Dr Welstead had snipped when he brought her into the world. Keogh had struck deep. 'Bloody idiot,' I said again and again as a teacher friend steered me towards the hospital. It was about 9.50 am when I walked through the

killings of the intimate kind   153

doors and explained who I was. In a plain little room outside which sat two idle trolleys we talked about what had happened. An unimportant family from the suburbs caught up in a domestic, we were left with not so much as an offer of tea or coffee. As the clock ground on I was sure she wouldn't die. 'She's tough. She'll survive,' I told Donna.

As Mum scurried up the hill to tell my brother Paul, she thought about the phone call the night before. If only I'd gone to Melbourne, she thought. If only Keogh had answered the phone he might have been stopped in his tracks. One thing's for sure. A bullshit provocation defence would have been absurd if he'd told Mum he had no intention of going near Vicki.

Unable to rouse the mob at Highview Road, Mum eventually began a frightful sleep that would have its climax at 8.25 the next morning. Lorna Cleary was a shell of herself when she set off up the paddock to bring the news to her son. In her mind was an image of a daughter captured against the backdrop of mountain and dam. In her blue summer dress, her body rich and curved and her hair long and luxurious, she had posed for one last photo on the rail that bordered the decking outside the back door. As Mum crossed the paddock, she thought of that girl. While Mum remembered, Paul sensed something was wrong.

'Vicki's been stabbed,' she told him.

'Keogh?'

'Yes.'

Before he rang me at school, Paul thought about all that had happened. The failed attempt at an intervention order at the Kilmore Court and the words spoken to Keogh after the attack on Vicki after Easter reverberated in his head. The shock and confusion at my end of the telephone was so at odds with his grasp of what had happened. On reflection it all made sense to Paul. 'I'd never hurt her. All I wanted was the vacuum cleaner,' Keogh had told our brother when he reminded the thug that his sister was not someone he could terrorise with impunity.

At the Homicide offices Keogh would tell a different story.

'What happened then, Mr Keogh?'

'Then the whole family broke off, they're pretty loud. The brother rang up abusing me, whatever... you know... I don't want to get involved in domestics. He said get back in your own... whatever.'

If only that were true!

'Any of 'em come near me and we'll see what happens,' he'd bragged to Vicki. She made sure none of her brothers took to him. In four years I'd said only a handful of words to him and when I wanted to speak with him Vicki said 'no'. It cost my sister her life.

At Homicide, his victim's tale made a mockery of the violent threats he had shouted down the phone after the attack on Vicki in their Broadford house. Fire and arson. That had been Keogh's drunken solution to Vicki's final flight from the house after the assault. 'I'll bomb ya dad's fuckin' butcher shop and set fire to your furniture,' he screamed as Vicki held the phone aloft for her parents and her youngest sister, Elizabeth, to hear. More than three months had transpired since those threats were made. As bizarre as it seems, they were never mentioned in the Court case.

As Lorna Cleary wound her way towards Melbourne, she prayed her daughter would survive Keogh's murderous attack. Meanwhile Dad set about closing the butcher shop he ran in the main street of the town. It was a morning of 'what if'. If only she'd told us. If only she'd trusted us to deal with him. If only we'd stopped him. Guilt was the card we plucked from Keogh's hand.

When she needed the company of old style, physical force men, our sister turned to the kindergarten and her new boyfriend and confided in those who weren't her flesh and blood. We weren't a bunch of thugs or standover men, but she was our sister and she needed help. 'This should all be done in a civilised manner,' Lorna had said to Keogh months earlier. For Keogh it was an invitation to do as he pleased. And so while we grappled with the confusion, Keogh and his mob considered the next move.

'Have the parents arrived yet?' a nurse had said, the significance of the question lost on us. It was now close to 11 am and the passing of time had given us hope.

'No, Mum's not far away,' someone had replied. Then, as if she'd heard the question, Mum appeared. Diminutive, sublimely courageous and energetic like her mother and her daughter, Lorna Cleary was the quintessential uncelebrated hero. As she swept into the hospital, she was immediately ushered into the waiting room. Now the doctor began his journey. At the door, he planted his feet and with the sister at his side, asked for Mrs Cleary.

'I'm sorry, we couldn't stop the bleeding,' was all he said. No fanfare, decorative words or expressions of grief accompanied the words. Just a simple methodical account of the cause of a girl's death was all there was. It was terrible. So began a wail, a horrible wail that must have reared through the corridors and stunned those waiting outside.

At 10.40 am, two hours and twenty minutes after she'd implored Ivano Forte not to let her die, Vicki lost her battle. From two wounds in the liver, the blood had now gushed for so long her strength was gone. Surgically cut from chest to stomach and with her liver sutured and clamped, she went into fatal hypertension and then her beautiful eyes dilated. Within five minutes her heart stopped, her eyes finally fixed and the operation was over. Keogh had won the battle. He had his revenge.

'Can I see her? She's my daughter, I have to see her,' Mum had asked the doctor. He stood motionless at the door and gave a gentle reply.

'I'm sorry. You can't, Mrs Cleary,' he replied. Now it was murder and the body belonged to others. From here, an abstraction, the state, and the men of the courts would take possession of Vicki's life. In Cameron Street, nylon ropes marked off the site where Keogh did his work and soon witnesses would discuss what they saw and a narrative would appear into which would step a brief, employed to explain away Keogh's cold-blooded attack. Bruce Walmsley QC would appear, a prosecutor forced to read from a script devoid of any understanding of the rights of the girl set upon in her car in Cameron Street. We would become nothing but observers.

While the doctors tried to save Vicki, two opposing journeys had unfolded. North of the city, the killer waited for Pat Cole while Lorna Cleary crossed busy Mahoney's Road only a few blocks away. By

10.15 am Lorna was nearing the intimate landmarks of her rich life. At Fawkner cemetery, she glanced sideways and wondered. As she passed Mercy College and the Mulqueen Funeral Parlour, the traffic thickened and she wondered if it would ever allow her passage to see her daughter. About this time, Cole pulled her car to a halt and beckoned to the man in the grotty blood-stained jeans. On his jeans and his Nike top and his runners, Cole saw Vicki's blood. He'd worn the size seven Dunlop volley runners for the occasion. The son of the man from Dunlop Rubber had done the hard men of the union proud.

From inner Melbourne, through the narrow streets of Richmond, to the shadows of the hospitals where Lorna had brought her girls into the world, Peter Raymond Keogh was only ever a step away. Now in the final act he would follow my mother's sad trip to the hospital where her daughter was about to be pronounced dead. Only an hour and a half before Vicki died, he'd walked through the back door of the rented brick veneer in Rosenthal Court, dumped his armour and gone to the phone in search of his solicitor.

'He's what? Left the fuckin' box in the garage?' Chamberlain growled as Cole delivered the startling revelation. From the phone box, she watched as Keogh took off with solicitors Robert Digala and Tony Nicholson for the Russell Street police complex. When she arrived home, it was agreed that there would be no mention of Keogh being in the house.

At 4.22 pm Chamberlain signed the sheet on which Senior Detective Hunter had dictated the story of how the dog pulled the overalls out of the box. The statement concluded, 'I hereby acknowledge that this statement is true and correct and I make it in the belief that a person making a false statement in the circumstances is liable to the penalties of perjury.' Without the box in the garage, Keogh's flight to the safety of the Chamberlain-Cole house might never have been documented.

With that done it was Cole's turn:

> At approximately 10 am I received a phone call from Kevin and he told me that a friend of ours Vicki Cleary had been stabbed. I rang several

hospitals trying to find out where Vicki had been taken and I found out she was at the Royal Melbourne Hospital. A short time later I left work as I felt sick at the news and I started to head home. On the way there I decided that I needed to get some cigarettes and I had decided to stop at the shop.

When I was near the shop in Hughes Parade I saw a male standing on the corner of Hughes Parade and another street I'm not sure of. He was standing near the Video Shop. I had a second look at this person and I realised it was another friend of mine, Peter Keogh. He was just standing there with his hands in his pocket, with a dazed look. He was wearing grotty jeans, and a grey and maroon zip-up tracksuit jacket.

I stopped the car near where he was standing and Peter got into the passenger seat. I said, 'Peter, have you heard?' and he replied, 'What have I done, what have I done?' It was then I realised it must have been Peter who had stabbed Vicki.

When they originally spoke with the police, Chamberlain and Cole didn't know that their little mate had already told Detective Jim Conomy how he roused Chamberlain from bed and then rang Cole at work to come and pick him up. When the police surveyed the Cole-Chamberlain account of the morning, something didn't look right. Once Keogh's statement was examined, Chamberlain's claim that he never saw Keogh at the house and Cole's story about stumbling upon the killer unaware that he'd stabbed Vicki were seen for what they were. The pair had lied under oath.

On Friday 4 September at 12.45 pm, ten days after their first set of lies were recorded for posterity Senior Detective Barry McIntosh pulled up a chair and gathered another version of the events of that morning. This time Cole said:

> I have made a statement to the Police previously... it isn't totally correct... I only left out some matters prior to the milkbar because I was afraid of being implicated in such a serious crime.
>
> Before 10 am I received a phone call from Kevin Chamberlain my de facto. Kevin told me that our friend Vicki Cleary had been stabbed and that Brian Freake had telephoned Kevin to tell him this. I asked Kevin

where she was. I telephoned PANCH, St Vincents and the Royal Melbourne. I was told at that she was in theatre and she was seriously hurt. I asked the nurse if she would be alright and she said, 'She's serious but she's not critical and we hope she'll be all right, don't we.'

I was in quite a state. I spoke to Kevin and I told him that I had found where Vicki was and that she was serious and in theatre. Kevin then told me that Peter was in the house and that he was trying to ring a solicitor and I told Kevin to get him out of our house, that I didn't want him in there.

I told Kevin not to tell him that Vicki was serious because I thought he might take off. I said to Kevin to tell Peter to go to the shops and I'll take him to the police. I started towards home. I wanted to go home and talk to Kevin. I thought we could ring the police and they could pick him up at the shops. I got lost and unfortunately ended up at the shops first. I saw Peter so I pulled over and I said to him, 'What have you done?' He kept saying, 'I don't know, I don't know.'

I said, 'Which police station do you want to go to, Russell Street or Coburg?' He said, 'I don't want to go to the police, I want to go to my solicitor's.' I thought if I couldn't get him to the police I should take him to the solicitors in case he took off. We drove around a few phone boxes. Some didn't work and the solicitor wasn't in on the other occasion. Peter made all the phone calls because I didn't want to leave him in the car in case he took off in it.

We drove towards the solicitors and finally Peter said after a phone call that the solicitor was in. I remember when we drove past the Royal Melbourne Hospital on the way in I told Peter that Vicki was in that hospital and I remember he crossed himself as we went past.

Peter and I went into the solicitor's office. Peter asked when we were in the office if he could listen to the radio to see how Vicki was. The news came over then that Vicki had died. Peter began sobbing and the solicitor said that this changes things and went to ring other solicitors. I left the room and left Peter on his own. Peter came out and said he wanted to go to the toilet. I stood outside the toilet because I still didn't know if he'd take off. I remember the solicitor said he would ring the Coburg Police to see if he should take him there or to Russell Street.

After this the solicitor came back in and told Peter that they were going to Russell Street and that he would call a taxi. Peter said he would rather walk...

I would say that Peter took the split up exceptionally hard and I think because Peter had to sell his antiques at the auction on the day Vicki was stabbed this might have triggered him off.

On Tuesday the 25th August 1987 I saw Peter at about 8.30 pm or 9 pm at Brian's place. I rang about 7 pm that night at Brian's to see if Peter wanted to come down for a drink but there was no answer. When we got there he was sitting there with a pizza and he appeared very quiet. We left shortly after this and he was still awake at this time. This was at about 9.30 pm.

A week had passed since she'd sat and watched Keogh deliver his explanation to the stalker, Brian Watson, from the confines of Pentridge. The apologetic 'I think because Peter had to sell his antiques at the auction on the day Vicki was stabbed this might have triggered him off' captured her warped understanding of Keogh's macho violence. If they knew about Keogh's words to Freake the morning he left to kill Vicki no one was prepared to speak. The cone of silence was up.

Chamberlain's new account of the morning was in stark contrast to that of Cole.

I have previously made a statement to police on 26 August 1987. There are a few matters that I would like to add. At about 9.45 that morning Brian Freake had rung and said Lorna Cleary had telephoned him and she said that Vicki had been stabbed. I think Brian said that Lorna had thought Peter had done it. After this call I rang Pat and told her, then I went back to bed and listened to the radio to pick up some news. The next thing I heard the back door open and I thought it might be Pat, but then I thought it would be a bit too quick for her to get home.

Then Peter Keogh came into the room and stood at the end of the bed. I said, 'What in the fucking hell have you done?' He said, 'I don't know.' Then he ran out of the bedroom. I put some clothes on and went out to find him and I saw him paying off a taxi. The taxi left and Peter came back inside. I went and put the kettle on and walked out.

Peter said he tried to ring a solicitor on our phone. I didn't know what to say to him, he was standing there shaking...

I just told him where Pat would pick him up and I think he was gone before I hung up the phone from Pat.

'No, he wasn't vague. He just had the solicitor on his mind and he knew what he wanted to do,' he told the court. Away from the court, Chamberlain would eventually tell it as it really was. It went like this:

'What have you done?' asked Chamberlain when the sweating and agitated Peter Keogh burst through the back door of the brick veneer in Reservoir.

'I dunno. I need a fuckin' solicitor. Where's the fuckin' solicitor when you need him?' growled Keogh as his stumpy fingers dialled and re-dialled Robert Digala's number.

'I'll put the kettle on.'

'Yeah, shit, I need a gun... her fuckin' brothers... they'll be on me tail.'

'Do you want to go to the police?'

'Mate, I need a fuckin' solicitor. Fuck the police. I need fuckin' Digala,' he repeated, placing the cup on the table and scurrying to the front window to survey the lie of the land.

At Homicide headquarters a little after 2 pm, Keogh would tell Detective Jim Conomy that he'd rung Kevin Chamberlain after the murder. Chamberlain later claimed it was Freake who rang him. To this day, Pam Duggan swears that Cole rang her from the house in Reservoir screaming about Keogh being there covered in blood.

In the aftermath of a brutal murder neither Freake nor Chamberlain nor Cole lifted a finger to help build a case against Vicki's murderer. Nor did Duggan. 'Vicki and me used to go to Ojas in Clifton Hill. He didn't like it. He was always talking about us meeting men. He was weird,' she told me years later.

'So why didn't you tell the police what you knew?' I asked.

'Dunno, love. Yeah, suppose I should have,' she said. While Cole prepared to help Keogh, Duggan lost an opportunity to show Vicki she cared. My sister had a right to expect better.

killings of the intimate kind

They say a coward never changes his colours. Keogh was every bit a coward. Rattled and desperate in the Chamberlain-Cole kitchen in Reservoir, he was plain scared. The only thing that could save him now was the law. Alcohol had saved him in 1964. He had an idea what it would be this time. But interception was a great threat. The thought that one of Vicki's brothers might appear at the door had transformed the man into a gibbering wreck. He wasn't dazed or distressed by the events of that morning. He was a coward frightened to death by what lay ahead. Gone was the brazen exterior and bluff.

By the time Keogh had made contact with Digala and set sail for Hardware Street, Vicki was gone. At approximately 10.30 am Paul Cleary's mate, Tony Bartham, a big genial bushy, dropped Lorna at the front doors of the Royal Melbourne Hospital. Three months earlier, Bartham had stood alongside my brother Paul at Keogh's front door in Broadford and warned him off harassing Vicki. At the front door of the house where he'd assaulted Vicki, Keogh stood frightened and repentant. 'Na, mate, there's no issue,' he howled.

As Bartham sat in the car outside the hospital, he reflected on the insipid man who'd protested his innocence that day in Broadford. Little did he know that as he waited for the news, Peter Raymond Keogh, killer and thug, was in the area. At around 11.20 am the Cleary family, weeping and distraught, emerged from the hospital. Not more than 100 hundred away Peter Keogh, said Cole, was making the sign of the cross with the same hand that that had rained devastating blows on our sister.

From Limerick, Ireland, through inner suburban Melbourne and claustrophobic Bunting Street in the heart of Richmond, to the hospitals where Lorna's daughters were born and her Vicki died, the demons that drove Peter Keogh were never far away from Lorna Cleary.

losing one of your own

St Paul's Church in Coburg is very much a product of the post-war exodus to the suburbs. A spacious place of worship in the red brick veneer of the era it has played home to some memorable priests. Childhood brought me into contact with the legendary Father Norris, whose Irish brogue and grumpy disposition was a relic of another time in the history of Catholicism in Australia. After I'd put the red brick temple behind me, the local parish was rocked by allegations that their spiritual leader, a bloke named Father Wallis, had been putting his hand in God's till. Soon the sexual proclivities of God's disciples would be splashed across the papers and we'd all begin to wonder whether Christ's sacrifice hadn't been in vain.

Perched alongside the Pentridge Prison wall made famous by escapees Ronald Ryan and Peter Walker, St Paul's was packed to the rafters when I was a child. Although I'd been sent to the local Catholic school, my parents weren't serious papists. On the rare occasions that my mother slipped into her orange mohair skirt and jacket, placed the pillbox hat on her head and joined me at church, I was overcome by the intimacy of the ritual. By the late sixties, church was a thing of the past.

Vicki's burial marked a sombre return to the old church. In the chaotic aftermath of her death, we'd gathered at my house in West

Brunswick. In order not to upset Dad, Mum had left him to finish up at the butcher shop. The news that his daughter was dead was a bolt from the blue. I'll never forget him arriving at the front door, his face contorted and his body shaking.

'What's happened, what's happened?' he cried. In the lounge room, away from the maelstrom, Vicki's brothers sought answers. When the police were eventually asked about the killer's history, they could only mutter something about him 'having a record'. How could any of us have imagined a man with this bloke's history of abject terror and sexual depravity being somehow connected to our family?

Amid the confusion, we talked and talked about a girl lost. Then began the mundane, humiliating task of the funeral. 'Stan Penn,' said Dad, in a throwback to happier times. It was almost childlike. Penn had buried a procession of deceased acquaintances of Mum and Dad in the old Brunswick of their early life and was one of the brightest lights in Dad's tales. It was as if the wisecracking undertaker might bring Vicki back to life. We settled on Mulqueen's across the road from Vicki's school.

Football and media work had ensured that I was sufficiently well known for the media to want a story. The phone rang incessantly. 'No, I'm not interested in being interviewed,' I would repeat again and again. We'd agreed there'd be no parading of the family's misery before the masses. Helpless victims we were not going to be.

Later in the day, Johnny Spencer arrived at the house. During a game of football at Millers Rope Works in Brunswick in 1954 Spencer had run onto the ground seeking retribution when a copper on the opposition team whacked Dad. Right now, there was nothing the Brunswick football legend could do for his mate.

On the evening news we saw the first terrible pictures of the murder scene and the killer being bundled out of Russell Street like some significant crook. Although there was blood all over Vicki's car we still had no idea of what had transpired. Vicki was dead—that's all that mattered. A trial and retribution was the furthest thing from our minds. My words for the reporter from the Melbourne *Sun* were brief and measured:

> She was a very gentle person. She lived for her family. She loved children and had always enjoyed the vitality of a large family. She called into training the other night and was just so happy. She was in the operating theatre when I arrived and about an hour later I was advised she died. They were unable to stop the bleeding.

As the news began to permeate the outside world, victims remembered the man with the tattoos and the strange eyes. The mother of the little girl assaulted in Richmond in 1974, the girl set upon in the T&G building in 1975 and a handful of ex-girlfriends imagined how lucky they'd been.

'Mum, I just heard on the news that a girl's been stabbed in Coburg. From the description it sounds just like Peter Keogh,' Terri McNulty told her mother by phone from work around 9.30 am. The RESI finance offices in South Melbourne were a long way from Coburg. But such was Terri's fear of Keogh, she imagined him running amok and coming after her. So too did her mother. Keogh had damaged so many lives.

Those who'd seen him in action knew Keogh was a time bomb waiting to explode. 'I knew it. I knew he'd do it again,' Judy McNulty told her daughter as they watched his latest act of violence unfold on the television set. Judy watched the reports then rang directory and scribbled the Cleary phone number in her diary. Many times she wanted to ring, but for now Judy would hold her peace.

I'd never really thought about taking one last look at Vicki before we lowered her into the Fawkner clay. Mum always knew it was something she had to do. She'd never been able to tell her daughter, 'Mummy's coming, it's all right, Mummy's here.' How much our mother wanted to be able to offer her grievously wounded daughter those protective words. At the hospital she'd been denied the chance to tell her how much she loved her.

'She'll be with us, Mum,' I'd repeated again and again as I stroked my mother's face and pressed her head against my neck. 'What am I going to do? Oh, Philip, what am I going to do?' she cried.

As the eldest child I believed I was the clan chief at 26 Shore Grove, North Coburg. When the police arrived one night declaring that my youngest brother, Perry, had been found driving Dad's car and was in big trouble I was equal to the task.

'Well, lock him up and we'll come and bail him out,' I told them when they tried to bounce Mum and Dad. They took their leave without my brother.

As the first child to go to university and to take the family name into public life, I thought myself a pioneer and a class above the Keoghs of the world, yet neither education nor identity prepared me to save Vicki from an illiterate loser. No matter what anyone said, I'd failed to save her. For the rest of my life, I'd never quite expunge that thought from my mind. In a sense it was why I felt so angry with Justice George Hampel. It wasn't just that he allowed Keogh a defence of provocation. I was convinced he led a hapless jury to a verdict of manslaughter. Ultimately he delivered the final insult. And as the eldest Cleary, I felt a responsibility to redress it.

At the Mulqueen Funeral Parlour, we had the opportunity to say all those things we couldn't say when the doctor sent us away from the hospital. And yet even as I moved towards the coffin I had no sense of all that had transpired and from what it was I should have protected my sister. If only someone had said, 'Hey Phil, that Keogh's a bad bastard.' And little did I know that a short distance away behind the bluestone walls of Pentridge, the killer was bragging to some loser from Port Melbourne that he'd killed Phil Cleary's sister. Oblivious to this, my mother was remarkably calm as she touched Vicki's face and shifted the errant strand of hair.

'Why didn't you tell me? Why don't women tell?' I wanted to ask Vicki.

Fourteen years later, I remembered Vicki's funeral and those thoughts as I sat in the office of the chief lawman, Victorian Attorney General, Rob Hulls. The day before, Hulls had announced there'd be no granting of clemency to convicted murderer, Heather Osland. Three years earlier, Hulls had publicly apologised for abusing a couple of pro-Liberal women in a bar. Today he listened intently as I put the case for Osland.

'The legal opinion from three QCs, one of whom is a woman, is that there are no grounds for clemency,' he told me.

'Do you expect the legal fraternity to damn a decision by one of their own?' I asked.

'I appreciate what you are saying but really my hands are tied. I put it to the Premier but he felt the same,' said Hulls.

'Weak as piss, Rob,' I thought, as he explained the government's position. I'd known Hulls from his days as a backbencher in the federal parliament. We often shared a laugh across the chamber when Prime Minister Paul Keating was in full flight during question time. A sometimes larrikin, delivering jibes about Tories with his cheeky angst-ridden mate Daryl Melham, Hulls was no crusader when I met him that day. Faced with a chance to show some moral courage against the misogyny of the law, the Melbourne Grammar boy and the Ballarat Catholic, premier Steve Bracks, were like a couple of stuttering public servants.

It didn't matter that my conversation with Hulls was frank and that he offered a sympathetic ear. The legal framework had to be torn asunder. Die a victim or kill and be damned. That was the option thrown at the feet of women confronted by violent partners.

On a piece of lined paper in sad but purposeful handwriting Heather Osland, inmate at Tarrengower Prison near Mansfield, told me what she thought: 'I'm totally devastated with the Government's decision ... sometimes it's very hard to endure ... I appreciate your support immensely.'

'She's a venal and evil woman,' someone close to the Office of Public Prosecutions had told me. Yet no one, not Justice George Hampel, not prosecutor Bruce Walmsley, nor anyone from the DPP had ever used those words when exploring Peter Keogh's character. Vicki at least could never be accused of being venal. She'd accepted her fate with the nobility of a martyr. That's how some men of law preferred it. But what would lead a man experienced in law to speak such savage, vitriolic words, I thought. Even if she over stepped the

losing one of your own 167

mark, was it true? Even if she had killed Frank Osland as a payback for all he'd done to her over the previous thirteen years, would she have deserved such a description?

'It'll be dark. He'll have the lights off,' Vicki had screamed hysterically when Perry had threatened to go and see Keogh after she arrived crying at his house. She didn't mention the knife or the wild claims he made when the drink seeped into his distorted brain. As with the savage in Heather Osland's life, only the sword was a match for the cowardice of Peter Keogh. But as Osland would discover, the sword was a blunt form of justice unless it was in the hands of a man.

At the church in Coburg, years before we'd heard of Heather Osland, a large eclectic assortment of friends had gathered to say their last goodbye. A local parishioner had assured us that Vicki's soul would be offered up in a special mass the night before the funeral. I only wished God had been more caring before Keogh struck. In our haste to bury Vicki, and because of the emotional turmoil, we'd forgotten that it was our prerogative, not that of some mindless cleric, to send Vicki off. As the priest droned on about the will and mystery of God the room became increasingly tense. Mum's uncle, Johnny Roberts, who, in his youth, had mixed fisticuffs at Festival Hall with singing on Graham Kennedy's 'In Melbourne Tonight', was so outraged we thought he might ask the cleric to step outside.

Nowhere in the eulogy could the man of cloth find the comforting words for a grieving family or remind a troubled society of the savagery of some men. Not even the sixth Commandment, Thou Shalt Not Kill, could find its way into the priest's story. 'It's not a time for anger or revenge,' he said searching for a subterfuge by which to pacify the anger. As with the victims of Hoddle Street, we all had suffering to bear, he reminded us. In the Catholic Church a martyred girl was a shadow of the Saviour captured in the stained glass windows along the walls of the church. There had been no such equivocation when communism threatened the church's spiritual heart. Nor were harsh words lacking when an abortionist killed a foetus or gay men sought the sacrament of communion. As Mum said, Vicki had made her bed and must lie in it. If only the priest had affirmed Vicki's rights as a woman and a human being. It was one more page from the parable that would accompany the ascent of Vicki's soul.

Years later when we lowered Jeff Angwin into the pristine dirt on a green, undulating hill outside Foster, there was purity in the grief and sadness. No such purity accompanied Vicki on her final journey. Vicki had died at the hands of a man she had chosen as her partner. And as long as Catholic priests, old men like George Hampel and Attorneys General such as Rob Hulls sat in judgment, she would bear some responsibility for her death. Having been deadened by the local priest's insensitive prattle, our turn to speak came at the cemetery. Against a threatening and overcast sky I paid my tribute:

> Vicki
> As a daughter were you not but a replica of a gentle mother
> Who ignited in her brood the passion of the ancient Irish clan
> Where the laughter and the spoken word were alive.
>
> As a sister you were what others could hardly be
> As an aunty and a teacher when did you not hold a captive audience?
>
> And when you graced the green abundant verandah of Broadford
> My, was your mother not happy and proud, and
> What of those fresh cut flowers in crystal vases on carefully
> chosen sideboards
> What charm!
>
> As for those five cats, who but my sister would find time,
> And when your big brother reached those two hundred games
> How proud you were.
>
> I don't come to whisk your soul away to heaven, my girl
> No, Vicki, God should have been more caring.
>
> Now the smile will be less visible
> But as the sun eases itself over that western shed
> Boys will talk loud and children will clamour
> And my sister's name will not fade
> Instead it will spring from the lips and hearts of all who say,
> 'I knew her'.
>
> Bye my love

On 11 September 2001, fourteen years and two weeks after Vicki's funeral, American President George W Bush spat out a set of words that sent my mind back to Cameron Street. 'These were innocent people going about their work,' said Bush as he declared war on the people of Afghanistan. 'Just going to work!' That's what Vicki was doing when Peter Keogh emerged with his knife. As the tragedy of each lost New York life passed across our gaze I thought again about Justice Hampel.

At services all over Australia, dignitaries and church leaders spoke of the terror and of the need for violent retribution. A week after the attack, the Prime Minister was joined by the conservative Catholic Archbishop George Pell and other church leaders in echoing the war cries of George Bush. As I watched the Old Testament response of these bastions of respectability, I wondered why the priest at St Paul's and men like Justice Hampel couldn't find the words 'terror, justice and retribution' when they spoke of the murder of a woman?

At the time, all that mattered to us was that we'd lost a beautiful woman. Revenge was a luxury. Like most people I'd never confronted this kind of violence. I'd seen the cockfights between strutting gangs in Lee jeans, listened to my parents' stories and confronted knuckle-heads on the football field.

In the days after her death a stream of letters and cards arrived:

> Well, what do I say after I have said how sorry I am to know of your sad loss of Vicki. I knew Vicki having met her at the shop of Ron's here. I thought her a lovely girl. She always had a chat, young or old it made no difference. To Vicki we were all the same...

> She'll be missed greatly by us and our children, Paul, Natalie and Christopher. Paul was in her kindergarten class last year, Natalie this year and although Christopher is not due to start kindergarten until next year, he has joined in her kindergarten group quite a number of times in the past. They all loved her.

> I'd like to say that she and all of your family has always stayed in my memory and heart over the years. Vick was such a gentle and beautiful

person, with a great sense of humour. This is how I am sure hundreds of her friends will remember her. I know I will. So please take care. Thinking of you ...

I was always the first to nurse the babies brought home to the brick veneer at 26 Shore Grove. I was nine years older than Vicki, so nursing her on the wrought-iron couch outside the rumpus room in October 1961 was a relatively easy task. Five years later, I stood in the very same spot with my hand on her shoulder as she prepared for her first day of school. Two years earlier we'd nearly lost her—the screech of rubber out front had been ominous. Dad had her in his arms in a flash, but her leg was broken. In the hospital her crying was so relentless and unnerving when the time came for us to leave, I never forgot it. She wanted her mother. She had always loved her mother. In the days and weeks after her murder I remembered how she loved her mother.

There was so much unfinished business. The difference in years meant I was just getting to know her when the bastard took her life. With Keogh gone from her life, Vicki and I had much to share. Suddenly she was there at the football and in the carpark before training. She'd began to blossom. Watching her play with my daughters outside the ground a week earlier, I was inspired by her vitality and lack of pretension. Their aunty Vicki was preparing to embark on a wonderful journey.

Among her possessions were bundles of letters and notes that captured the spirit and the warmth she generated in others. 'Dear Chris ... I didn't get to hang out the washing, but there's always tomorrow. All my love, Vicki', she had written only weeks before she died. Whimsical and free spirited yet so kind it captured what a gorgeous girl she was. However it was the letter she left on Chris Wheeler's windscreen, a letter I didn't see till years later that drove me to anger and thoughts of revenge.

Dear Chris

Thank you for a great couple of weeks. I'll miss you something terrible but I'll be with you in spirit. Hope you work everything out in New Zealand. Don't be too cruel to poor Ross.

I hope the night is a real success anyway. Have a good flight make the most of the break. I can't tell you enough how happy I've been. It's a great feeling. I'll miss you but I'll keep in touch.

All my love

Vicki

A collection of words that spoke of redemption and love, the letter offered a profound snapshot of where she had been and was now going. Keogh had been an aberration in her short life. Like others before her, Vicki had stayed with a bad man out of pity and maternal obligation. Eventually, the absence of intimacy and warmth made the relationship a farce. Torn by a desire to protect him and a need to liberate her soul, she flirted with freedom.

A series of letters dating from 1983 to an ex-boyfriend camouflage her cry for help.

> When I spoke to you over the phone we were to shift on the 29th of November but since then the sale on the house has fallen through. I'm a little disappointed as I was looking forward to moving—my attitude towards moving has changed now. I don't even know ...'
>
> P S. Give us a ring sometime.
>
> Love, Vicki

The truth was, the purchase of the house in Broadford hadn't fallen through. Always modest and uncertain about the love of men, she couldn't bring herself to say exactly what troubled her. Instead of saying she didn't want to go to Broadford to live with Keogh, she fumbled with the words, 'I don't even know'. Then she stopped midstream, crossed out that line and left her fate in the hands of the gods. While her ex heard but didn't understand, Vicki's sister listened to the unabridged story.

'I don't want to go to Broadford, Donna. I told him that. But I'm worried about him. He's too old for me, but he doesn't have anyone else. And I know he'll cause trouble,' she'd confided in late 1986. Within a few months the relationship would be over. Although Broadford was home to our parents, it meant isolation from her friends and an hour's drive to the kinder in Coburg. For the moody and indolent Keogh, a home in a rural town was ideal. At the local pub he could indulge himself with pool and drink, while the 'little woman brought home the bacon'.

In January 1987, the man in her letters arrived on the doorstep of the semi-detached brick veneer they rented at 463 Gilbert Road, Preston. With Keogh away in Broadford, she had hoped her ex-boyfriend might offer a way out. Any sign would do. When he kissed her on the cheek and said, 'All the best, kiddo,' she went close to telling him the whole truth. As always, a mixture of pride and uncertainty conspired against her. As she shut the door and watched him disappear out of sight, she struggled with the possibility of asking what he thought about her. Then she quietly cried about her plight.

Vicki, Keogh and Donna had been in the Gilbert Road house since moving from Beauchamp Street in January 1985. In the final year of the relationship, the house had become a hellhole for Vicki. Late one night in 1986, the brooding Keogh had awoken in a state. Angry that she hadn't gushed over the roast he'd pulled from the oven, he was in a vengeful mood. 'Cop that, ya fuckin' bitch,' he growled as he poured the contents of a rubbish bin over the girl in the bed. 'What's going on with Vicki?' asked Donna when she stuck her head in the bedroom door and found the bully drunk on the bed, with rubbish strewn everywhere. No matter how much she shook him he refused to open his eyes. Vicki was nowhere to be seen.

The next day Keogh was abjectly apologetic, and Vicki laughed about how she'd slept in the 'summer residence'. In Gilbert Road, that was the garage. As with the black eye she once explained away, this became another event to be hidden from her brothers. Donna had never seen anything like this in her own life—she was only 22 and unsure about what to do. Angry that Vicki appeared to take it lightly, she wanted to tell someone, but Vicki would have none of it. She was always desperately worried about troubling our dad or embroiling her brothers in her affairs.

It was different on the final Monday of her life when she spoke to

Donna. Suddenly she grasped the danger and, I believe, was as close as she'd ever been to telling us what she feared.

It wasn't till 8 October, a full six weeks after the murder, that Donna was asked what she knew about the crucial last weeks of our sister's life. In a sworn statement, Senior Detective Barry McIntosh received a telling account of the terror experienced by Vicki before she died. The most chilling event was the phone call from Keogh on the Monday before she was murdered. That day, Keogh and Freake dined on a counter meal of steak and mash at their favourite haunt, the Council Club Hotel. Known locally as Cramers, it was here on Monday at lunchtime that Keogh rang Vicki at the kinder and delivered his final threat.

Although Keogh's calls to the kinder had been screened, on this occasion a staffer inadvertently called Vicki to the phone. While he lit up a fag and sipped his stubbie the sociopath went to work on his victim.

'Hello.'
'Where's my fuckin' things?'
'Peter, what are you doing ringing me?'
'I want my fuckin' things.'
'What things, Peter? I don't have any of your things.'
'I'm sick of your fuckin' childish games.'
'What games, Peter? I haven't hassled you about anything.'
'What about the fuckin' car? I want the fuckin' car back, that's one thing I want.'
'The car isn't even mine. I've taken out a loan for it with the bank at Broadford. It's worth nothing, Peter.'
'Fuck the bank. You'll get a solicitor's letter about the car anyway. Think you're so smart using that car to see your new boyfriend. You're not so smart I've had you followed.'
'Followed?'
'Do ya think Watson and I spotted you by accident, do you?'
'Why do you need to follow me? What have I done? You've even got some of my furniture at the Auction Rooms.'

'Listen. I've told Bob not to let any of your lot near it and he said the job's done.'

'But some of that furniture belongs to me.'

'Too bad. Listen, the only place for you is to get your arse to Broadford. And if you don't bring my things around by six o'clock Tuesday night you'll be hearing from me.'

Like so much that transpired, I had no idea about this phone call or the fact that Freake had often rung the kinder and passed the phone to his mate. Years later when I found a piece of paper in Vicki's belongings with the scribbled words 'Vicki, ring Brian. Urgent', I went mental. Freake had a silent number but fortunately Mum had it.

'You bastard. You were ringing Vicki for Keogh, weren't you!' I told him when I got him to the phone in 1997. As always the informer displayed the kind of cowardice for which he and Keogh were legendary.

'It wasn't me, believe me, I had nothing to do with it. I didn't ring the kinder. I promise,' he bawled down the line. When it was all said and done, they were so pathetic.

'If I find out you were a party to this murder you're in trouble,' I told him. Ironically he was and I didn't even know. Soon he would die a violent death.

As the full story unfolded over the ensuing years I imagined revenge almost every day. I just still couldn't understand how this could happen to the beautiful girl I'd nursed as a baby and had begun to know after her split with Keogh. The thought that this miserable coward could terrorise my sister with impunity was simply unbearable. I wanted my day with Freake and the mob. I wanted Keogh, Freake and Watson alive.

At 1.50 pm on Sunday 18 September 1988, I planted my feet on the old floorboards under the Hird grandstand at the Windy Hill ground and prepared to deliver my final thoughts as coach of the Coburg Football Club. In 1986 Williamstown had stolen the VFA premiership from us after I was controversially ordered off in the third quarter. This and the turmoil of Vicki's murder in 1987 meant life just hadn't been smooth sailing. This was more than a football match for me. I knew a victory would bring some emotional relief to my parents and my brothers and sisters. As I thought about the place of this ritual in the context of what we'd endured over the last year, I became convinced of its significance. We must win. I was sure of that.

To my left in the rooms was the Prime Minister of Australia, Coburg's Number One Ticket Holder, Bob Hawke. The arrival of Hawke and his entourage a few minutes earlier had added a layer of drama and suspense. Now we steeled ourselves for another assault on the flag. With the Committal over and only the trial to come a loss against Williamstown would have deepened the despair. I decided to be frank.

> I would like to acknowledge the presence of the Prime Minister Bob Hawke. It's great to have you with us, Bob. Everyone knows this has been a difficult time for my family. Nothing will ever bring my sister Vicki back. Nor is it your problem or something you can rectify. Nevertheless it will mean something if we win this grand final. I know it will bring some happiness to my parents and ease their sorrow. I've dedicated everything to my sister. This game is for her. She is my inspiration. And one thing I've always said to you blokes is that we are like a family. We're committed to each other. That's what has made us a great side. We're going to win this one. Remember what Terry Wheeler said. 'We're ready for them but the question is, are they ready for us.' Are we fucking ready for them?

As we collectively drew breath and imagined what lay ahead, a wave of confidence swept through the room. As I followed the players down the race and headed for the coach's box I knew my sister was with me.

When Greg Reynoldson steered through a goal at the grandstand end of Windy Hill as the clock hit time-on in the 1988 VFA grand final, the relief was indescribable. Another goal by Reynoldson a few minutes later and the premiership was Coburg's to celebrate. When I took the cup from Premier John Cain and held it aloft with club captain Brad Nimmo, I could see Vicki's sparkling eyes in the crowd. Mum saw them too. A year earlier in that barren room at the Royal

Melbourne Hospital I'd told my fractured mother Vicki would always be with us. That day I knew I was right.

Fifteen thousand people were at Windy Hill and several hundred thousand watched the broadcast on ABC TV. Bruce Walmsley, a mad Essendon Bomber supporter, was among them. Walmsley had grown up in Moonee Ponds before being shunted off to Wesley College by his parents. He wasn't the first Walmsley to go to war with a Keogh. In 1952 his father had formed part of the Chambers, Wallis and Carmody legal team that represented the employers in a dispute with Jack Keogh's Rubber Workers Union.

At the time of the grand final he had no idea he would end up with the brief to prosecute R v Keogh in February 1989. In the whole scheme of things, prosecuting for the Crown is no plum job. Eight hundred dollars a day might have been a king's ransom to a Coburg labourer or a butcher like Ron Cleary. It wasn't big end of town stuff for a QC. And garden-variety domestic murders, even when the girl is the sister of a well-known local football identity, are no career-boosting event.

Coburg's premiership had come one year and one month after Vicki's murder and three months after the conclusion of the two-day committal at Hawthorn Magistrate's Court. After studying the evidence, Judge Jillian Mary Crowe had declared:

> Vicki Maree Cleary aged 25 had arrived at work about 8.10 am and was straight away approached by Peter Raymond Keogh who stabbed her a number of times to the face and chest region and thereby contributed to her death.

Despite defence counsel, Mr Kriss, flagging the argument that Keogh had the DTs, was a chronic drinker and didn't know what he was doing when he stabbed Vicki, Crowe committed Keogh to stand trial for murder. Yet even Magistrate Crowe seemed to have overlooked the detail. Why didn't she note that Vicki was murdered on the passenger side of the car? Why didn't she say that witness Suzanne McKay saw Keogh dragging Vicki to the passenger seat of the car? Why did everyone ignore the fact that the stabbing occurred some time after the initial confrontation?

The desperate little petty thug from Westgarth never left anything to luck or chance. From the bare-faced lie to Paul Cleary that he wouldn't stalk Vicki, to the meticulous planning of a provocation-style murder, Keogh was the master of his destiny. By the time he appeared in Hawthorn Magistrate's court he had begun bombarding those who sat in judgement with a defence.

In Ms Crowe's possession was a submission from his defence team Jerry Prus and Consultants, solicitors of Frankston. They were seeking to have the charge of murder reduced to manslaughter. Mr Prus' office had this to say about what happened in Cameron Street:

> It is quite evident, your Worship, that the Defendant was in a depressed state of mind as a result of the break-up of a four and a half year relationship. You have heard from both the Defendant and witnesses of excessive drinking of alcohol for periods of seven to eight hours per day, both in hotels and drinking in the home. You have heard that the Defendant used drugs and alcohol prior to the attack on the victim.
>
> The defendant dressed in bright yellow overalls ... and carried a Stanley knife, a fishing knife and a set of pliers ... You have heard from the Defendant's record of interview that the defendant and the victim had an argument and that the victim had used provocative language to the Defendant.
>
> From the evidence he quite clearly loved the deceased, Vicki Cleary.
>
> I submit that in light of the current evidence, read in conjunction with the current law, the defendant is not guilty of murder.

Included in the submission under the heading, 'Defence of Self Induced Intoxication', was a ruling deemed to favour the killer. In the R v Keogh of 1964 that had made its way into Victorian Case Law, a fifteen-year-old boy had beaten attempted murder. Unfortunately for the defence, it was the very Peter Keogh who killed Vicki Cleary. It was a strange strategy by Prus. The sight of Keogh arguing that just as he beat attempted murder in the knife attack on a cop, so he should be reprieved for the knifing murder of Vicki, would have excited the boys in the tabloid press and raised a few eyebrows on the bench. And in any case, without alcohol or drugs in his blood, Keogh could never run an automatism defence. The whole submission was plain stupid.

Without a weak jury, a sympathetic judge and prejudice on his side, Keogh was gone. Although the submission devoted only one page to the provocation defence, Prus had begun the argument that would save him. It mattered not that there was no evidence of an argument or that Vicki said 'fuck off!' or 'piss off!' Nor did it matter that Keogh was armed to the teeth when he flung open Vicki's door and grabbed her keys before she'd even finished parking. She either agreed to his terms or she was dead.

Everyone, even the mass murderer, Julian Knight, must be defended. When Knight faced George Hampel in 1988, Robert Richter QC, the avowed civil libertarian, took on the job. Having decided against provoking the society any more than he already had, Knight pleaded guilty and avoided the acrimony. No matter what act of inhumanity Keogh committed, there was always someone there to support him.

Jerry Prus' submission was more provocative than anything Vicki could have said that morning. It made my blood boil. I had no difficulty explaining Keogh's mode of operation that morning. I knew why Keogh wore bright overalls—they were both a disguise and an alibi. Before the murder he was an ordinary railway worker. Afterwards, he was a man who'd drawn such attention to himself he couldn't possibly have gone to Cameron Street to kill his ex. Prus never mentioned the hat on Keogh's head and the packing tape in his pocket. And we know why he described the weapon as fishing knife. A fishing knife's not for killing the ex. Is it?

'She's a dog and a cunt!' Was it his favourite old saying he offered Freake before he took off that morning? Two weeks earlier, he had marshalled another set of words for Vicki. This time it was Chamberlain who heard them. The run of the mill atmosphere in the Magistrate's Court had been pierced by the words of the last witness on 17 June 1988. 'Keogh threatened to neck Vicki if she didn't pull up,' Chamberlain told Keogh's mouthpiece out of the blue. As the ripple of shock ran through the room, defence counsel Mr Kriss searched for a response. Nearby, Keogh feigned a look of contempt for what he'd eventually call 'a lie'. The spectre of a debilitated and pitiful killer who knew not what he'd done was emerging over the dead girl's body, but Chamberlain, we thought, had buried his drinking mate. We hadn't counted on a couple of psychiatrists saving him. Hidden from the story to this point, they would make their cameo when the show trial hit the Supreme Court.

Stigmatised as the kind of outrage the hoi polloi visits on its own, 'wife' killing doesn't excite the top prosecuting silks. When the accused is the pathetic grubby Peter Keogh and the dead girl is his former lover public sympathy is confined to the close circle of friends and relatives. It was one thing for Princes Di to choose a bad prince. It was another for the butcher's daughter from Coburg to choose a bad man. It took me until 1997 to ask Bruce Walmsley what he thought about the outcome of R v Keogh. His description of the trial as 'a lemon' seemed sublimely cute. Later I'd run my eye over his letter to the DPP following my request for a review of Hampel's handling of the case. I wasn't impressed.

Walmsley struck me as a good bloke and by all accounts is a fine defence barrister. But was he a take-no-prisoners, killer prosecutor? I thought not. He was approachable, but there was never sufficient opportunity to explore the background matters we knew would have weakened Keogh's position. It remains one of my great regrets that I didn't adopt an old style working-class approach to the matter of R v Keogh. Instead of asking politely whether the defence was aware of certain matters, I should have grabbed hold of the team as they wandered by and told them straight. Constrained by bourgeois notions of propriety I let them do the thinking when it should have been us. As a consequence, Freake got away with murder in the box, while Pam Duggan and parole officer Margaret Hobbs weren't called. With Keogh in the dock and George Hampel on the bench, we needed a ruthless wig and gown with a grasp of every nuance of the case dominating the floor of the court, but that's not how it was.

When Walmsley led the prosecution against the boy from

Westgarth, it was before a cultural backdrop that treated 'domestic murders' as just another little murder, in a profession that looked down its nose at prosecutors. Sending someone down for killing the ex-missus was not the sort of success to be celebrated by a round of drinks at the Melbourne Club or the Christmas break-up.

Neither prosecutor Walmsley nor defence barrister John Champion was like the theatrical Bob Vernon QC. Declared bankrupt on several occasions, when the taxman called Vernon didn't always play by bourgeois rules. For Keogh, there was only ever one rule: lie your way out of a fix. Funnily enough, both men were loners.

'He's by nature not a vicious or violent person. Whatever he may be, he is not the sort of person who would normally take a dagger and attack people with it,' Vernon had told Justice Monahan on Monday 25 May 1964. One wonders what he might have said about his client had he risen to defend him against the stabbing murder of Vicki Cleary.

Keogh was taken by Vernon's grasp of the spoken word and how he'd convinced the bigwig high above the court to unburden the jury of a need to return a verdict of guilty of attempted murder. Watching Vernon spice his plea with images of a boy mesmerised by the power of the bottle the petty thug knew he was the man for all seasons. 'Burst of larrikin behaviour.' I like that, he thought, when Vernon splashed those romantic images of his client across the court. With Justice Monahan accepting that automatism precluded intent to murder, only the sentence remained. To help the judge, Vernon opened up the kitbag of deprivation Keogh carried and found a troubled, fatherless boy from the wrong side of the tracks. Nagged by a shrewish mother, poor young Peter had done it hard. Still, the old, Catholic judge wasn't convinced.

'What worries me is this boy's mental state and that reference to the "gunnie" uncle. Who is this uncle?'

'This was a complete straw clutched out of the wind.'

'I am going to get a report and see if there is any truth in that… if he is hero worshipping a gunman he has to be stopped.'

'I can tell you, Your Honour ... it did not make any sense to him ...'

'That may be ... I want to find out the truth about that ... this chap has to be stopped. He is a real menace ...'

'If it were found out to be so—on my instructions Your Honour will find it not to so—but even if it is so, might I put this to Your Honour. It is perhaps understandable how a young lad of that age could come to wrongly hero-worship some uncle. Uncles have been seen to have a very natural way of obtaining the affection of youngsters. On instruction there is no such uncle. You will notice there is nothing against this lad so far as violence is concerned. If he were gaoled for any length of time at his age, he might very well come into association with the very worst types to influence a fifteen or sixteen-year-old boy,' said Vernon.

'He'll go away from this court and tell his mates, "You don't want to worry about having a go at a bloke. You only have to be full and you're out of it",' bemoaned Monahan as he looked for Vernon to allay his fears.

'With respect, I don't think so, Your Honour.'

'I think he will ... I had a close look at him at close range, and I think that is what he will be inclined to do, to go away and skite.'

Two days later, armed with K J O'Sullivan's pre-sentence report, Justice Monahan secured his place above the body of the court and took the accused and the public on an erudite excursion through the law as it pertained to intent. First, he congratulated the jury then moved on to cite the words of wisdom of British luminaries Lord Devlin, Lord Sankey, and that sworn enemy of Irish republicanism, Lord Birkenhead. Well-versed in the effect of liquor on the behaviour of British gentlemen, they could hardly resile from the proposition that uneducated working-class boys might be beguiled by the foxy devil.

As Justice Monahan positioned his notes, Keogh rearranged his demeanour and stood to attention. Then came the moment of triumph:

> Mr Keogh, the truth is you are an unhappy and misguided youth just approaching manhood in a world where if you can adopt a healthy

attitude towards life you can achieve great happiness and success. If you go around with a song in your heart rather than a dagger in your belt you may realise the advice I'm offering is sound.

'Get on with it you old bastard, what's the damage,' he thought as Monahan continued with his sermon. When the words 'probation', 'good behaviour for three years' and 'abstain from liquor until you are nineteen' rolled off the judge's tongue, he secretly revelled in the moment. He'd loved to have shot the words 'fuckin' ripper, take that copper' from the corner of his mouth. Now wasn't the time. He'd save the bragging for his mate, Larry.

'Yes, Sir,' he said nodding obsequiously.

'Very well, come down, Mr Keogh. Now, you are going away on probation, and if you break the terms of this probation order you will be brought back to me to deal with you in regard to these matters, so do not forget that.'

'No.'

'So take my advice and look after yourself. Good luck,' concluded Monahan.

On 3 October 1966, a little over two years after the compassionate Justice Monahan wished him good luck on his journey through life, Peter Keogh joined his mates Mario, Robert and Colin in Bendigo Magistrate's Court following a bit of biff and bash after a dance in the town. On the police brief, it was claimed Keogh had stuck the boots in to the victim. As Monahan had predicted, nothing had changed for the would-be tough. Keogh added three months gaol to his Curriculum Vitae and immediately appealed. On 2 May 1967 his appeal was dismissed and nineteen-year-old Keogh was shunted off to Pentridge for his first real burst of gaol. Down the road from the gaol, five-year-old Vicki Cleary was a joyful face in a sea of laughing girls behind the walls of Mercy Convent School.

Ask a man of law about Peter Keogh's journey through the system and the needle goes on the record. 'Keogh wasn't much good. Usually I think one thing or another. With him I felt nothing,' Vernon's associate, Peter Berman, would tell me. Son of Peggy Berman, a substantial figure in ALP politics in Richmond and the woman who blew the whistle on police corruption during the abortion scandals of the 1960s, Peter Berman had boarded at Xavier College. A staunchly anti-Liberal Party defender of the ordinary punter, Berman enjoyed the craic.

'So what was it like defending a bloke who's committed buggery on a nine-year-old girl,' I asked.

'Everyone deserves a fair trial and the presumption of innocence,' he told me.

'Do you remember much about the case?'

'Bob Vernon must have been busy or Keogh couldn't pay. That's probably why I finished up with it. I was cheaper. One thing always troubled me. The girl never mentioned his tattoos. He was covered in pictures and I had him strip down to his jocks so the jury could see how obvious they were.'

'Well, maybe they meant nothing to her.'

'Yes, I don't know. It was just odd.'

'So what about the case, was Keogh guilty?'

'He was very lucky to get only eighteen months for that assault. Professionally, I had to be very happy with that result.'

Too often, truth and morality was the first casualty of adversarial law and the farce of reasonable doubt. Keogh was plain bad and every barrister must have known it. Like the hand wringers in the civil liberties push who defended the rights of refugees but said nothing about the human rights of Christine Crowe or Vicki Cleary, Karl Marx, too, never seriously tackled the political dimensions of male violence. Patriarchy did none of us any good—he did note that. Abolish capitalism and the family, and women would be liberated, he said. Maybe he was right. What to do with Peter Keogh while we waited for the family to disappear? That was the question.

Parole officers turning a blind eye to violence or blaming hard-working mothers and Bob Kent splashing nude photos of Christine Crowe across the court needed to get their marching orders. Instead of excusing kids from the housing commission, the ordinary punter should have been outlawing the violence. It wasn't what Bob Vernon told the boys.

Twenty-three years after Justice Monahan implored Keogh to set out with a song, not a dagger, in his heart, the knife man was ensconced in remand in Pentridge preparing to explain away the murderous actions of his blade. He was a nervous man.

'Gotta delay the trial,' he told them at the Legal Aid Commission. Little did we know that delayed trials were a signature of the devious Keogh. After a succession of delays, February 1989 was set aside as the trial date. It had taken the criminal justice system a disgraceful seventeen months to finally put him in the dock. There had not been one phone call from the DPP as to the circumstances of the case or whether any of Vicki's family might give evidence. 'Time has probably been a wise factor in assuaging one's outrage at the indecencies you perpetrated on the young girl', Justice Rapke had told him in 1976. Keogh hoped it would be the same when the girl's name was Vicki Cleary and the charge was murder. As the trial approached, Keogh rehearsed his defence. Alcohol, amnesia and the victim's crown were back on the agenda. By January 1989 his defence had assembled a host of letters that carried the expert opinion of sympathetic shrinks and social workers. Keogh knew the value of a good shrink. In 1976, psychiatrist Dr Allan Bartholomew delivered a classic vignette. 'In my opinion this prisoner is an alcoholic. He claims amnesia for the present offence. I do not consider this prisoner sexually deviant in the accepted sense of the word, but rather a man who, under the influence of alcohol, may behave in a sexually deviant manner', he told Rapke.

In 1989 there was no Dr Bartholomew or Bob Vernon to defend him. He was in the hands of Legal Aid, and John Champion would pick up where Vernon had left off. Dour but persistent, Champion was on top of his brief. In place of Dr Bartholomew, the defence team had resurrected the eccentric-looking man with the funny name, Dr Thomas Oldtree Clark, and found the neat, carefully scripted Dr Lester Walton.

Not long after Clark had begun treating Keogh in 1981, the Preston Law firm, Cain and Lamer, needed his help to defend the sexual assault charges over the two young girls. When I took the VFA premiership cup from the hands of Victorian premier John Cain in

September 1988, at Windy Hill, I never imagined that locked away in the High Street files of the firm he'd established were a stream of letters and records documenting Keogh's troubled mind and his assaults on the unsuspecting. Those records show that Dr Clark was exceedingly sympathetic to Keogh. 'He was feeling suicidal, had terrible feelings of doom and kept breaking into tears', he would write two months before the case went to the Preston Court. Not one of Keogh's drinking mates noticed that Keogh was close to necking himself.

If Dr Clark knew about Keogh's primitive rampage against Judy McNulty in late 1981, and subsequent stalking throughout 1982, he never mentioned it in his letter. 'Throughout the last six years he has had one further relationship which foundered when his girlfriend heard of the present charges. This had been steady for three years. He has no present partner and currently lives by himself in a house in Preston', wrote the psychiatrist. In my opinion, all he'd done was recite Keogh's lies as told to Margaret Hobbs.

In reality, Judy McNulty had ended the relationship with Keogh after a terrifying night in St David Street, Northcote, in late 1981. The terrorising of McNulty and the claim that he was living alone in Preston in 1983 were not an innocent oversight by Keogh. Only by the use of complicated subterfuge could his real life be hidden from scrutiny.

What might Clark have thought had his 'disturbed' client told him that he was sharing a house with two naïve young girls more than fourteen years his junior? And how prophetic that the murder of one of these girls four years later would bring the psychiatrist to the court as a witness for the defence.

In October, a year after she had left her husband and moved into St David Street, Judy McNulty grasped the depth of Keogh's savagery. It was a night Judy's daughter would never forget. Even through her young eyes, twelve-year-old Terri spotted something disturbing in her mother's boyfriend.

'I don't want to go home, Mum,' she said as they prepared to return home from their Auntie Dot's home in South Melbourne.

'Don't worry, everything's all right,' Judy had assured her daughter. When the mother and her children arrived home, Keogh was seated imperiously in the family armchair with a full view of their entry into the house. Whether his brooding mood was a consequence of what Dr Clark attributed to 'psychological problems in relationships since adolescence' was inconsequential. Affronted that his girlfriend of eighteen months had tired of his emotional immaturity and obsession with a sexual act to which she objected, Keogh had arrived at a place he'd visited many times before. The man that sobbed into Margaret Hobbs' blithely uncritical ear and wallowed in her gentle, comforting presence was about to reveal his real self.

Within minutes of drinking the nightcap Keogh had prepared, Judy felt her head spinning. As she struggled with the whirlpool, the muffled sounds of Terri's cries outside her bedroom door drifted into her consciousness. Only moments before, Terri had woken to find Keogh pouring Panadol down her three-year-old brother's throat, as he lay asleep next to her. Neither the girl's hysterical protests nor residual morality could impede the predator's obsessions. With the little boy removed to his unconscious mother's bedroom, Keogh was ready for another savage sexual assault. 'I must wake up, I must wake up, my daughter needs me,' Judy thought as she fought to free herself from the Rohypnol he'd slipped into her coffee.

Outside her bedroom door, Keogh's fingernails were tracing a line down his young victim's arms as he attempted to drag her back to the bedroom. 'It was God's will that I should wake up,' Judy would tell Lorna Cleary years later. Amid a rampage during which Keogh ripped the phone from the wall and knocked her across the kitchen floor, the children took flight. Somehow the gods decreed that she would be reunited with her children at the Fletcher household across the road. Vomiting and catatonic, Judy thought about all she'd done to protect the man who would have raped her daughter. What to do? That was a question a terrified woman just could not answer. Men knew what to do.

'I'll go and fix the mongrel up,' a tall Essendon footballer dining at the Fletchers had cried. He never did fix him up—Keogh was lucky like that. Judy's words of thanks to the Catholic god who rescued her family didn't surprise her daughter, but something else did. Years later, Judy told her daughter that had she not woken up, she'd have been raped and murdered by Keogh. Terri blanched. Rape she understood. Murder was different. The day the news of Vicki's murder broke, the words made perfect sense. Whether Margaret Hobbs knew about this night of terror and the stalking that followed is open to speculation. What the letters confirm is that Hobbs continued to coax McNulty to stay with the madman.

With Keogh on the prowl, McNulty regularly stayed with a sister. On a warm summer's morning she and her children returned to St David Street. There was an eerie silence in the double fronted brick Victorian house on the edge of the dogleg, east of High Street. As always the family began a quick search under the beds. Almost simultaneous with Judy opening her wardrobe, Terri spotted a disused packet of tobacco and the sheath of a knife under her mum's bed. A startled Judy was about to exclaim 'He's slashed my shoes and dresses!' when the room imploded.

'Quickly, get out!' she screamed as Keogh, knife in hand, sprung from the cavity between the wall and the wardrobe. Somehow the kids found themselves in the sideway grappling with a gate. Eventually it was prised open and they again made it to the safety of the Fletchers'.

As Terri banged on the Fletchers' door, she watched in disbelief as her mother flew out of her house with Keogh in pursuit. In the middle of the road he threw his left arm around Judy's head and placed the knife at her neck. By now she was on her knees and he was dragging her towards the side street where he had parked the car that might well have been McNulty's coffin. At first, the blokes on the garbage truck didn't know what to make of the commotion in the street. Children screaming, a woman on her knees in the middle of the road and a bloke brandishing a knife. It was no ordinary summer's morning in Northcote. For now Keogh would be defeated.

By the time Judy's friend, Des Powell, and his mates arrived at the house, there was no sign of Keogh. Armed with baseball bats they searched the house but found nothing. Bold as brass he would return. When Powell's brother spotted him in his white Ford parked around the corner from the house Keogh took off. After a brief chase Powell lost sight of him. History had taught him that terrorising a woman was not high risk. No one tells of him getting a whack or having a gun at his temple as retribution for attacking someone's sister. When cornered he was truly a coward. I'd seen genuinely tough, incorrigible blokes who couldn't be stood over. Keogh wasn't one of them. As his suicide confirmed, he was acutely susceptible to a counter terror.

If only one of those letters from Clark or Hobbs had met the eyes of our family, Vicki would be alive today. While a growing circle of people on the street talked of his violence and of the mad stare, Margaret Hobbs continued to fall for his lies. In one letter after another on Victorian government Social Welfare letterhead, Keogh's lies were perpetuated. A government department entrusted with community safety had been an abject failure.

Just over a year after the knife attack Dr Clark offered one of the most staggering assessments of Keogh ever recorded. How, in 1983, he could tell solicitors Prus and Markopoulos he found it 'difficult knowing him not to believe his story' is almost beyond comprehension. How could he say it was difficult not to believe a convicted child molester cum rapist had tampered with two young girls? Four years later Dr Clark's client would walk into Markopoulos' city office with my sister's blood on his hands.

On 10 January 1989, a month before the trial, Clark would write, 'I understand that he was in a very curious state of mind, apparently smashing a car up when he "went blank" and stabbed his girlfriend'. He described Keogh as 'a man of good intelligence and high self-esteem who strived to overcome great mood changes through various means...' He said Keogh did not fit the picture of the 'old style psychopath who does impulsive anti-social acts for no other reason than self-gratification'. As Dr Walton had done, Clark also claimed that Keogh's family had no history of alcoholism or trouble with the law. Parole reports indicate that this was patently untrue. And if there were no childhood neuroses, what were the traumatic childhood episodes about which Clark spoke at the trial? Had the prosecution challenged Clark's evidence, god only knows what might have happened. So why didn't someone show that the psychiatric evidence was at best careless? And why didn't Margaret Hobbs, who proudly claimed to know so much about Keogh and who was on record as saying she respected his honesty, give evidence for the defence? Keogh had reasons for not calling her. The murder of Vicki Cleary must have been a devastating and humiliating blow for Hobbs. In one fell swoop it exposed the lies she'd been fed by Keogh since 1975. Had she been asked to give evidence, Hobbs might well have been forced to unveil the real truth and repeat her damning accusations of 1980.

What must Hobbs have thought when psychiatrists Clark and Walton took the stand and dragged the court on an emotive trip through Keogh's alleged history of alcoholism, depression and childhood trauma? In the years before the murder and the weeks before the trial, Clark had described Keogh as 'aloof and assertive, intelligent and a man of high esteem'. I now wonder whether this was the same Keogh he offered the court a month later.

An expert witness for the defence, Clark painted a picture of a pathetic, chronically depressed man with an emotional illness, experiencing what is called 'psychogenic wipe-out of memories; the emotion so overwhelms the whole laying down mechanism for memories'. In layman's terms this meant the poor bastard was so devastated by what he'd done he had erased it from his mind. I believed this was absolute bullshit. Keogh was ill, true. He was a psychopath who deserved not a sliver of sympathy.

At the Homicide Offices, six hours after the killing, Peter Keogh told of the man who knew not what he'd done.

> 'I was standing in a driveway ... she pulled up and I walked across the road ... past the kindergarten ... the car was straightening up ... it was five past eight or something ...'
>
> 'What happened then?'
>
> 'Well I opened the car door ... the driver's door ... she said "fuck off" or "piss off I don't want to talk to you" ... and I don't know what happened ... everything just fucken blurred, ... just fucken cracked ... next thing I'm in Moreland Road, fucken covered in blood.'

'Did you see what happened to Vicki?'
'No, I don't think so, I don't know.'
'What time was it?'
'I wouldn't have a clue... this morning...'
'Was there anyone in the car with her?'
'I don't think so, I don't think so...'

The varying accounts of those who met Keogh that day and the stories he told give some insight into how he planned to explain away my sister's murder. Not until he spoke to Detective Jim Conomy at Homicide did he mention Vicki swearing, or flag amnesia.

'Fuck, you're in trouble. What happened?' Freake had said, when Keogh rang at 11 am.

'I just cracked. Don't worry about that. Have the coppers been?' Although they talked for some time, Keogh never once mentioned the words he would later attribute to Vicki. His vast experience in the criminal justice system taught Keogh not to make statements that might be used against him. Today was no exception.

Had Vicki seen Keogh? That's a question I still can't resolve. Keogh gave a clue. 'Oh, yeah, I think so,' he told Homicide detective Jim Conomy, who, spotting the equivocation, repeated the question. 'Ambush! If I say she hadn't seen me it will sound like an ambush,' Keogh would have thought. There was only one appropriate answer.

'Yeah, she seen me,' he added with a nod of the head. The truth was more problematic. Maybe the acute nature of the angle of her car reflects the fear she experienced when she saw him there in the overalls. The overalls and the cap meant business. Or, as is more likely, she was oblivious to him hidden there in the driveway of number 38 Cameron Street or behind a tree. Intent on parking the car, Vicki wouldn't have noticed Keogh as he set off towards her.

When asked whether anyone else was in the car with Vicki when he opened the door, Keogh was again coy. 'Yes', of course, would be incorrect. He knew there was no one else in the car and that the correct answer was 'no'. However, an unequivocal 'no' would have indicated a clear memory of what happened. 'I don't think so, I don't think so' was the perfect answer. True, yet replete with the confusion of a man who can't quite remember everything. The killer knew exactly what he was doing.

When Pat Cole swept Keogh up that morning, he was in a panic. The terror he'd contemplated during the 50-minute wait for Vicki to arrive in Cameron Street was now murder. During the taxi trip north from the Auction Rooms, he worked and re-worked his story. At Russell Street he described the wait in Cameron Street as brief. About ten minutes, he said. Again he was well aware of the correct answer. The shorter the wait the more plausible Keogh's account of the 'incident' being a spontaneous and unplanned response to Vicki's arrival. Premeditation had to be cast from the story.

Nowhere in her account, tendered that afternoon, did Cole corroborate the words attributed to Vicki. And without them there in her first statement, there was no way she could insert them once Keogh had settled on his story. Had she really said 'Fuck off'? And if she did, why did Keogh say it was either 'Fuck off' or 'Piss off'? Why didn't he stick to one set of words? And why did she get out of the car and leave her bag behind? The truth was, Vicki didn't say the words. When she saw him in the battle gear and was confronted with his demands, all she could think about was escape. Trapped between the cars she was soon under siege.

The minute she refused his demands the die was cast. Not until he'd dragged her to the passenger side and overpowered her in the front passenger seat did Keogh put the knife to work. Where Walton and Clark saw an impulsive man propelled by a depression, history spoke of a man obsessed with violence. Where Champion saw a pitiful alcoholic, everyone who knew Keogh saw a vicious man who wouldn't let any woman go free.

When I first laid eyes on Dr Lester Walton on Friday 10 February, the fifth day of the trial, I had no idea that among the trial documents was a report he'd written on Keogh based on four visits to Pentridge after the murder. All these years later, I remain astounded that the prosecution didn't take to it with a blowtorch. For the proceeding two days we'd been subjected to the sight of the killer fumbling and bumbling his way through an unsworn statement that accumulated 27 pages of transcript.

Unsworn statements are no longer allowed in Victorian courts, but Keogh's must rank as one of the most obscene. So humiliating was it, I don't know how we sat through it without screaming. For those two days, a criminal had lied every time his counsel, John Champion, had asked him a question.

In Champion's monologue, there had been no killing. An incident in Cameron Street had engulfed Vicki. Like George Bush discussing slaughter in Baghdad or on the plains of Afghanistan, Vicki emerged as collateral damage in Peter Keogh's search for justice. 'Did you challenge her about this other man?' asked Champion, as if she had no right to another life after Keogh. Poor Vicki! How hypocritical that her relationship with another man, begun as a consequence of Keogh's violence and savagery, should have been used in this way.

Coming on top of two sessions of Keogh's unsworn lies, Dr Walton was a body blow for the prosecution. The Keogh he met after the murder was sick, depressed, suicidal and pitiful. This picture, coupled with a doctor's prognosis that Keogh was hurt by 'a deteriorating relationship' and was, therefore, 'prone to impulsive behaviour', was dynamite. A violent man had killed his ex-girlfriend, and become a victim worthy of sympathy.

Deteriorating relationship? What a lie! Vicki had left Keogh more than three months before he killed her. 'Feminists would have your balls,' I'd said when Walton happened to sit next to me in the foyer outside Court Three. I vividly remember the anger I felt towards him. The next day Hampel reminded the court that we were not allowed to speak with a witness.

When I finally spoke to the two doctors in February 2002, neither could identify the 'traumatic childhood events' alleged to have been the source of Keogh's problems. To say they were sheepish about what had happened in George Hampel's court would be a gross understatement. To Dr Walton's credit, he did express amazement at his fellow psychiatrist's written defence of Keogh over the sexual assault of the girls in 1982. As for Keogh's alleged amnesia, Dr Walton said, 'So much depends on the prosecution questions' and that had the prosecution asked him directly whether the 'amnesia' defence was a lie, he'd have told them that it might well have been. And his view of Keogh? 'Evil might be a better term than sociopath' was his telling answer. A bit late now, I thought.

The report Dr Walton compiled after his three chats with Keogh in Pentridge is gripping for its leaps of faith and offers an insight into how this violent man had survived. When the psychiatrist put the tape recorder on, Keogh went into overdrive:

> He could recall saying 'Hello, I want to talk to you' and the alleged victim replied 'Get fucked, piss off, I don't want to talk to you.' He stated 'I just snapped' and his next recollection is of standing up in Moreland Road, becoming aware of the blue light of a police car then noticing blood all over himself. Mr. Keogh stated that he crossed the road and walked up to the drive into a carpark, observed a tap and he proceeded to wash his hands. He stated, 'I just couldn't think. My vision was blurred. I had bad stomach cramps and a lump in my throat. I was trying to figure out what could have happened.'
>
> He stated that the next thing to occur was that he took off his coat and overalls and washed his face, 'wrapped the clothes up and walked along the laneway hearing police sirens.' He made his way to the back of the tram depot and observed that there were police everywhere and that they drove past him.
>
> He stated 'I ended up in the auction room where I expected to be later in the day. I was in a daze sitting in there. Police were going up and down Sydney Road. I left the clothes on a bench. A chap knew me, a worker, he commented "Something is going on outside, they're looking for somebody, something near the kindergarten, it's all blocked off" and I thought "Hang on, I was up at the kindergarten, police, blood all over me" and I grabbed the clothes, put them in an empty box and left with the box. I wandered around in a daze. Got on a bus and then got off and got on another bus. I got off again and walked along in Northcote somewhere. I took a taxi to Reservoir to find a friend. I was looking at the clothes, the blood, I tried to recall what had happened.'

When Detective Jim Conomy interviewed Keogh at the Homicide Offices, the cop asked the questions. When Walton met Keogh in remand, the killer had carte blanche. The result was a report that contained nothing more than Keogh's lies. A caring doctor fashioned by the nobility of a Hippocratic oath had transformed the killer into a patient. In something akin to a Freudian slip, Walton consistently referred to Vicki as the 'alleged victim'. It seemed to have escaped him that there was no dispute regarding who had died. The body hadn't gone missing, and there was no suggestion she'd stabbed herself. But it was more than an issue of semantics. As events unfolded, Vicki did become 'an alleged victim'. Before the case was over she'd be neither a victim nor a murdered girl. In Hampel's court she'd be virtually accused of abandoning an alcoholic depressive and causing him to lift the knife that killed her.

'I ended up in the Auction Rooms.' I wondered what Dr Lester Walton must have thought as he repeated Keogh's cunning defence. Isn't the planning of a murder bizarre? Isn't murder always bizarre? Once we accept that, everything about the murder—his decamping from the scene and the tearful theatrics for the social worker Cole and the psychiatrist Walton—bear the hallmarks of a meticulous assassination. Across Moreland Road and up the lane he went, disappearing like Jack the Ripper in the London fog. With the camouflage gone, he was just another bloke in an urban morning. At the Auction Rooms he made himself a coffee and eyed Sydney Road for his pursuers. 'Mind if I use the toilet, Graham?' he calmly asked employee Graham Jones. 'Impressive sale,' he said when he returned from washing the last vestiges of Vicki's blood from his hands and fingernails.

Jones had been ensconced on his own in the rooms since 7 am with only one visitor, Cornellius, who'd brought his truck to a halt at the back roller door, minutes before Keogh arrived. Unless Cornellius told him, Jones wouldn't have known anything about events near the kinder. And even if Cornellius had seen the police car in Moreland Road, he'd have had no idea about the details. Only Keogh had the knowledge to declare, 'Something's going on outside, they're looking for somebody, something near the kindergarten.'

To reach the Auction Rooms, Keogh had to negotiate the 250-metre stretch from Vicki's car to Moreland Road. Then, once he was out of the lane, he had to reappear on the corner of Cozens and Cameron Streets. From here, he was exposed again, until he passed the Tram Depot and reached the lane, 170 metres away, that led to the Auction Rooms. Although it left him vulnerable, it offered him a chance to take in proceedings outside the kindergarten.

It was now 8.17 and Constable Tim Highett was bringing his police van to a halt alongside the girl lying in the gutter outside the kinder. To the north, the sound of an ambulance pierced the morning air. Keogh took it all in and proceeded to his refuge. At Pentridge Prison he cunningly transposed what he'd seen to the lips of Graham Jones, a man who'd seen nothing.

> Having arrived at his friend's house, Mr. Keogh found him asleep and was unable to wake him so he rang his friend's girlfriend. She agreed to meet him at nearby shops. Before leaving he placed his clothes in the garage and when he met up with this woman friend she said, 'I didn't think it was you, the wrong description, what happened?' and he replied, 'I don't know.' Following further discussions a telephone call was made to the hospital and Mr. Keogh was informed that his de facto was in a very serious condition but, evidently, she was not dead. He drove around with his female acquaintance, consulted his solicitor by telephone and went to visit him. He arrived there around 11 am and on the midday news he heard that his de facto was dead and he stated, 'I couldn't believe it.' Around 1 pm Mr, Keogh turned himself into police at Russell Street.

It's hard to believe Dr Walton's ears didn't flap when Keogh told him he couldn't wake Kevin Chamberlain. Keogh had already told police at Homicide that he and Chamberlain shared a cup of tea while Keogh waited for Pat Cole to reach the shops up the road. The semi-literate Peter Keogh had a history of lying to educated professionals.

Although I could accept Walton's argument that so much of what he said depended on how the questions were put, I could find no justification for the interpretations offered in his report.

> This man's motive for committing the alleged offence remains obscure. There had been arguments following the break-up of his relationship with the alleged victim over property and, in particular, the use of a motor vehicle. And Mr. Keogh, somewhat foolishly, appears to have armed himself intent on doing damage to his own car that was at that time being used by the alleged victim. This man does have a past history of assault but, as far as I'm aware, the incidents have not have been of serious assault. He has also been convicted of sexual assault and these offences have usually occurred when he has been intoxicated.

Is it any wonder I told him he sounded like a witness for the defence?

How could Dr Walton so willingly sanitise the lies of a killer and conclude that the motives for Keogh's violence were obscure? Keogh was angry because Vicki didn't do as she was told and visit him the night before. Throughout his life that had been motive enough for Keogh to use violence. If this wasn't bad enough, how could the doctor describe Keogh as 'somewhat foolishly arming himself'? Without recourse to all the facts, Walton was indicating that there was no premeditation in Keogh's actions. This was, I told him, prejudicial to my sister. How could he say Keogh's past assaults had not been serious? No one who'd read Keogh's criminal sheet could conclude that his assaults weren't serious. This was a man described by a learned judge in 1974 as 'a menace that must be stopped' and in 1976 as 'a man of violence'. This was a man who'd done time for bodily and sexual assault. It was plain wrong to say he wasn't violent. And no disclaimer such as 'as far as I'm aware' could camouflage that.

> Mr Keogh believes his de facto had been unfaithful ... the motor vehicle owned by Mr. Keogh ... He had had not seen the alleged victim since 24 August, 1987 ... The damage (to the car) was to be inflicted as some form of retaliation.

The careful use of euphemisms to sanitise the violence, and the reconstruction of events, made me so angry. Keogh had retaliated. For what, doctor? That's what Walmsley should have asked him. Then he should have asked why the word revenge didn't feature in his report. After all, wasn't it all about revenge? And didn't the doctor understand that Vicki was not his de facto? They were well and truly separated. Or was she, like the car, just another chattel that could never be alienated from the spoilt prick who plied Walton with lies?

Unlike Dr Lester Walton, Bernie Bell saw the killer in action. Today he can't be sure of all that he saw. The realisation that just maybe he and Stephen Docherty might have been heroes had they jumped from the privacy of their car into the public territory where Vicki struggled, probably crosses his mind. 'It brings back bad memories. I can't tell you any more,' he said in his customary quiet voice.

'I just need to know. That's all, Bernie. Nothing will bring her back. I just want to know what happened,' I told him.

By talking to Bell, Docherty and Giuseppe Piccolo I came to understand the pain Vicki's murder inflicted on all of us. I know, too, that those men would have loved to have saved her. The problem is few of us think like Peter Keogh. Before anyone grasped what was happening he'd secured his revenge. Today I still visit Cameron Street and speculate about what happened when that door was ripped open. I see the killer's face, hear the words and the sound of my sister' heartbeat as she felt the knife and saw her dreams blown away.

the final insult

I'd never set foot in the Supreme Court until that day in February 1989. Among my Irish antecedents, there was a deep and documented mistrust of British law. Under the Galtees in County Limerick, the clan had put the Queen's law to the torch. I understood why Celts such as Frank Galbally and the Xavier College boys felt compelled to speak on behalf of troublesome Catholic lawbreakers. But flouting the Queen's political laws in occupied Ireland, on the union picket line or in an anti-worker Royal Commission was a far cry from robbing and thieving from your own class and terrorising the weak. It wasn't something eulogised in the Cleary home.

Fronting up for a murder trial at the Supreme Court seemed so at odds with our destiny. The whole setting was so absolutely foreign to Mum and Dad's purpose in life. There was no role for bourgeois law in their lives. Their possessions were meagre and Dad's one-man butcher shop required no more than the services of an accountant once a year. The moment the family walked through the austere brick doorway into the cold little anteroom, all of us felt a sense of foreboding. Prosecutor Bruce Walmsley was genial and polite and told us provocation was a live issue. But we already knew it. That's why Mum desperately wanted to sit down with the prosecution and tell them everything she knew.

Walmsley seemed to be in a hurry. If the prosecution team had listened to what Mum wanted to say, a different set of questions might have confronted Cole, Chamberlain and Freake on the stand. Although I threw snippets of information in the path of the prosecution team as it skirted past, somehow my pride was an obstacle. There was something demeaning about constantly trying to catch the eye of the smooth, urbane barrister in what was his territory, after all. We soon discovered that domestic murder wasn't like real murder.

Not only isn't domestic murder sexy, it bears a stigma. Had a mysterious stranger murdered Vicki, or had the killer been a self-mutilating Van Gogh with tats, aka Chopper Read, or a swarthy dark-eyed Italian in a long black coat, the media would have been riveted. Because her killer was her ex-boyfriend, the dead girl and her family were firmly implicated in the murder. What was she doing with him? Guilt by association! Too often this was the judgment made of a woman killed by the violent man in her life.

Once the case began, it was as if Vicki's guilt was the real subtext of so many of the questions asked. It seemed as if that would be enough to explain away Keogh's crime. Inside the imperious doors of Court Three, we all watched as Keogh exercised his legal discretion and dismissed five prospective female jurors, leaving his fate in the hands of seven men and five women.

The foreman of the jury, a neat and proper man from the suburbs, troubled me. Wife murder has everything to do with politics and power. For all its haughty assertions, all the law does is trot alongside like a compliant dog. The jury wasn't likely, I fancied, to put the blowtorch to Keogh's underbelly. In a society where a woman killed by the man in her life is seldom innocent, it would take a burst of dissidence to get a murder conviction against the whinging hypochondriac in the dock. Nothing I'd seen in the court imbued me with such confidence.

Within a few minutes of the opening of proceedings, defence Counsel, John Champion, told Hampel, 'The question of loss of control is an important one insofar as the running of the defence is concerned.'

'So you will be asking for provocation to be left to the jury?' asked Hampel.

'Yes,' replied Champion.

From here we moved to the question of whether photos of the dead girl's wounds and the surgical incision made by Dr Flanagan in an attempt to stop the bleeding might not be prejudicial to Peter Keogh's rights.

'They're emotive and prejudicial,' said Champion.

'Well, the Crown does seek to rely upon the nature and extent of the injuries,' replied Walmsley.

Why, I thought?

'It might be relevant to both sides in a sense,' noted the judge, conscious that a wild attack might imply loss of control.

After this initial skirmish, I sensed the Crown was labouring under a misunderstanding of the circumstances of the Cameron Street murder. In the barbaric actions of the killer's knife, Walmsley imagined he had a watertight case for murder. On the final day of the trial, he would wave the knife around as if acting out a role in a Hollywood movie. Four inches of black handle and eight inches of glistening steel, it was the same weapon Mum and Dad had seen on the bench when they rescued Vicki that day in Broadford three months before he struck. It was a big knife, said witness Geoff Berlowitz when he relived the story of how he almost jumped from the car as Keogh finished Vicki off.

Waving the knife at the jury was a waste of time. Defence barrister John Champion had already conceded on the knife. He was fixated on provocation. Vicki Cleary's words, not Keogh's intentions, were the reason the knife emerged from the scabbard. The prosecution needed to forget the knife and convince the jury that no civilised society could live with itself if it believed an ordinary man might do what Keogh did. Yet so often when Walmsley spoke, it seemed the prosecution was down the wrong path.

'And you are aware that after being, on one view, told to "fuck off" by her, he then took from somewhere on his body a knife and stabbed her repeatedly?' he asked Dr Clark. It proved nothing. The real facts were that Keogh didn't stab her immediately. I believe the prosecution should have hammered this fact and used it to blow away the provocation defence.

Within an hour of the beginning of preliminary discussion, George Hampel had assured Champion that Keogh's arrival at the kindergarten in the month prior to the murder was not prejudicial to his case. It was not unusual for 'one person to be intense about seeing the other' and 'there is nothing terribly harmful about that', said the judge. It took only that long for me to realise how prophetic was my conversation with Detective John Hill minutes before the trial began. The deep unease I was feeling had already swept through my family.

A man prising open a workplace door was not some romantic lover, but a potential stalker or, worse still, a killer. If Hampel didn't see that, then he didn't understand Keogh or the helplessness felt by a woman when confronted by a man's physical intimidation. Moreover, when two co-workers offered the view that they were scared when Keogh barged into the kinder, their feelings were ruled inadmissible. Hampel's stated position, I believed, was blind to Vicki's human rights. Framed within provocation Keogh's aggression was legitimised.

Until Detective John Hill grabbed a seat alongside me and said, 'George Hampel's known around the traps as Father Christmas', I'd never heard of the judge. A finely built, small man with a bony face that kind of poked out from the decorative wig and voluminous red gown, Justice Hampel, I eventually discovered, was a darling of the civil liberties set. Little did I know that only three months earlier, on 10 November 1988, he'd delivered the following words to mass murderer Julian Knight:

> The answers to what you did lie in your background, your fragile and disordered personality, and in your inability to cope with the accumulation of pressures and stresses which operated on you.

That said, he sentenced the murderer to 27 years.

The words used by Hampel would form the basis of the narrative during Keogh's trial. Everyone, Adolf Hitler or the next mass murderer, is a product of their background. But there were more sinister layers to Hitler and Knight, and Hampel surely knew it. Young Suzie's comments at Avondale High on the day of the murder were more incisive. She had looked deep into the social construct for an explanation. Most blokes who ran the eye over Knight's insipid face knew what kind of bloke he was. The gun and the fatigues, like Keogh's knife, were a substitute for what, in football circles, we called character and intestinal fortitude. Like Keogh, Knight was a selfish bloke with nothing but contempt for the life of others. On the street they knew it. But did George Hampel?

Hampel was only fifteen years of age when he arrived in Melbourne in 1949. While Keogh's father powered away on his tyre drum in the suffocating heat at Dunlop Rubber, Hampel began the schooling that would propel him up the social ladder. An education at Melbourne High and the prestigious Haileybury College was the first step. By the time the doors of Melbourne University opened for the Jewish refugee from Hitler's genocide, the bench was a formality.

Whereas union man Jack Keogh fought for a wage that would advance the lot of Labor's downtrodden, Hampel spoke of their right to equality before the law. For all his theoretical principles, Hampel didn't know Jack Keogh's mob like I did. The rough and tumble of football and the banter of a Northcote pub, were not the social setting for a judge's life.

All of this and Hill's quip that Hampel was no hanging judge and had divorced his first wife and married a woman more than twenty years his junior should have been irrelevant. We'd not come to court to hang Peter Keogh. And anyway, if, as Hill said, Hampel's wife was into women's rights, I thought he'd look after Vicki. An armed man had murdered a girl as she went to work. All we wanted was justice and a sentence that was appropriate to the crime. But Hill had a story to tell. He'd heard exactly how Keogh planned to beat murder.

Oblivious to the eyes and ears of Hill in the adjoining room at the

Homicide offices, Keogh mumbled, 'I remember nothing from the time she said she didn't want to speak to me until I was in the lane covered in blood.' said Keogh. That done, the cameras prepared to roll on another little murder

'He's gunna plead provocation. He'll claim he can't remember anything. It's a lie,' Hill had told me as we sat in the foyer

'And we can't use it in court?' I asked somewhat naïvely. I didn't need an answer, but Hill gave it anyway.

'No, it's illegal.' A hard-nosed cop from City West, Hill would shoot himself dead in September 1993 after being charged in relation to the shooting of armed robbery suspect Graeme Jensen in a stake-out in 1988. It seemed a terrible waste.

I didn't bother to tell Hill I wasn't an advocate of increased police rights, draconian sentencing or demonising the accused. The courts were tools of the ruling class. Every kid from the northern suburbs who read Karl Marx knew that. Even without the writings of the great father of dialectical thinking, they knew the coppers were on the other side. That was one thing the killer Keogh and I might have agreed on if we'd ever shared a beer or a few minutes of conversation. Even then the words we'd have used, the reason for uttering them, and the look in our eyes would have been very different. My problem with coppers was that they were too much like the blokes they chased, and were asked to spend too much time protecting the property of the big-end-of-town mob. The coppers were a problem for him because he was a sexual pervert, a bully and a murderer. Peter Keogh was no Ned Kelly.

Ned Kelly! I've thought a lot about the famous bushranger from the North East Victorian hamlet of Greta since that trial. At the time I didn't know that, like Kelly, Keogh had bitten the dust after a round of police gunfire crashed into his lower limbs. Nor did I know that Bob Vernon's creative defence of Keogh in 1964 had earned him a citation in Victorian Case Law.

Such were the colourful words Vernon found for Keogh, it was as if he believed Keogh was of the ilk who might have ridden with Ned and Dan, spoken the language of rebellion and died for a mate. After all, was he not, like the man in armour from Greta, a widow's son who refused to buckle under a copper's command? Like Constable Hall in the main street of Greta 100 years before, Detective Kim West was under no illusion as to the power of Keogh's defiance. 'He was like a raging bull when I tried to arrest him in the sixties,' the thick-set, bull-necked West told me years later. In his time West bore a fearsome reputation at Northcote CIB.

Like Kelly banging a clenched fist on his suit of armour and stumbling into inevitable defeat, Keogh had roared at the 'copper cunts' before falling to the gun at Preston Station. The difference was, Kelly didn't call the poor 'dogs and cunts'. In the Jerilderie Letter he spoke only of defending the poor and orphaned of Greta from injustice and never thought of abusing women and children. When he went to war against the state, the Kelly boy dreamt of a new political order where the squatters and urban financiers took their place alongside, not above, the settler and itinerant bushmen. Keogh didn't care about such lofty ideals. Oblivious to the political morality of his father, the Keogh boy was a ruthless exploiter of the innocent. A man of the shadows, he preyed on those who spoke the language of kindness. Women, not the rich and powerful, were his enemy.

Faced with the attempted murder of Constable Bellesini, Peter Keogh was every bit a lagger and a coward. Ned Kelly would never have allowed his mother to take the blame for his breaches of bourgeois law. Keogh had no qualms about defence barrister Bob Vernon sheeting home the blame to a mother they cynically labelled 'possessive'. When murder called again in 1987, it would be the same story. When Kelly had his day in court, no tears sullied the truth. He pointed his rifle at police officers McIntyre, Lonigan, Kennedy and Scanlon. About that there was no argument. No legal ruse or smart-arse lawyer was going to camouflage Kelly's war against an unjust state and a corrupt police force. Keogh, by contrast, lied like a coward and cried like a dog when asked to explain what he'd done. Never would he admit that rage had so consumed him he wanted Vicki to either come to heel or bear the full force of his law. Hampel must surely have known that.

When Kelly stood before the Irish loyalist, Redmond Barry, he had no hope. No matter what the sexual sins perpetrated against Kelly's sister by Constable Fitzpatrick in the Kelly home, or the intent of the armed, disguised troopers at Stringybark Creek, Kelly was a condemned man. Justice Barry's contempt for those Irishmen who refused to don the English yoke worn by the Barrys of County Cork, was there for all to see. Yet, by some paradox, Barry, the ruthless hanging judge, and Hampel, the protector of the rights of those less fortunate than him, shared so much. Had Kelly stood before George Hampel, he'd have felt the full weight of the law. So, why was Peter Raymond Keogh allowed a defence of provocation, and why did Hampel give a sentence that would see him walking the streets a mere three years and eleven months after he brutally ended Vicki's life?

Keogh's victim was not the state, a stranger or bourgeois decency. Nor had he struck out 'in the name of the white races'. His was an act of appropriation against a woman who dared challenge the property laws of the bourgeois state. In Keogh's eyes and the patriarchal justice system, women were little more than a chattel to be used at the discretion of men. Vicki's death and the verdict that followed had nothing to do with cars, houses and provocative words. Vicki Cleary flouted the law that governed relations between men and women. That's why she died, and that's why the jury lost its way.

What thoughts must have crossed Hampel's mind when he discovered he was looking down on one of his mate's great success stories? Bob Vernon QC, the man who ran the automatism defence that saved Keogh from attempted murder in 1964, was a mate of the bloke high above us. Vernon had travelled to France on a holiday with George Hampel, and the two great advocates shared a love of language and the art of legal defence. The more I searched, the deeper became the questions. Although a judge is constrained by legal rules and precedent, how could he have not reflected on the arguments of the much-feted Bob Vernon all those years before?

Alcohol, amnesia and shameless grovelling had saved the knife-wielding Keogh in '64. If Justice Monahan believed alcohol was the reason for Keogh's actions at Preston Station in 1963, then why not 'alcoholic depression' when he killed Vicki Cleary? Peter Keogh was a man once proclaimed by Hampel's mate and certified by a brother judge as a victim of alcohol. Did this influence Justice George Hampel when legal argument turned to the question of provocation? When the provocation defence finally arose, Hampel's explanation for making the ordinary man in Cameron Street a replica of Peter Keogh labouring under alcoholic depression was bizarre.

For all the myths about Hampel's generosity and respect for human frailty, he shared much of Redmond Barry's Old Testament righteousness. After a couple of Aussie thugs bashed an Asian man to death in 1996, in the days before Pauline Hanson's racism peppered the airwaves, Hampel spoke a language unlike anything I heard from him in 1989. On 15 May 1997, Hampel's office advised the media that His Honour had some important things to say about the case. They duly looked on as George delivered the following thoughts, before sentencing the men to a minimum 16 years:

> The whole event is an ugly demonstration of unprovoked violence, accompanied by an attitude of bigotry and racism, especially by you, Briggs. The attack happened at a time when right-minded members of this community are struggling to combat such views and attitudes.

It begged some serious questions. If it was important to declare his public opposition to racism and assert the role of the courts in combating it, why did he not speak with the same conviction against women killers? When he sentenced the serial thug on Wednesday 15 February 1989, George Hampel could find not one word of condemnation or of moral guidance.

'Do you know what you've done? You've let a murderer go free.' It was a tragic cry that so consummately captured what had happened to Vicki. Those were my mother's words when she walked into the jury in the foyer after the foreman delivered the verdict of 'not guilty to murder' on Tuesday 14 February. I was so proud of her courage and her intelligence. Not one expletive or a word of sarcasm did Mum need to capture what had happened. How succinctly she explained for George Hampel what should have been the inalienable rights of a woman.

On reflection, I'm probably angrier now about what Hampel did than I was then. Sure, I'd given Keogh a mouthful as I passed him slouched there in the dock at five minutes after six on Tuesday 14 February. He was a monster. A monster excused by a court in a society that boasted about how it had liberated women from oppression. How could I not tell him? Mum had simply walked out the door into twelve men and women who we believed had defiled her daughter's character.

At 6.02 that evening, after seven days of evidence and six hours of deliberation, the jury had reached a unanimous decision. In their eyes the Crown had not proved beyond reasonable doubt that an ordinary man like Keogh wouldn't have lost control and done what he did in Cameron Street. Stripped of the legal cant was the proclamation that it had been within Vicki's power to avert Keogh's act of murder.

The verdict was an act of unforgivable hurt to my family and unequivocal brutality to Vicki. I blamed Hampel unreservedly, felt deep animosity towards Champion and harboured grave reservations about the prosecution's handling of the case. For Keogh I felt nothing but abject hatred. A lying, conniving coward, he deserved some rough justice. To walk past him in silence would have compounded the injustice and humiliation. I wanted to point a gun at his ugly head and bury a bullet in his criminals mind, as Bellesini should have done in 1963. Instead, all I had was a bundle of words. It was water off a duck's back for Keogh. When I delivered those words, no one spoke. Not Mum, Dad, my sisters, my brother Paul, or the security men who stood alongside him. In the anteroom I cried in anger and sorrow for my sister.

'You're nothing but a fucking murderer. You're a fucking murderer!' Talk is cheap, but I've imagined some reckless solutions to what Keogh did. So many times I imagined killing him. When word arrived in 1996 that his mate Brian Watson had been seen at 463 Gilbert Road, Preston, the house Keogh and Vicki shared before they moved to Broadford, I went looking. So many times I parked outside, hoping Keogh or Watson might appear. Then I'd drive down Rathmines Road, Fairfield, searching for the car they'd used to stalk Vicki. I'd rung the phone number of the house where Watson's car was registered, but the woman who answered claimed he didn't live there.

At the trial, Watson's name was carefully withheld from the public gaze. The driver was a lucky man. Had the police put the blowtorch to him for stalking Vicki, who knows what he might have told? On 1 September 1998, four months after I named him in *Cleary Independent*, Watson drove his Ford Fairlane into Bundoora Park near La Trobe University, downed a few beers, connected a hose to his exhaust and started the ignition. When Senior Constable Ellis found the car, he was dead. In the previous weeks, he'd been accused of sexually assaulting yet another female.

Had Keogh been found guilty of murder, the sentence would have been irrelevant. The Cleary family would have walked from the court with not a word. The jury's decision changed all that and led me on a strange journey that unearthed profound conclusions and the worst thoughts. What if I'd happened upon him after the revelation that he'd told Freake he was going to get Vicki? I gave up fistfights when I was sixteen and, apart from a few skirmishes on the football field, haven't laid a finger on anyone since then. If he hadn't gone to Tyers in 1995, I'd have run into him one night. I'm sure of that. I dreamt about it. That's what it's like when a murderer goes free.

I'll never forget that final day in George Hampel's court. At the doors to the courtroom an apologetic security man was there to greet us when we arrived at 10.25 am.

'Sorry, you'll have to sit in the public gallery,' he told us.

'Why is that?' I asked.

'Orders of the judge,' he replied.

Our family had been reduced to a reckless proletarian mob. For my parents, who'd never harmed anyone, it was soul destroying. Lorna and Ron Cleary had opened their home to the kids of Shore Grove and bestowed unlimited affection on everyone who entered their lives. What Hampel did, I believed, was cruel and insensitive.

From the isolation of the balcony, we watched the judge enter the court on the morning of Wednesday 15 February 1989, and deliver his sermon.

It was reported to me that after the jury left the court and after the court adjourned, there was an outburst in court that resulted in the abuse of the accused and abuse of jurors outside the court.

I think it outrageous that a person can't stand trial in these courts and the members of the public who sit as jurors can't do their job without being abused by people who have access to what is an open courtroom. They should not be exposed to such conduct.

I think perhaps, in the context of this trial, it may be significant to realise how little ordinary people are able to control their emotions and prevent themselves from unsuitable outbursts. It's for that reason that, in order to preserve some sort of calm in this courtroom today, I have ordered that members of the public should not be sitting in the body of the court. Any such further outbursts will be dealt with severely.

It was a very disappointing response from the judge. 'It was as bad as the day Vicki died,' Mum would later remark. Couldn't my family's frailty have been met with greater understanding?

When the moment came for the judge to sentence Keogh, there was nothing of the anger he had found for our act of frustration. In his two-and-a-half-page statement, there was not one word of sympathy for the family of the dead girl. Nor was Keogh admonished for the 'loss of control' that led to Vicki's death. Sure he was bound by the verdict to treat this as murder reduced to manslaughter because it was said to have occurred during a state of 'loss of control'. But should that have meant he couldn't say anything about Keogh's tolerance level and his refusal to accept Vicki's flight to freedom?

'Given the degree of provocation, it is a serious crime that must be met with a substantial term of imprisonment,' said Hampel when he reached the final paragraph. How could three years and eleven months in gaol for killing a woman be classed as 'substantial'? A drunk would do worse for knocking someone over in his car. When George Hampel sentenced Peter Keogh at 2.30 pm on Wednesday afternoon, he repeated so many of the assumptions that had dogged Vicki's trial over the preceding days. Admittedly, it was a truncated version of the facts presented by him to the jury before they considered a verdict.

However, I felt it encapsulated his version of the facts. A host of unsubstantiated claims made by Keogh were repeated as if they were fact.

> You put the house in which you had both lived on the market and went to live with a friend. You drank heavily. You hoped for reconciliation, but shortly before 26 August, you believed she was living with another man. You felt let down and angry; you saw the motorcar in which you had some interest and which your de facto was using as a focus of your anger and a source of your problems.

Keogh was never led to believe, nor was there a sliver of evidence, that Vicki had indicated to Keogh she was interested in reconciliation. Brian Freake, with whom he lived for three months after the separation, could remember Vicki coming to the house maybe once or twice, and never once in his evidence did he suggest Keogh believed there was a chance of reconciliation. Nor was there one shred of evidence produced at the trial that Keogh had a financial interest in the car. Vicki purchased the car with a loan from the bank in her name. He had no legal or moral right to it at all. She was working, he wasn't. She never sought to take from the sale of the house what was legally hers. And how much was he really drinking?

> The night before the stabbing occurred, you expected the deceased lady to visit you following some telephone arrangements but she, in fact, did not do that. You appeared to be withdrawn and upset about that. Next morning, you picked up a knife... told the police your intention was to damage the car and not kill the deceased.

Again, unsworn evidence aside, there was no evidence that Vicki was going to visit Keogh on the night before her murder. Why would she? And what did it matter if she didn't? Did he own her? Had she broken some moral code by not visiting a man who claimed, in order to attract pity, to have been drinking all day? He threatened her on the phone on Monday, and she was upset. It was established in Hampel's court and accepted by defence barrister, John Champion, that Vicki was crying at work after the phone call from Keogh at midday on the Monday before he murdered her.

Hampel told the jury before they retired to consider a verdict, 'The accused received a phone call from the deceased woman saying that she'd be visiting on the Tuesday night'. How at odds this was with the girl cowering in the kinder, frightened by Keogh's threats, about to be killed by him. Brian Freake, who was with Keogh when he made the call from Cramer's Hotel, never suggested Keogh was crying or upset. The tone of Hampel's words and the slip-up about the call only added veracity to my argument that it was Keogh who'd attracted victim status. Freake's evidence as to his mate's disposition on the night, for example, painted Keogh as brooding, not sad. My view was that George Hampel delivered only one narrative and it favoured the accused.

> When she arrived you approached her car in a busy street and shortly after stabbed her a number of times, apparently on the passenger side of the car. You were then seen by a number of people in the vicinity walking away in a blank or dazed state.

It was an indisputable fact that Vicki was stabbed on the passenger side and that Keogh had been seen to drag her there, push her into the passenger side seat and stab her repeatedly. So why did Hampel use the word 'apparently' and why didn't he mention how long Keogh had waited? The location of the stabbing made a farce of the 'sudden loss of control' argument. And why did he ignore Bernie Bell's observation that Keogh 'wiped the blood from the knife with a handkerchief'? At the Committal Hearing, Bell used the expression 'callously wiped the blood'. Bruce Walmsley never asked him to repeat or elaborate on that observation. Equally, Hampel forget to mention that Keogh changed his overalls in a lane and had a coffee at the local Auction Rooms.

> You have for many years been an alcoholic and you suffer from a serious depressive illness. These factors were, I think, relevant to your conduct during the separation and to the way you reacted on August 26. I accept that you have been remorseful and that what you did has had a profound effect on you.

When Keogh assaulted nine-year-old Valerie in Richmond in 1974, he initially told police he'd not been drinking. When he was convicted of assaulting two girls in 1982, he claimed, and Dr Clark confirmed, that he'd not been drinking. When he killed Vicki he was sober. When he drugged the McNulty family and attacked Judy McNulty with a knife in 1981, he was sober. The attack on the girl at the T&G building in 1975 and in Coburg in 1970 had nothing to do with drink.

Keogh would not take 'no' from a woman. Vicki said 'no'. This, not alcohol or depression, was why she died. Hatred of women, not addiction to alcohol, was Keogh's cross. I believed that, as a wise man of the bench, George Hampel had a responsibility to comment on this social malaise. If he felt the need to sermonise when it was a couple of convicted racists in the dock why not do the same to a violent misogynist? And what evidence was there that this chronic offender was remorseful?

When I came across George Hampel and his wife Felicity in the Bangkok Thai restaurant in Carlton, a couple of years after the trial, I had to tell him what I thought. 'That was such a bourgeois decision' was all I said. The meaning was simple.

Vicki's death had violated no sacred tablet. She'd stepped beyond the sensibilities of polite society and chosen a relationship with a tragic deprived man. That he was incorrigibly violent seemed to count for nothing.

In the eyes of patriarchal law, she was just another girl from a class that married and bore children before their time, spoke funny and left the justice system to pick up the pieces when their man went off his head. During the trial I wanted to tell Hampel and the others that Vicki wasn't like that. She'd been a good student who loved painting and talking and tended the children of others as if they were hers. Soon she'd have been a trained kindergarten teacher. Vicki was from a solid working-class family with a father who bought a set of Encyclopaedia Britannica for his six children and never raised his voice to his wife. Our parents were as pure as the driven snow. As the days in Court Three rolled on, it seemed Vicki, like young Jean in the lane thirty years before, was on trial.

On Monday 13 February, the foreman asked the question that convinced me Keogh would be found not guilty of murder. Justice

Hampel was half way through summing up, when the foreman said, 'Is there any law about the degree of provocation?'

In my view, the meaning of the question was unmistakable. The jury could see no provocation in Cameron Street, but because the judge had indicated that it was a matter to be considered, they mistakenly spotted it.

At 2.15 pm on 14 February, after three hours of deliberation, the foreman returned to the courtroom to ask a further question of the judge. The coup de grâce was about to be delivered.

'We have a query from one or two of the jurors on the point at which provocation becomes a factor. If it is proved that it was a conscious, voluntary act—that would constitute murder?' asked the foreman.

'And that it was done with the intent to kill, yes,' replied Hampel when he concluded his initial explanation.

'Does provocation become a necessary point of discussion?' asked the foreman.

'Yes,' said the judge, before stepping the foreman through the critical issue of whether Keogh lost control, and whether an ordinary man with his characteristics might have done the same.

'Does that include alcoholism and...?' asked the foreman.

'Yes, transient conditions such as the "blues" or feeling down don't count, but if you accept the evidence from the medical practitioners that his alcoholism and depression are permanent characteristics, it becomes part of the characteristics, the make-up of the man,' said Hampel. In the dock, Keogh listened intently and wondered whether another triumph was around the corner. Deep down, he knew he was now a chance.

When the exasperated Bruce Walmsley suggested Hampel clarify the issue of loss of control for the jury, the judge delivered a direction that should have set a fire in the prosecutor's belly. Hampel found these words to describe what happened in Cameron Street that day:

> The issue of provocation has nothing to do in law with the finding of the deliberate, conscious and intentional act of murder. The issue of

provocation is based on the concept that this is an act of intentional, deliberate, conscious killing, but done at a time of loss of self-control.

In other words, looking at a totally different case, to give you an example, supposing someone gets into a situation where an acquaintance, friend or spouse, uses the most provocative comments and gestures, and he goes into the bedroom and picks up a firearm and kills that person. There may be no doubt whatever that he intended to kill them; there may be no doubt at all he was acting consciously, voluntarily and deliberately, but because of the provocation that was offered, the act was in a loss of self-control.

It was a truly absurd example by which to explain the profound question of provocation in Cameron Street. Hampel had compared 'the most provocative comments and gestures' in a hypothetical case involving overt aggression in a situation of implied cohabitation or a relationship, with the actions of a girl set upon by her armed ex-boyfriend outside her place of work, three months after she ended the relationship. Keogh did not 'go and pick up a knife or gun and kill her'. He already had the weapon on his body, and didn't draw it until he had dragged my sister to the passenger side door of the car.

In essence, Hampel's analogy seemed to imply that Vicki had sworn at Keogh and that these uncorroborated words might constitute the kind of provocation that could cause an ordinary man to lose control. Hampel might have starred in matriculation English, but his logic cut no ice with my family. Keogh wasn't some bloke quietly sitting in the lounge room before being verbally set upon by a wilful wife. He was an armed man who waited an hour for the arrival of his prey, then prised open her door with murder on his mind. The reason Hampel offered such a ridiculous comparison was because it was almost impossible to find an analogy for what happened in Cameron Street that met the legal definition of provocation.

The ordinary man about whom George Hampel spoke wasn't my father or me. So who was he? Was he George Hampel? The answer was found when the 56-year-old judge wove his version of provocation into the events he imagined that morning in Cameron Street.

But the provocation issue does arise and, because it arises, it is for you also to say whether the prosecution has disproved provocation, in other words, proved that there was no provocation beyond reasonable doubt...

You can have that sort of situation arise from just a single, provocative act which causes a person to lose self-control. It can arise because of a series of acts and events that build up a situation of pressure where a person, at the time of committing the killing, is acting out of control.

Usually, and this is the case here, it is said that such a state existed where there were acts and circumstances existing for some time beforehand which, in culmination, their cumulative effect produced a loss of self control because of the trigger comment that occurred that day by the deceased lady. That sort of situation, the law says, is capable of raising a situation of provocation.

Did all that is relied upon occur here. Namely the build-up during the previous couple of months right up to the evening and the morning before and the words uttered, the whole situation, did all that cause him to lose self control and did he commit the act which killed her in such a state?

So the question you ask yourselves is this. Has the Crown proved beyond reasonable doubt if he did lose self-control that the conduct was such that it would not cause an ordinary man with his characteristics to lose his self control? Or that having lost self-control, an ordinary man with his characteristics would not react like this?

The words, 'that sort of situation, the law says, is capable of raising a situation of provocation', left Vicki with two choices. She either stayed put or as Heather Osland had done, killed him. Instead, he killed her, and was excused.

'She won't be free of him until he's dead,' Dad had said after the sexual assault in Broadford. Sadly, he was right.

Where people of experience saw macho power and revenge engulf Vicki that morning, Justice Hampel imagined love gone wrong.

In *Cleary Independent* I described what happened in this way:

The circumstances were, that three months after the ending of a relationship, not two months as Hampel said during the trial, an armed man had gone after his ex-girlfriend and fatally invaded her private space. To conclude that one woman's quiet, gentle and unostentatious pursuit of personal freedom should qualify as an 'act' which might cause an ordinary man to do what Peter Keogh did, was to plunge the society into moral barbarism.

When Nicole Kidman stepped out as Isabelle in Jane Campion's film adaptation of the Henry James novel *Portrait of a Lady*, her character was eulogised as 'a romantic with a strong sense of independence'. When Vicki Cleary sought romance and independence free of the clutches of a pathological bully, a century after James' Isabelle, she was cast as a working-class femme fatale.

In the aftermath of Australia's sanctimonious condemnation of the Afghanistan government's treatment of women, those words seem even more fitting. The 'small L' liberals at the bench were among the first to defend the rights of refugees. And when it came to women denied an education and forced to wear the burka they were unequivocal about a woman's rights. They were nowhere to be seen when the violent Peter Keogh was granted a patriarchal provocation defence.

Hampel's decision to grant provocation came on Friday afternoon after five days of eyewitness evidence and the medical opinions of Doctors Walton and Clark. Apart from those who'd stood within metres of Keogh as he set to work, there had not been one witness to tell Vicki's side of the story. Not even Chris Wheeler, with whom Vicki had shared her last intimate moments in Montmorency, was asked to give evidence. All we heard was hearsay evidence and the personal opinions of Keogh's mates as to the nature of the relationship and Keogh's state of mind.

When Kevin Crowe appeared in the Supreme Court on 5 September 1988, charged with murdering his ex wife, Christine, the Crown called her sister Carmel, her brother-in-law and her mother. Not one had been privy to the shooting. All gave evidence about the nature of the relationship and the circumstances preceding the murder. With Keogh's provocation defence heavily dependent on the circumstances leading up to the murder, every issue had to be fought. The length of separation, ownership of the car, Vicki's relationship with Keogh prior to the murder, and finally, the minutiae of what happened in Cameron Street; all this needed a fine toothcomb approach.

So why didn't the prosecution call Vicki's mother or father, boyfriend Chris Wheeler and her sister Donna? Mum, Dad and my youngest sister Elizabeth would have sworn on oath that it was Keogh's voice booming from the phone threatening arson and murder when Vicki told him it was over. And why was Suzanne McKay, who saw Keogh dragging Vicki towards the passenger side door, deleted from the witness list? And where was Margaret Hobbs when my family needed her?

George Hampel had based his granting of a defence of provocation on Justice Lush's 1982 ruling in R v Dincer. Zerrin Dincer was only sixteen when her father pulled a knife from his sock and stabbed her to death in her boyfriend's bedroom. Unlike Keogh, the killer didn't inflict multiple wounds. Lush ruled that Dincer, an allegedly devout Muslim, carried permanent cultural characteristics that made the alleged sexual behaviour of his daughter more likely to cause him grief.

Prosecutor Jim Morrissey, who defended one of the 'Fairfield rapists' in 1960, was astounded when Lush allowed provocation. Dincer was found not guilty of murder. He wouldn't be so lucky after the September 11 attack on New York. No bloke today would be so silly as to cite love of Islam as the reason for stabbing his daughter.

'There must be some real connection between the nature of the provocation and of the particular characteristics of the offender by which it is sought to modify the ordinary man test, and the law will only concede provocation if there is some kind of proportion between the provocation and the act.' Although Lush set this as the test for granting a provocation defence, Hampel adopted a different approach. As irony would have it, I had taught Zerrin at Sunshine West High School the year before she was killed.

The idea that a Muslim had thrown him a life raft must have

intrigued the petty suburban racist, Peter Keogh. The non-drinking Muslim and the alcoholic depressive had much in common, said Justice Hampel. If nothing else, both believed that a woman should do what she was told, and both carried a knife. The knife! So often during the trial I remembered that short story, 'The Knife,' and Judah Waten's gripping defence of the immigrant boy with the knife.

A Palestinian Jew, Waten understood what it was like to endure the bullying of brazen racists like Keogh. A committed communist, Waten's sympathies were on the side of the oppressed ordinary man, not the storm trooper. Like many Italians in post-war Melbourne, Waten's character, Plinio, struggled to understand why the Aussie boys felt the way they did towards him.

'Don't fight wogs, they'd stick a knife in ya guts as soon as look at ya.' It was a favourite expression of the young Peter Keogh, whose menacing ilk Waten captured in his story. One day the provocation and humiliation overtook young Plinio. Out of his sock he ripped a knife, an emblem of his father's work, and drove it into the gut of his traducer. I was on the side of the young Italian.

The knife man, Keogh, wasn't Plinio the Italian. And Vicki and Zerrin weren't anything like the mob that taunted and bullied in Keogh's Fairfield or Waten's North Melbourne. The girls were on the side of the angels. Not because they were girls, but because they were in the front line in the fight for independence. Zerrin cared about her dad and didn't intend to shame him. But what was she to do? Subject herself to her father's law just as an Aussie mob demanded Plinio live by their rules? The young Italian waved his knife in the name of freedom. The racist Keogh and 'Dincer the Turk' struck out in the name of power. And no law should ever reward that.

By way of Dincer, George Hampel had legitimised the right of a man to walk over any woman who said 'no'. Vicki Cleary, Zerrin Dincer and Jean in the lane were testimony to the Marxist dictum that the law serves the ruling class. The capitalist was above the worker. Men were above women. Alcoholic depression wasn't the source of Keogh's violence. Even the shrinks told the judge that suicide, not violence, was the modus operandi of the alcoholic depressive. Keogh's violence was a product of the kind of patriarchy the west bemoaned in the mythical Islam.

'The sentence handed down and the period of incarceration is an obscenity. It is in your hands to rectify this appalling miscarriage of justice,' I'd concluded in a letter to John Coldrey, Director of the DPP on 24 February 1989. On 17 March, Coldrey responded. Apart from explaining that in the absence of the death penalty the law of provocation—a common law concession to human frailty—was weakened, and conceding that the sentence was lenient but not manifestly inadequate, Coldrey had this to say on the matter of provocation:

> Whether he (Hampel) was correct or incorrect in that ruling (evidence of provocation capable of being considered by a jury) the verdict of acquittal for murder cannot be reversed. What the Crown could do, and I am currently considering whether it is legally appropriate, is to refer His Honour's interpretation of the law relating to provocation to the Court of Criminal Appeal. Such a process, which is known as Director's Reference, would enable the court to rule on the law and pronounce afresh on the ambit of the concept of provocation.

That was all there was to the murder of Vicki Cleary. Although the Crown Prosecutor had told him, 'His Honour's ruling that the jury must include Keogh's "alcoholic depression" in the ordinary man test had made a nonsense of the test...(and)... it was time to step back and see if anything is left of the ordinary man test,' Coldrey never did explore the matter.

Although he told me he could, and Bruce Walmsley said he should, refer the ruling to the Full Court pursuant to section 450A of the Crimes Act, for whatever reason he just didn't. Two years later, Coldrey was elevated to the bench. Known for his impersonations of the British comedy troupe the 'Two Ronnies' there was nothing funny about Coldrey's refusal to test the logic of Justice Hampel. Walmsley wasn't laughing either, but he just didn't carry the fire that burnt in my belly.

'The accused was very fortunate in persuading the jury to return a verdict of manslaughter... (but)... there was sufficient evidence to raise the defence of provocation ... (and) ... the result was mildly surprising without putting too sharp a point on it,' Walmsley had written when Coldrey requested an opinion. Nowhere did he question what the judge ruled as constituting provocation or take exception to Hampel's analogy about the bloke pulling a gun from the bedroom and shooting the 'recalcitrant woman'. Nor did he take exception to the gaol sentence, saying instead that it was within the range given to 'instant killings' in the domestic manslaughter context.

As considered as his thoughts were, Walmsley failed to grasp the real problem. Of course Hampel should not have turned the ordinary man into the sociopath Peter Keogh. But this was only part of the problem. It was Justice Hampel's words and the assumptions that underpinned the words that was the problem. Provocation wasn't meant to extinguish the inalienable right of a woman to go to work. It wasn't meant to relegate a woman to the status of a chattel. The verdict was 'mildly surprising' to Walmsley because the men at the Bar don't understand how discriminatory the law is. Ask the legal fraternity about the rights of women and children asylum seekers locked behind the concentration camp wire and you'll be moved by the passion. But if a woman's on the end of a Keogh knife or a Crowe gun, the silence is tragic.

Although criminal barristers consider themselves an urbane and larrikin mob that won't be lauded over by parliaments or the coppers, apart from Justices Alastair Nicholson and Frank Vincent, there's hardly one who consistently talks like he understands what should be the inalienable rights of all women. That's why not one bloke at the Bar has ever publicly railed against the manslaughter verdict in R v Keogh or said a word when the Victorian Law Reform Commission delivered a majority report in 1991 claiming that provocation carried no gender bias. Provocation wasn't meant as a defence for a man who kills his ex as an act of revenge, but that's what it has become. And that's what the verdict meant for my gentle sister.

Justice Vincent has damned the law of provocation, and Nicholson has held the line against those who blame his Family Court, and women generally, for male violence. But too often it's the jury or the so-called complexity of the law rather than the institutionalised bludgeoning of a woman's rights, that is blamed for the manslaughter verdicts of the kind delivered to Keogh.

Today I still wonder whether Justice Hampel expected the jury to find Keogh guilty of murder. I wish he'd said no to provocation and it had been left to an Appeal Court to deal with Keogh's violence. I believe that that would have settled the matter.

As for John Coldrey, well, I never heard from him again until his office responded in April 2002 to my request for an explanation as to why he didn't refer Hampel's ruling to the Court of Appeal. 'It was His Honour's view that it would not be appropriate for him to make any comments additional to those in his letter of 17 March 1989', said the letter. Nevertheless, Coldrey did forward me two recent cases where provocation was referred to the Court of Appeal. One involved the killing of a woman during a Family Court adjournment in 1997. The woman was stabbed 48 times by her ex-de facto.

If the killer, Robert Parsons, hadn't read Keogh's evidence, his defence must surely have done. Parsons could remember nothing from the time of his ex-wife's smile and the abusive words, 'We've got you now, you bastard' until he was in the police station. He couldn't remember using the knife or running across the road. As Keogh had done, the killer claimed that the woman's uncorroborated abuse had provoked him to lose control. Although Crown Prosecutor, Bill Morgan-Payler, a vehement critic of provocation, had not opposed its use in this case, Justice Cummins would have nothing of Parson's lies. Provocation was denied and Parsons was found guilty of murder. He was sentenced to a minimum of 25 years gaol, and appealed.

In the Appeal Court, Justice Brooking was unmoved. 'To hold that provocation arose in this case would be to encourage savagery at the expense of civilised behaviour', he had written.

'To conclude that one woman's quiet, gentle and unostentatious pursuit of personal freedom should qualify as an "act" which might cause an ordinary man to do what Peter Keogh did, was to plunge the society into moral barbarism.' Those were the words I'd used in my book, more than a year before Justice Brooking delivered his damning assessment of the provocation argument in R v Parsons.

Appeal Courts are comprised of three judges. Brooking provided a detailed judgment that was supported by Chief Justice Phillips, who said that the killing was one of 'pitiless violence inflicted on an innocent, defenceless woman'. He went on to say it was 'one of the most heinous single murders' he had encountered. I wondered whether he'd ever spoken a word about Vicki's murder.

The third judge didn't explore these issues. Instead he simply said, 'For the reasons given by the Chief Justice and Brooking JA, I agree that both applications (provocation should have been left to the jury, and the sentence was excessive) should be dismissed.' That judge was George Hampel.

Unaware that Hampel had so ruled, on 28 March 2001 I wrote to him at Monash University and asked whether he might forward me anything he'd written or said on the law of provocation generally, or articles by anyone else on R v Keogh. A couple of weeks later, his secretary wrote, 'I have asked around and the best I can offer is the new edition of Waller & Williams *Criminal Cases* (sorry I don't know who the publisher is)'. Why didn't she refer me to R v Parsons? I wondered.

Hampel's refusal to engage me on the question of provocation, and John Coldrey's reluctance to explain why he didn't refer Hampel's ruling to the Appeal Court in 1989, beg some profound questions. If Brooking was right, and George Hampel agreed, that granting a provocation defence in R v Parsons would have 'encouraged savagery', why was it allowed in R v Keogh? Equally, isn't it perfectly understandable that my family remains outraged by Hampel's ruling and Coldrey's refusal to refer that ruling to the Appeal Court?

Ned Kelly didn't share the privileges of the men of law. Life under the jack boot of the squattocracy was the genesis of his wisdom. In the Jerilderie Letter he found a simple set of words to explain it:

> ... there was nothing such a thing as justice in the English laws, but any amount of injustice to be had.

If I were able to entice Justice Phillips to reply to my questions, he'd probably tell me Keogh's chronic depression made him a special category. But wasn't Parsons a special category? I'll bet I could have found a shrink to say he was chronically depressed before the murder. Poor Vicki. Attacked as she parked her car for work. Not in the Family Court in the midst of a bitter dispute that involved children, money and pride. Poor Vicki. A young woman outside her place of work, warding off a sadistic man with murder on his mind is said to have provoked her death. Tell me it wasn't wrong. Tell me Coldrey shouldn't have been reprimanded for not referring the ruling to an Appeal Court. Tell me something. That's all I want one of them to do. But do you think that's possible?

The legal system is a maze of interconnected themes and players. I shouldn't have been surprised to discover the name Lester Walton in the second case sent to me by Coldrey's office. But I was. The defence had called Dr Walton to give psychiatric evidence for a Turkish man, Ali Tuncay, who had killed his wife in the kitchen of their home in Melbourne's western suburbs, in March 1995. Tuncay had bashed her with a range of kitchen items, including a crystal bowl, after she said she was leaving him.

As he'd done with Keogh, Walton attested to the killer's chronic depression, and attributed Tuncay's relentless bashing of his wife's head to an intense state of rage, brought on by the 'wellings of emotion, anger and distress'. These personal factors were identified as being relevant to the accused man's loss of control. Tuncay was granted a provocation defence, but was found guilty of murder and sentenced to a minimum fourteen years. In the Appeal Court, it was agreed unanimously that the trial judge erred in allowing a defence of provocation. If only John Coldrey had allowed my family the possibility of hearing an Appeal Court say what we knew to be true about Vicki's trial! It's no wonder I wanted my day in court.

As I lay in bed on the night of the verdict, I thought about what might have been. Deep in the night, I strode into George Hampel's court and took my place in front of the jury.

'Thank you, George,' I said when the judge gave me leave to address the jury.

Ladies and gentlemen of the jury.

The man at the rear of the court is a liar and a bully. Justice Hampel has twice asked you to consider the so-called, 'trigger comments' made by my sister and on three occasions has referred to her allegedly insulting or abusive words. Ladies and gentlemen, forget the so-called abusive words. It would be an obscenity to conclude that what this man did with his knife was anything less than a cold-hearted assassination. More importantly, if you aren't convinced he went there to do Vicki harm, let me ask you this question. Don't answer me or nod your head. Just whisper it to yourself.

What kind of society would we inhabit if we believed that a woman parking her car three months after separating from a man labelled a drunk is somehow responsible for his stabbing her? Yes, we've heard about the alleged words. But let's be serious. What would any of you do if a man ripped open your door, pressed his arm against your chest, then threw the car into park, grabbed your keys and pulled the handbrake on? Yes, he had the keys. That's a fact. It's also a fact that Vicki left her bag on the console before she was dragged or fled from the car. You know, she didn't even have a chance to park her car properly. I don't give a fuck what George Hampel says about the law. The law's not supposed to condone this kind of violence and thuggery.

Mr Champion would have you believe that Vicki swore and his client suddenly stabbed her. But why, then, was he seen dragging her on the passenger side of the car? I don't know why the prosecution didn't call Suzanne McKay. She was in the car with Mr Berlowitz and was adamant that Mr Keogh was dragging Vicki towards the passenger door.

Just a minute, I'll take advice on that. 'You needed to hurry things up, did you?' I won't repeat that, I think you heard it yourself, ladies and gentlemen. What a shame time was so pressing. Anyway, trust me, at the committal, Miss McKay was quite definite about that.

The upshot is that her eyewitness account, along with that of Mr Bell and Mr Docherty, confirms that he didn't begin stabbing my sister until he had her screaming in the passenger seat. Doesn't that strike you as odd? Why didn't he stab her at the front driver's side door where he reckons she said 'piss off', 'fuck off' or 'I don't want to talk to you'? Do you think she might have made a run for it? I wonder.

You know what I've always wondered? I've always wondered what she really said. Just imagine she said, 'Leave me alone, I don't want to talk to you.' Just imagine she said, 'Give me back the keys.' There are so many possibilities. How unfortunate that no one actually heard what she said. Whatever she said, in not one of these scenarios do we have a man suddenly stabbing a woman at the door immediately following insulting words. And don't you just admire her courage for telling him to go away?. This little 25-year-old girl who had the courage to tell him it was over.

Of course he didn't go there to hurt Vicki. No. Peter Keogh's not that kind of bloke. If he were going there to hurt her, why would he wear yellow overalls and draw attention to himself? You know, I've just thought of something. With the overalls on, Peter Keogh could pass as a bloke working on the railway line. That's what the signalman said. Without the overalls and the cap on his head, he'd have been Peter Keogh, and someone might well have raised an alarm.

And you know, once he'd stabbed Vicki, what did it matter what he was wearing? I reckon the overalls were a disguise. Better still, they hid the big knife, the Stanley knife, the wire cutters, the gloves and the roll of masking tape. He was well prepared, Mr Keogh. For a sook who cried when he told us how much he loved Vicki, he had a strange way of showing it. Jesus, imagine if he didn't like you. She took a bloody risk leaving him, I reckon. It's a wonder he didn't kill her. Of course! Of course! I'd almost forgotten. That's exactly what he did do.

Masking tape! What was the reason for the masking tape? Funny, isn't it, that he never did explain why he had masking tape. Nor did Mr Champion ask him why. Excuse me, John. Is there any reason why you didn't ask Mr Keogh about the tape? Sorry? Didn't fancy the answer would have done him a lot of good. Too right, John. Good call. Someone might think the tape was for binding up the bloody victim. And then this silly mob might have put two and two together and concluded that's why he was dragging her to the passenger side.

I see, John. You think, maybe he was going to cart her away and kill her. Knock her out and kidnap her and drive her away with the keys he pulled from the ignition. What a shame Vicki Cleary put up such a fight! Maybe he'd have just raped her. Didn't have any Rohypnol on him, though, did he?

Excuse my musings, ladies and gentlemen, I seem to have been sidetracked by my learned brother's prognosis. You know, separation was good for my sister. She didn't want to die. Ambulance driver Ivano Forte would have told us how much she wanted to live if he'd been here. Unfortunately, the Crown didn't call Mr Forte. I don't know why. Which reminds me. Mr Forte donned his gloves when he tended to Vicki's wounds, didn't he? As for the rubber gloves found in Mr Keogh's overalls, well, your guess is as good as mine. Why didn't he put them on? Gloves? Bleeding brake lines! Bleeding tyres! A bleeding bound victim! You be the judge.

Now, if Mr Keogh thought the tape and the gloves incriminated him, he could have thrown them away when he changed out of his disguise up the lane, couldn't he? Let me put myself in Mr Keogh's blood-spattered Dunlop volleys for a minute. I'd have contemplated throwing the tape away. Ah, but what if the police found it? That would have looked like a cover-up and blown the bullshit cover about me being in a daze and not remembering anything. That's why I'd have kept them in the overalls.

'Impressive sale, Graham.' Tell me. Does that sound like a bloke in a daze? Funny! Peter Keogh in the Auction Rooms didn't strike me as a bloke who'd lost his marbles. Interesting how he remembered that Vicki swore at him and couldn't remember a thing after that until he was cleaning himself up in the lane. No problem with amnesia when he was hiding out at the Auction Rooms! Then the minute he's in Pat Cole's car, he's like a zombie. First she lied about picking him up, then she went and visited him in gaol. No, sorry. It doesn't ring true to me.

Keogh's a liar. Look, I've got a letter here from Dr Jack Wodak, written a month after the murder. Someone dropped it in the bar at the Melbourne Club the other night when we were having a yarn.

I'll read you a few lines, and you can tell me what you think.

He (Mr Keogh) claims to have no recollection of the activities that formed the basis of the charge against him. You asked me to see if I could find a neurological basis for his impaired recall ... I saw Mr. Keogh at Pentridge Prison. He was very co-operative. I was dependent, almost entirely, on the information he provided. Mr. Keogh claims he can remember nothing of the events that followed immediately after his de facto told him to leave ... Mr. Keogh had no difficulty in recalling any of the events from the time he found himself walking along Moreland Road with his blood-stained overalls up until his meeting with the police some hours later ... he has no difficulty in remembering the events immediately leading up to that incident or those that followed it. He left carrying the tools he had brought with him even though he was allegedly amnestic at the time.

His amnesia provides an extremely convenient explanation for the events he is charged with. There is nothing inconsistent in his story but, equally, there is nothing to confirm that he was either amnestic or confused at the time. I must confess I found it impossible to totally deny the possibility that his amnesia is genuine, but I would not be prepared to accept his assertion without some further evidence to indicate that his memory was impaired.

In short, I do not believe there is a neurological explanation for his amnesia although I cannot totally discount the possibility that he is unable to recall the activities that he is charged with.

I must tell you, I wish the Crown had called Dr Wodak as a witness. You don't have to guess why the defence didn't call him.

Yes, I know Pat Cole reckons Keogh was all over the shop when she picked him up. He pulled so much wool over her eyes she even went into Pentridge to visit him with that piece of low life, Brian Watson. Imagine fronting up to Remand to visit a bloke who stabbed a girl you regard as a friend. Could you do that? Seriously, you need to have the hide of a rhino to do that. As you'd expect, when Vicki was murdered there was a page of notices in the paper from her friends. But nowhere to be seen on the page were the names of Kevin Chamberlain, Patricia Cole or Brian Freake. Does that tell you something?

In law it's appropriate to explore the credibility of a witness. You'll remember Mr Champion asked the director of the kinder, Maree Matthews-Jessop, whether she liked Mr Keogh. He was trying to suggest she wasn't well disposed towards him and that's why there was a minor altercation when he went there to see Vicki. Fancy asking a woman who's seen her friend dying in the gutter, whether she liked the man that did it. Fancy suggesting that a good and decent woman who'd seen the murderer's aggression at the kinder a month before the murder was a hostile witness. And poor Maree wasn't even allowed to say she was scared, that Vicki was scared, that another woman at the kinder was scared. You might have noticed she was allowed to repeat anything Vicki said if it put the murderer in a good light.

Remember when she told us, 'Vicki said Keogh was upset about the break-up'? Didn't hear anyone say that wasn't admissible, did we? Upset, my arse. He was angry that my little sister wouldn't do as she was told. It's a family trait, that. If only she'd told her brothers, then we'd have seen how tough he was.

I'll tell you about credibility. Ask yourself this. If Miss Cole were prepared to visit Keogh in gaol with the stalker, Brian Watson, and Freake, what conclusion would you come to as to her objectivity? To quote from His Honour Justice Hampel when dismissing Mrs Seirlis' talk about Keogh being like a vicious dog, 'I'd be very wary of placing too much store on the opinions of Patricia Cole'. And would you believe anything this little prick at the rear told you? I wouldn't.

Ladies and gentlemen of the jury. No ordinary man could do what this monster at the rear of the court did. If you believe that the law of provocation should save him then imagine my sister was your daughter, your wife, your sister or your mother. Should this be a woman's lot?

If you don't find this man guilty of murder, what are we to do with him? If you don't find him guilty of murder, you'll have trammelled on Vicki's life, and he could be out in three and a half years. Can you imagine that? Less than four years in gaol for doing what he did. Is that what my sister's life is worth?

If you show some courage and send him down for murder, he'll finally have been told that he can't do this to any woman who leaves him. There's only one choice. If you let this man off, then what happens to the next woman? Will he stick a knife in her if she gets tired of him or drug and rape her daughter? His brother reckons he killed a bloke in the bungalow in Northcote and burnt it down. Maybe he'll burn the next sheila's house down. I reckon he's dangerous. And I reckon he's a murderer. I wouldn't mind betting he's done it before.

a noose around a coward's neck

When Peter Keogh appeared at the Committal in 1988, Terri McNulty thought she should be there. With a friend as a backstop, she set forth to tell the Clearys what she knew about the man in the dock. She'd lived with the fear of Keogh for so long she felt the need to tell someone and unburden herself of the terror. With him in gaol, at least, she and her mother would put the past to rest. En route to Hawthorn her car broke down, and so her opportunity to tell me what she knew was thwarted. When the *Herald Sun* ran the piece about Julie McAllister having sought an intervention order in 2000, she knew what she had to do.

> I felt the need to write to you. I read your book about two years ago. I was hoping to speak with you about some things discussed in your book. I was a bit apprehensive writing this letter, but I feel now is the right time. Hoping to hear from you,
> Regards
> Terri McNulty

By then her mother had been claimed by cancer, and so could not answer all the questions that had come to light. Margaret Hobbs, Judy

McNulty, Brian Freake, Brian Watson and Peter Keogh, one after the other, someone or something claimed them.

Judy McNulty thought long and hard about ringing Lorna Cleary in the days and weeks after the murder. The problem was what to say. Catholicism had embedded in her soul a rich vein of guilt that corralled her every time she reached for the phone. 'I'm so sorry. I was the lucky one. He's got away with murder before.' That's what she wanted to tell our mother. Time after time, she reached for the phone, only to stumble over the lines. Then came the verdict of 'not guilty' to murder. Judy could no longer hold her tongue.

At first Judy withheld her name and would only say that she'd been Keogh's girlfriend before Vicki. It took a few years before she finally announced who she was, then she dropped the bombshell. Some time in 1993, Mum rang to tell me what she'd heard.

'Phil, I've had a call from a woman who claims Keogh might have killed the Thornbury Bookshop woman.'

When Mum told me, I neither believed it nor wanted to pursue it. My anger was with the law of provocation and how Hampel had applied it. Whatever Keogh had done before was of little consequence. It was just too late now to be dragging up his sordid life. Nevertheless, I owed it to my mother to find out whether Judy's story might be true. And there was one thing about which Judy was adamant. Keogh had been interviewed and some people reckoned he'd done it.

So was it true? Once Detective Jack Jacobs told me Keogh had a watertight alibi, I considered that the end of the matter. Yet there remained a nagging doubt. And what was Judy trying to tell Mum when she described Keogh's demeanour in the car on the day of the murder? 'Hang on, I want to hear this,' he had said as he reached for the volume switch on the car radio, then the minute the broadcast finished, began changing channels in search of the latest news. If Judy was with him on the day of the murder, then who was the woman who provided him with the alibi? I had to find out. It wasn't until 1997, four years after Judy McNulty died at 47, that I found my way to the offices of the Homicide Squad in St Kilda Road.

The Thornbury Bookshop file is like so many others from the

days before computers and online technology. Endless pieces of paper, notes and snippets of information, almost randomly piled into cardboard boxes, tell the story. Detective Ron Iddles had been a pup when he worked on the case. Tall and engaging in a minimalist sort of way, he'd had an interesting journey since the days of Maria James. By the time we chatted about James in 2002, he'd added Alphonse Gangitano and Victor Pierce to his list of unsolved murders.

In 1997 he was non-committal about Maria James. He vaguely remembered interviewing Keogh, but details were scant. As for who did it, he felt there were a number of possibilities. One bloke, who was very hot, committed suicide. Another had a jacket dry-cleaned on the day. And anyway, Keogh was never linked to Maria James. He might have drunk beer up the road at the Junction Hotel and worked locally, but no one ever said he knew the dead woman.

As we talked, I wondered whether he thought I was some kind of interloper with a bit of an education who fancied he was going to waltz in and show the coppers what they should have done. Bit by bit I suspect he came to understand that I just needed to know whether Keogh really did it and that my sources were pretty good. As I riffled through the papers in the little room at Homicide, Keogh's sordid journey appeared more and more bizarre. Now I knew why I'd met him only three times during the four years he spent with Vicki, and why I had never seen him at a family function. He knew it was only a matter of time before I discovered his secrets and told him he had no place in our family's life.

In the years after Vicki's death, Margaret Hobbs was one name that kept bobbing up. I'd never heard of her until Vicki was murdered. A parole officer cum psychotherapist, Hobbs' relationship with Keogh, said Mum, had always been a mystery to her. When I came across her name in the James file, I was absolutely flabbergasted. It was now 1997, and ten years had passed since Vicki's murder. But there it was in black and white. A parole office named Margaret had told police a woman-hater she knew, a man who carried a knife, was worth looking at over the murder of Maria James. That man, she said, was Peter Keogh.

The woman Keogh bragged to Mum about having her wrapped around his little finger had fingered him. Wouldn't it be nice to tell him that? I thought. And the smart arse didn't even know it. Or did he? According to the file, on Monday 11 August 1980, Jim Goulding rang a police associate, Inspector Liddell, claiming Hobbs had said Keogh should be treated as a suspect in the murder of Maria James. Not only did Hobbs believe Keogh was the killer but she went on to say he'd raped a woman two-and-a-half months earlier.

From here the mystery only deepened. For some reason, Hobbs was reported as telling Goulding that the woman raped by Keogh would have consented if the rapist had asked. It was illogical. How could Hobbs say this if she hadn't spoken to the woman who made the rape allegation? Given she hadn't done this, then the only answer was that this was Keogh's version of events. And if she believed he was a murderer, why did she accept his pathetic lies about the rape?

The woman raped by Keogh, I would discover, was Judy McNulty's sister. And never did she ever say she wanted sex with Keogh, or that she would have consented. She said she couldn't stand Keogh. When she rang Pampas Pastry that night to tell her sister what Keogh had done, she was hysterical. If the police records truthfully reflect Hobbs' view of the rape, she has much to answer for.

Despite the astounding revelations concerning the rape of Judy's sister and the murder of Maria James, neither Hobbs nor her teacher, Jim Goulding, were ever interviewed by Homicide. Dr Clark named both in passing at the trial in 1989 in relation to Keogh's battle with depression. But that's all we heard of them. And as with McNulty, Hobbs had fallen to the Keogh curse before I could ask her what she really knew. Vicki Cleary, McNulty, Hobbs, Freake, Watson, and Keogh. So many people had died. It was weird.

Within three years of Hobbs' damning revelations about Keogh, Hobbs and Lorna Cleary would meet to discuss the health of one of my sisters. At other times they'd talk by phone about the matter. Never once did Hobbs say a thing about the danger Keogh posed to Lorna's young daughter. One sentence would have alerted my family to Keogh's real disposition. One sentence would have saved her life. To this day, Mum can't understand why Hobbs said not a word about the danger Vicki faced. Today, my mother blames Margaret Hobbs.

When Vicki fell to Keogh's dagger, Hobbs said not a word to our family. How could she? Instead, she chose to pursue absolution by way of a letter to the Melbourne *Sun,* a week after the trial.

> Sex offenders: An inside view
>
> I have been 'treating' sex offenders and victims for years, and conducted a group therapy program in Pentridge for four years. With about a quarter of the jail population then in jail for sexual offences, it was possible to isolate a very small proportion of rapists 'diagnosed' as being the type that might be conducive to therapy. Overriding features of the treatment-resistant majority were alcohol abuse and particular socio-economic backgrounds.
>
> There was a trenchant belief that there was 'nothing wrong with them', so the question of voluntary participation did not arise. These are representatives of a much larger group in the community we cannot statistically analyse. Not only haven't they been convicted, they've not been reported.
>
> This is due to often-horrendous consequences for a victim. I see this victim in later life, now in chronic psychological torment, without even the minimal consolation of justice being meted out. Only a small proportion of sex offenders will submit to therapy. The majority has an absolute belief in their lack of culpability. This is perpetuated by a community with horrendous double standards in sexual mores and the treatment of its women, often reinforced by some of the judiciary and police. The 'she asked for it' scenario is alive and well and effectively blocks any offender's acknowledgment of responsibility. Worse still, it gives them 'permission' to do it again.
>
> Margaret Hobbs
> Consultant psychotherapist

Hobbs didn't name Peter Keogh as the source of her 'revelations'. Missing also was the name of the girl raped in the lane in Fairfield, the murdered Vicki Cleary and Christine Boyce, and the terrorised Judy

McNulty. These were the women about whom Hobbs wrote. Now it was too late. We needed to know these things before Keogh set out that morning, armed to the teeth.

As I ran my eye over the police file, I began to wonder just how deep was the mystery of Peter Keogh. What was the real story? I thought. Incompetence, a cover-up, or plain lucky? A woman-hater. How those words jumped out at me. If Hobbs were right when she said he hated women, what did this say about the granting of a provocation defence by George Hampel? Provocation was meant to deal with the frailties of an ordinary man, not the demons of a disturbed sociopath. If Keogh was truly unhinged, then insanity was an appropriate defence. Yet here on an unremarkable piece of paper filed under 'Maria James', Margaret Hobbs was confirming what we all knew. Keogh had got away with murder. Never mind whether he killed Maria James. The woman-hater had killed my sister and walked away with an obscene verdict and a contemptible sentence.

Why didn't Hobbs tell Vicki's mum what she knew? I still can't resolve that question. Not surprisingly, this was not the only time Hobbs furthered a damning view of her client. Not until I'd searched through the full brief with a fine toothcomb did I unearth the depth of Hobbs' complicity in Vicki's death. Did Hobbs tell the gentle and sublimely caring Judy McNulty that Keogh was a danger to women? Or did she congratulate Judy on being the first woman to expunge this hatred from his soul? Eventually I discovered that she had flirted with McNulty's life.

When Homicide re-opened the Maria James case in 1998, I stressed the importance of finding Margaret Hobbs' reports on Keogh. Although Detective Steve White received permission from the family to do that, his search was fruitless. I thought that would be the end of it. Imagine my disbelief when I happened upon a Pre Sentence Report from the Probation Service of Victoria, dated 11/5/76, in the R v Keogh file at the DPP. Four years before the Thornbury Bookshop murder, Hobbs had delivered an astonishingly damning account of Keogh's character. The report never appeared at the trial.

Thus Keogh demonstrates a low frustration tolerance and a progressive inability to profit by experience or to circumvent the lies. He continued to display his overall defiance and hatred, which, it is noted, is not invariably dictated by alcohol. The presence of heavy drinking and sexually aberrant behaviour in other siblings is further evidence of a disturbed family...

Concern is expressed by the disproportionate use of violence and pathological hostility which has invariably been a feature of his offences and which he claims is alcohol-induced. It may well be that Keogh does not remember these offences, which would suggest alcohol-induced amnesia. Keogh has an underlying personality disorder characterised by hostility and sexual immaturity, which is exacerbated by alcohol.

This offence of sexual abuse must give rise for alarm, as it is suggestive of an excursion into an area he has previously suppressed, but there seems little doubt, on sexuality, in his long record with this Department, that he has an unconscious antipathy towards women. His insistence on the child performing humiliating and degrading acts with him perhaps illustrates the contempt in which he holds females.

A disorder such as Keogh's is considered untreatable, and there is little psychiatry can offer.

Hobbs' assessment of Keogh's ailments was at odds with those offered by Doctors Lester Walton and Thomas Clark. Hatred of women, not alcoholic depression, was the reason he killed my sister. In 1976 a parole officer in the employment of the Cain Government was unequivocal about the danger Keogh posed for women. So why didn't someone at government level act on that danger?

A decade after Walton and Clark had their day in Justice Hampel's Court, Justice Philip Cummins told Robert Parsons what I wish somebody had told Keogh:

> I regret that I am not assisted by the evidence of the psychologist who said you had been suffering a long-standing depressive illness (presumably meaning depression as the witness is not a psychiatrist). The psychologist had not examined you at the time or before the time of the

murder. The psychologist said 'it may well have been that this tragedy could have been averted if this man had access to appropriate mediation and appropriate counselling when the problems were clearly starting to be flagged up in terms of his deteriorating mood state, his depression'. You were not depressed, Mr Parsons; you had a cold anger that no one was going to cross you, least of all the deceased.

If only Cummins had been looking down on Peter Keogh, or Margaret Hobbs' damning opinions had been used to challenge the views of psychiatrists Walton and Clarke.

It is plausible that these thoughts so confounded Hobbs in the weeks after the murder of Maria James in High Street that she named Keogh without good reason. That he lived nearby and was known to react badly when a woman left him could well have influenced her. So, too, would his penchant for knives and his work as a meat boner have weighed on her mind. Peter Raymond Keogh was a prime candidate for mistaken identity. The man with short legs and thinning hair seen running across High Street by Jeanette Hodson bore an uncanny resemblance to Keogh. Yet, maybe Peter Raymond Keogh was a man in the wrong place at the wrong time. Maybe that's all there had been to it.

And was torture Keogh's modus operandi? I wasn't sure. 'He's done things to me I could never tell anyone,' Vicki had told her sister in the weeks before her murder. Just what she meant remains a mystery. What's not speculation is that in 1986 Keogh cut the whiskers off Vicki's cat in Gilbert Road, Preston. Was it an act of revenge against his girlfriend? Did it indicate a capacity for torture? Who knows? One thing's for sure. His actions outside the kinder showed that he carried the same hatred for women and love of the blade as the man who murdered Maria James. But was it he who dragged James to the backroom and systematically inflicted more than fifty wounds on her?

'Get it yourself.' These were the words Maria James' husband heard just after the phone fell from his estranged wife's hands around 12.30 pm on the afternoon of Tuesday 17 June 1980. Words! It was said that Vicki's words in Cameron Street in 1987 had been the reason

Keogh took her life. There's little doubt Vicki would have told Keogh she didn't want to see him. Like Vicki, Maria James wasn't exactly asking her killer to enjoy a romp in the bed. History shows that if Keogh had been the man in the shop that day James' words would have been enough to stir him to retribution. The man who killed James was not a man to be crossed by a woman. If he wasn't Peter Keogh, he was a man of similar character. Maybe that's why Hobbs named him. Maybe!

Whatever Hobbs thought, there's no official record of her ever again raising the issue with police. In fact, her opinion of Keogh only improved the longer he stayed under her care. By April 1983, having tried unsuccessfully to cement the relationship between Keogh and McNulty, Hobbs delivered a new assessment of the man she said had murdered Maria James.

> In spite of these problems the union was a warm and a close one at this time. This climate initiated the revelation to Mrs McNulty and the writer of hitherto closely suppressed and traumatic events which had occurred during Mr Keogh's childhood, and which would have had a direct bearing upon his subsequent behaviour.
>
> The Court will be aware from this report that Mr Keogh has been known to the writer for some eight years during which significant information and impressions have been gained. The writer has intensive experience in working with sexual offenders and Mr Keogh has not been categorised as demonstrating sexual psychopathology. He has impressed over the years with his genuine desire to resolve his personal difficulties and most certainly, this overt expression of severely traumatic, and hitherto unrevealed childhood trauma together with the existence of hypoglycemia state has done much to explain previously gross ambivalent behavioural patterns... Above all the writer has been impressed with Mr Keogh's honesty.

I can only imagine what Keogh might have done, had he known it was his confidante, Margaret Hobbs, who sent the coppers to flat 3/223 Westgarth Street after the murder in High Street, Thornbury. What stories he must have fed Hobbs and McNulty for them to show him so much compassion. Nevertheless, not everyone was beguiled by Keogh's criminal charm. In the box of records at Homicide are the identities of numerous people named by do-gooders and sometimes hysterical or malicious neighbours as the likely killer of Maria James. As late as 1982 names were still being forwarded to Homicide.

The records show that on Thursday 14 February 1982 at 5.30 pm, police took a call from a woman by the name of Josephine Reedes of 3 Henry Street, Balwyn. Reedes was responding to a 'Most Wanted', on Radio 3KZ. The man described on the broadcast, she said, 'sounds like Peter Raymond Keogh, who you have already spoken with about this murder and once attacked my sister with a knife.' It was a compelling accusation. At 7 pm Mrs Dorothy Miles of 2 Cecil Street, South Melbourne, rang Homicide and named the same man. Miles was more forthright. 'He's a slimer, a butcher who carries a knife and likes women,' she told the person on the end of the phone. So why did Detective Legg stamp 'no further action' on the file? And how did this tally with the notation 'Keogh would walk with a limp as the suspect did'? That piece of information had come from Detective Bellesini, the man who could have killed him.

As I riffled through the papers, I looked again at the name Josephine Reedes and wondered how she knew Keogh had been interviewed over the murder. Then it dawned on me. The name had been transcribed incorrectly. It should have read Josephine Reeves. This I somehow knew to be Judy McNulty's maiden name. 'Reedes' was Judy's sister, Josephine Reeves. It was astounding. The alibi's sister reckons he's the murderer. How can that be, I thought?

So what about Dorothy Miles? Then it sank in. Of course! This was Judy's sister, who'd married a bloke called Miles. A slender elegant woman with a face to match any Hollywood starlet, Dorothy Reeves never liked Keogh. But that wasn't why she rang Homicide. She rang because Judy asked her to. And if Judy thought he killed James, then why did she provide him with an alibi?

Dot couldn't understand why her sister spent time with the tattooed, aggressive Keogh. She knew her sister wasn't in love when she married, but why leave for Keogh? she asked. The thought that the carnations he placed in her hand might be enough to woo her sister or that he might find the kind of romantic words to touch a sexual nerve mystified Dot. What she didn't know was how the ubiquitous Margaret Hobbs was soothing the waters and preying on Judy's desire to transform the savage beast in Peter Raymond Keogh.

When Dorothy Miles and her husband appeared at Pampas Pastry in the aftermath of the knife attack, demanding Keogh return money he owed Judy, the colour drained from the thug's face. Gibbering and pathetic, he pulled the money from his pocket without as much as a question. It was a far cry from the man who drove Judy and her family into a Women's Refuge and ultimately sent his ex to an early grave. After the knife attack in 1981, Judy had spent some time with Dot in South Melbourne. It was here on the night of 4 February 1982, an hour and a half after Josephine dialled Homicide, that Judy asked her sister Dorothy to ring Crime Stoppers and name Peter Keogh as the killer of Maria James.

'There are things I can't tell you, Dot,' Judy had said when her sister returned from the bedroom after making the call. So many women had lived in fear of Peter Keogh. And when the police had a chance to take Keogh to task, they failed. Not one conversation with the women who fingered him. So why did Judy want her sister to ring Homicide? She wasn't a vindictive woman. And it brought inherent danger. There must have been a reason. Whatever it was, Dorothy never found out. Well, not until I told her nearly a decade later.

Judy McNulty knew where Keogh wasn't when Maria James was murdered. He wasn't with her. But that's not what she had told Detective Ron Iddles. After the tip-off from Margaret Hobbs via Jim Goulding, the tall fair-haired Ron Iddles and his senior, Detective Brian McCarthy, called at Keogh's flat in Westgarth Street, Northcote. It was now Monday 11 August, and six weeks had passed since the murder of Maria James.

'Just inquiring as to your whereabouts on Tuesday 17 June, Mr Keogh,' said McCarthy.

'My whereabouts? What's this about?'

'We're investigating the murder at the Thornbury bookshop. We need to ask a few questions and we have a warrant to search your premises, Mr Keogh.'

'Terrible business, that. I remember the day. Heard it on the news. I was with me girlfriend, Judy McNulty. She's a married woman. She wouldn't want her husband to know,' he told them with characteristic confidence.

'Judy McNulty, was it?' asked Iddles, his inquiring blue eyes sparkling as he scribbled the name and address in his notebook.

Exactly what Judy said to Iddles when he and Detective Brian McCarthy called at her 75 Arthur Street, Fairfield house, is unclear. The last thing she wanted to tell her husband was that a couple of Homicide cops had called at their home to verify that she was the alibi for a suspected murderer she was seeing on the side.

'We work night shift together at Pampas Pastry, but I often meet him around midday.' Was this all Judy told the cops?

There are no records to indicate that Judy offered police anything approaching a watertight alibi for Keogh. The best I could find in the records were the words 'Peter Keogh was probably with me'. Whatever she said, it was enough for them to write 'eliminated' on the file. Keogh was never questioned again on the matter.

Was it enough to exclude him? I think not.

If Keogh were having a fling with the attractive married Judy, then an ordinary person might well conclude there was no reason for him to be chasing Maria James. Better still, the police reckoned the killer was on their shopping list. And those suspects were at least known to have a connection with Maria James. Keogh by contrast was never linked to Maria James. If the police had interviewed Hobbs and Goulding god only knows what they might have discovered.

When I finally tracked Goulding down in 2001, he was adamant he had told Inspector Liddell more than was recorded in the files. '"I'm gunna kill the bitch." I remember Margaret telling me Keogh used those words about the murder of the woman in the shop.' Was he gilding the lily, or was his memory playing tricks with him, I wondered. Naturally it was what I wanted to hear. But they weren't my words.

'She was a brilliant woman. She was genuinely concerned about confidentiality. That's why she asked me to ring someone. If Margaret thought it was Keogh, then it was. She knew these people,' he explained with not so much as a moment's equivocation. On 27 January, 2002, a year after I found him, Goulding died of a heart attack. He was 74 and had carried Hobbs' words for 21 years. Detective Dave Rae heard the same story and said he believed him. But did Keogh do it?

If you believe the stories, Fred Tyrrell has had a colourful life. Carrying a pistol for notorious Richmond criminal, Dennis Allen, whose family had been linked to the murder of Constables Tynan and Eyre in 1988, had to be a risky business. Along the way it was alleged a Bikie had been chain-sawed so his body could be squeezed into a drum dumped into the Yarra River. Drugs were dished out like lollies and guns were always going 'pop' in the Richmond house bulldozed by police after the barbaric Walsh Street murders of the two young policemen. Fortunately, a stint in the clink in 1985 for heroin-trafficking meant Tyrrell wasn't around when the police went on a rampage after the murder of their two colleagues.

None of this had anything to do with why I arranged to meet him in 1997 at the Reservoir home of a bloke who'd known Judy McNulty. Tyrrell had been a drinker at the Junction Hotel and heard stories about the murder. When we met in the front room of a house in Reservoir, he was on the wagon. Specific times, dates and names weren't a feature of his version of life. It was simply a matter of 'a bloke said this', or 'someone said that'. No name, no pack drill, was the expression used around the northern suburbs. Although Tyrrell had never met my sister, she'd heard stories from Keogh about the man they called the 'frog'. In the weeks before her death, she relayed the stories to Chris Wheeler. Years later he passed them on to me.

As Tyrrell sipped his cup of tea and began his story, I was reminded of how strange was the whole business of Keogh and my sister. He reckoned he didn't like Keogh. That was a good start. About the rest, I wasn't sure what to believe.

'The blokes said she was his missus.' I didn't need to ask about the meaning of 'missus'. But what blokes? I thought.

'The blokes?' I asked.

'Different blokes in the pub. It was the word around the pub. She was his missus and he killed her.'

Just who told Tyrrell I never discovered. The alcohol-damaged 'Billy' was one possibility. After a skinful of drink, he would prattle on about the bookshop murder to the barmaid, Julie McAllister. Julie has vivid recollections of Billy's meanderings. Every time he said Keogh killed the woman in the bookshop, she told him it was Vicki and that it was at a kinder, not a bookshop. Oblivious to the rumours about the murder down the road years ago, Julie had no idea what Billy was trying to tell her. Only after the arson attack would it dawn on her. Tyrrell knew Billy from the Junction Hotel. And there's no doubt the word that Keogh 'did the business' was rife in the pub. So why didn't it find its way to Homicide before I discovered the flaws in the investigation? Why indeed.

When Detective Dave Rae asked Billy what he knew, he played dumb and said he didn't know what the cop was talking about. Then when I needed Tyrrell to repeat his story, he went missing. Was it any wonder the killer of Maria James didn't have his day in the witness box? In the aftermath of the trial, Judy gradually opened her heart to Lorna Cleary. The two women developed such a bond that after Judy was diagnosed with incurable cancer, she rang for one last conversation. Yet even then she couldn't bring herself to tell my mother how she'd protected Keogh. All Judy would say was that her own mother believed he'd killed the woman in the bookshop. It was a ruse. This and her part in the calls to Homicide naming Keogh led to one conclusion. The alibi must have been false. If it weren't false and she was with him, then he couldn't have killed Maria James. So he must have done it.

Ask Chris Wheeler today and he'll tell you that Vicki told him Keogh bragged about killing Maria James. In the final weeks she revealed more and more about Keogh's bragging. One word to her family would have broken his cover. One word was all we needed. Yet when I asked her if there was a problem, she refused to utter the words she found for others: 'He's violent and disturbed.' How the words she'd found for workmate Tina Trajanovski would have set the dogs barking! 'He wouldn't hurt me.' How could my sister tell me that when she knew otherwise? I still don't understand.

Damien Keogh, the son born to Marilyn Reeves and Keogh in February 1971 is nothing like his father. A quietly spoken boy, he's had to shelter from his past. Unlike his father, it's not a past of his own making. As a boy of three years and ten months, he was there in Canterbury Street in 1974 when his father humiliated and sexually abused a nine-year-old girl. So, also, was he in Broadford visiting his father during the Easter of 1987, just before Vicki walked out. So worried was his mother about leaving him with his father that she demanded he take a friend with him. At Broadford he saw the aggression and the hatred alcohol generated in his father. He remembered Vicki as a lovely girl. When she drove him back to Melbourne after Easter, he told her to look after herself. She told him everything would be fine.

Following Keogh's death I spoke with Damien on the phone. These days he works a crane at P&O on the wharf, not far from where his grandfather toiled at Dunlop Rubber. Although he had virtually no contact with his father, he and his mother, Marilyn, went to the funeral. When he told me his father talked about going out with a girl from a pizza shop in High Street in 1980, my ears pricked up. On closer scrutiny, he identified the shop as being south of the Junction Hotel. Although the Thornbury Bookshop meant nothing to Damien, the location he gave indicated the pizza shop was across the road. It remains yet another unexplored piece in the jigsaw puzzle left by Peter Keogh. After our initial conversation Damien chose not to return my calls.

The Peter Keogh I know could well have been telling his son half the truth about his association with the street and the shop. Maybe the woman he was really talking about was Maria James and young Damien got mixed up. Whatever the truth, it seems Keogh had a connection with someone near the bookshop. Ask Ron Iddles, and he'll tell you Keogh was never linked to Maria James. But was he? Was he the man who bought carnations for Maria in the days before she was murdered?

Make no mistake, if Keogh knew about the bookshop woman's separation and her sexual liaisons, he'd have been on the prowl.

On the day James was murdered, Peter Keogh was working nightshift at Pampas Pastry in Separation Street, Northcote. Work began at 4 pm and finished at 1 in the morning. According to local gossip, Maria James sometimes entertained a man in the early hours of the morning. Night shift meant it was possible for Keogh to do that. With McNulty still living with her husband, Keogh had to either spend his nights at his Westgarth Street flat or wander the streets. He had the personality, the experience and the opportunity to kill Maria James. So many people reckoned he did that it's hard not to think likewise. After months of searching records and listening to the stories I decided to write to the Chief Commissioner of Police and express my concerns. On 30 September, 1997 Neil Comrie replied.

> Dear Phil
>
> Thank you for your letter of 24 September, regarding the murder of Maria James in 1980. I have read your letter with great interest as I have some memory of this case.
>
> Given the passage of considerable time since that crime occurred, I felt it was necessary to have the relevant file reviewed. I am unsure that any of the investigators from the Homicide Squad who were involved in the James case are still in that Squad or, indeed, still in the Force.
>
> I have passed on your letter for consideration by the current Officer in charge of the Homicide Squad. You can expect contact from that Squad in the near future.
>
> Yours sincerely,
> Neil Comrie

Detective Steve White, a young enthusiastic bloke from the Homicide Squad, was assigned the task of sifting through the material and interviewing the appropriate people. Marilyn Reeves, who'd split up with Keogh three years before the murder, claimed to know nothing about the event. And with McNulty dead, and no direct link between James and Keogh, the case fell silent again. Then I found Jim Goulding. By the time he walked back into the story, another three-and-a-half years had passed since Comrie's letter, and Keogh's joust with destiny was on the horizon.

Goulding's evidence was stunning. With the *Age* exposé pending and Keogh's picture about to explode on the front page, the boys at Homicide knew they had to move fast. But no sooner had I started the ball rolling with Detective Dave Rae than news of Keogh's suicide arrived. Rae was from the Cold Case Unit and had the job of looking into unsolved murders. A man with a handsome and sublimely innocent demeanour, he was anything but your average cop. I couldn't imagine him barrelling some crim in an interview room or chasing a bloke in a balaclava down a dark lane. Maybe he's the new breed of cop, I thought, as I told him Keogh was worth another look.

Unbeknown to me, Rae had arranged to bring back into the picture the woman who'd seen the killer's escape. Jeanette Hodson paused momentarily as he spread the photo board across her table. With hardly a moment's reflection, she spotted her man. 'Am I in danger?' she said as she prepared to point the finger at the man she believed she saw running across High Street that June day in 1980. As the tears welled in Hodson's eyes, the kindly and considerate Rae assured her that all would be well. 'That's him. I have absolutely no doubt about it. I've never forgotten that face,' she said as her trembling finger edged towards the image of the man responsible for one of Melbourne's most brutal revenge killings. The man she identified was Peter Raymond Keogh.

The day after Maria James was murdered, the *Herald* carried the gruesome headline, 'Woman stabbed 50 times', alongside her photo. The killer is 'some kind of perverted sex maniac and the motive is clearly sexual', said Chief Inspector Paul Delianis. On the night of the murder a man had won $16 000 at a Pyramid gambling night in a Fitzroy Hotel. Pyramid, with its 'last in, you lose' approach to making a quid, was the perfect metaphor for the murder and the craven individualism of the eighties. Didn't it help explain how the killer simply disappeared in Hutton Street, and why so many men refused to give him up? Soon everyone between Coburg and Preston, Peter Raymond Keogh included, was talking about who killed Maria James.

Twenty-one long years after Maria James paid with her life for refusing a violent man's advances, a witness had identified Keogh as that man. In the Junction Hotel, in the McNulty family and on the lips of Margaret Hobbs and Vicki Cleary, the name Peter Keogh had been synonymous with the Thornbury Bookshop Murder. But did he do it, or am I just a man on a mission?

'The murder was poorly investigated. They had tunnel vision,' was the opinion of one experienced cop in Homicide. All that was left was the DNA and one last witness.

On 2 February 2002, Detective Ron Iddles boarded a plane for Ireland. It was a trip that would culminate in a meeting with the man who'd seen the killer minutes after the murder. On a dairy farm near Mallow on the south-western edge of the Galtee Mountains, a mere 30 kilometres from the field the Cleary boys left behind in 1863, Patrick Cashman eyed the photos laid out by Iddles. From number 14 Hutton Street, Cashman had seen a plump balding man with hairy arms scurry down the street, step under the boom gate and flee. Cashman noticed that the man walked with something akin to a limp. It was enough for Frank Bellesini to ring homicide and name Keogh as a suspect.

Georgio Martini was one serious suspect. Martini lived with his mother in Hutton Street and had visited the shop that day, trying to entice James to purchase the American magazine *Parade*. Although she had men in her life, Maria told Martini the sexually explicit nature of the material was not to her liking. Ron Iddles has never completely given up on Martini. He has good reason. The tape used to bind James was similar to that used by the loner to tie his tomatoes. That afternoon he had a jacket and a pair of trousers dry-cleaned, then claimed he didn't know about the murder until the next day. The truth was, newsagent Terry Gannon told him of James' murder a few hours after the event. Worse still, the dry cleaner said she thought the clothes were blood-stained.

Martini now lives in Victoria Street, only a short walk from where Keogh committed suicide. If he didn't kill James, then who did? Was Peter from Telecom, the man James had talked about beginning a relationship with, really Peter Keogh? And did he do it? And why did Jeanette Hodson identify Keogh as the man she slammed on the brakes to avoid running over outside the shop? Some people, including Detective Iddles, reckon Father Bongiorno holds the key. Bongiorno had heard Maria James' confession at St Mary's Church on the adjacent corner in the months before her death. Nothing Iddles said went close to enticing Bongiorno to share the confessional information that might shed light on the murder.

In tiny Ballinguile, on the Cork-Limerick border, Patrick Cashman was unequivocal about what he saw. The killer had hairy arms, but no tattoos, and although he was about the same right height, was too fat to be Keogh, he told Iddles. An angry Georgio Martini? A spurned Peter Keogh? The mystery continues. So it was that a man from the place where the Cleary-Keogh journey began had compounded the uncertainty. It hardly surprises me. A year after Keogh's death there was still no word on whether Keogh's DNA matched anything found at the scene of the crime or when the inquest would be held. Answers have never come thick and fast where Peter Keogh is concerned.

In 1855 John Keogh and Julia Gleeson from County Limerick arrived in Victoria with their seven children. After striking gold in Fryerstown, the Keoghs would assume a position of prominence in Glenlyon. Down the road was the goldmining town of Daylesford, where they'd eventually own the Farmer's Arms Hotel. To the west was the basalt plain that led to the Irish enclaves of Eganstown and Blampied, where the Clearys would soon be flourishing. In Daylesford their distinctive Limerick brogue produced a familiarity that would bring the two families into deeper and intimate contact. Early this century Dorothy Cleary, granddaughter of the immigrant, Dinny Cleary, would marry Tom Keogh, grandson of the immigrant John Keogh. At funerals the Clearys and Keoghs shared the burden of caskets and stood shoulder to shoulder in wedding photos. Vicki Cleary and Peter Keogh shared a common history.

In 1960, Peter Keogh's aunty returned to Glenlyon to announce the death of her brother. Some believe she laid his ashes on the old ground where his father had been buried. Maybe it's all just coincidence. Or is it? The philosopher Carl Jung might have explained it by way of the theory of synchronicity and the preordained nature of things. The trajectory that brought the brooding killer into the life of the ebullient Vicki Cleary now looks so clear. It's as if it was almost inevitable. But was it?

Tom Keogh and Dorothy Cleary's marriage and Eileen Keogh's visit to Glenlyon were apparitions that carried a warning no one could see. Among my family records are pages from the *Creswick Advertiser*, the local newspaper that recorded the births and deaths of the clan. On 3 November 1932 it offered a full column obituary to John Cleary, son of the Fenian immigrant, Dinny Cleary. Old Dinny had fought with the Pope's forces against Garibaldi in 1860 and his family was highly regarded in the district. Among John Cleary's pallbearers was his son-in-law, Tom Keogh. When I first laid eyes on the secretive Peter Keogh in 1983, I never imagined he was from my tribe. I could imagine he'd been a bad bastard. But one of us? No.

Vicki Cleary had developed a keen interest in her Irish heritage and the Clearys of Blampied. Yet although she often talked about her Irish antecedents, Peter Keogh never uttered a word about his. Keogh could never risk discussing history. With so much to hide, the mere mention of the past might trigger questions and a narrative capable of unearthing a tale of sexual violence. Peter Keogh was a man without a history. It's highly unlikely he knew that his own great great-grandmother was a Cleary from Limerick. Although they emerged from almost identical origins the Keoghs of Fitzroy and the Clearys of Blampied were a different people. Our people were a proud Fenian clan that produced men and women with spirit and talent who saved their guns and rage for the British invader, not a neighbour.

In the Glenlyon Court on 16 May 1877, James Dier sought and won a £5 damages claim against Thomas Keogh for assault. It was a lot of money for the times. Some might say, and history is their ally, that it was this spirit that beset the boy from Westgarth. On 26 August 1987 Keogh stepped from a dark, slow-moving shadow that had risen in the Limerick fog and followed Vicki to Cameron Street, Coburg. Then and there he struck with the force of his great-uncle. That much we do know.

Violence was the only way Peter Raymond Keogh could make his mark in the world. As Margaret Hobbs had written in 1977, he played down his offences and blamed others for his sins. The Clauscen and McLachlan Streets of his childhood were not the trendy enclaves they are now, but neither were they hellholes of deprivation. In the Glenlyon cemetery his paternal great grandfather and the rest of the clan lie beneath a beautifully cast granite headstone. There is nothing cheap or common about the stone or the Latin embellishments. Nor was his father, John Thomas Keogh, a thief and criminal. Exactly what went wrong in the little single-fronted house above the Merri Creek in Westgarth remains a mystery.

Keogh gravitated towards men with a look of alienation in the eye. While his childhood associate, 'Eddie', was collecting twelve months for the 1966 rape in Broadmeadows, Keogh was staring at three months for kicking a bloke senseless at a dance in his father's hometown of Bendigo. Three years later one of the boys who helped do the kicking in Bendigo was in the court facing sexual assault charges after a gang-bang. Violence and sexual assault was part of the landscape and the modus operandi of Keogh and his mob.

There was a certain symmetry and predictability in the journey of Keogh and the boys. One after the other, they stepped in and out of a criminal justice system that knew so little about them. There was nothing romantic about the violence and thuggery. Two years after Maria James was murdered, Larry, one of the blokes in the gang that came face to face with Constable Bellesini on Preston station, stuck a knife in an enemy's back. Enraged that his ex-girlfriend had gone out with another man he crashed through her back door like a raging bull.

'I'll fix ya, ya took my girlfriend,' he roared as he punched and attacked the man. Described as violent, explosive and psychotic, he was a man cast in Keogh's image. Sentencing him to two years gaol for attempted murder, Judge McInerney said the difficulties of his early life in Plant Street, Northcote were partly to blame. It was all so familiar.

Romanticising the violence of Keogh's mob is a luxury for many a silver-spoon barrister or judge. For the women who live with it, it's a different story. Too often the light that shone on Labor's Hill cast only shadows on union maids. It took a brave man to extend the hand of solidarity to the factory girls set upon after dark by the marauding mob that Keogh inhabited.

'Reckons he's a jack. Get back or I'll smash your head in. You're going to wear this billiard cue for dobbing us in. You're gone, little black boy,' he had told a young copper in the billiard room in 1972. In his bone Crestknit shirt and jeans, his muscled tattooed arms flexed like weapons, Keogh was no boy suffering from disadvantage or upholding the principles of solidarity. He was a lumpenproletarian thug at war with his own, not the class above him.

In a little street in Richmond four years later, with a frightened naked nine-year-old girl on his lap, he was the embodiment of an evil spirit.

'Scream and I'll smash your head inside out,' he told the child girl as he humiliated and abused her.

'Get to my place on Tuesday, or you'll be hearing from me.' That was the last threat he made to Vicki before he flung open her door in a quiet Melbourne Street. How did he get away with it? I still don't know.

More than anyone else, Margaret Hobbs knew why. After the degrading assault on Valerie in Richmond, Hobbs had said there was little psychiatry could do for him. Keogh was what Sigmund Freud might have called a rampaging primitive id. He revelled in assaulting and degrading women and children. His mother had tried to stand over him and every other woman was going to pay for it. Yet when the battle was over and the jacks had him corralled, he became a cringing diminutive sook with a yellow streak down his back. 'He presents as contrite and frightened, yet he re-offended with an act of aggression against a female only a month after the assault in Richmond,' wrote Hobbs in 1977.

While awaiting trial for the sexual assault in Richmond, Keogh flirted with suicide. An overdose had some thinking he was truly remorseful. Hobbs was more circumspect. 'It cannot be ascertained whether a suicide attempt he made while awaiting trial was a genuine guilt-ridden impulse or a manipulative gesture. Considering Keogh's psychopathology, the latter is more likely,' she had written.

It was an opinion supported by Dr Canning, whose caustic description of Keogh at the racetrack one Saturday afternoon after his release from gaol in 1978 captured the real essence of Keogh.

There were now so many questions I wanted to ask Margaret Hobbs. The problem was she couldn't answer them. In January 1996 Hobbs' husband lost control of their car and ran off the road. The acclaimed friend of a string of prominent sex offenders had become one more obituary in the life and times of Peter Keogh. In April 1994, three years before I unearthed the real facts of Keogh's alibi for the Maria James murder, cancer got 47-year-old Judy McNulty. Then, in March 1998 Freake was murdered and five months later Brian Watson committed suicide. One after another, the people who knew the real truth about Peter Raymond Keogh had died before I could have that one last conversation.

So much had happened since 31 May 1989, the day I took Mum to the Melbourne Town Hall for a commemoration of those women killed by the man in their life. I still remember the passion, the emotion and the tears inside the Town Hall. I'll never forget watching a policewoman nearby crying as the stories unfolded. I've rarely, if ever, spoken with more emotion than that day. It had been less than four months since the trial, but from the moment I stepped from the stage I knew the pursuit of Keogh would only end when he was dead. I had no idea it would take until June 2001 to reach its climax.

In Mansfield Street, Thornbury, on a cold winter's afternoon, with arson, murder, and an impending 0.05 swirling in his mind, Keogh was finally cornered. On the previous day he'd dropped coins into the slots with the panache of a casino highroller. Intermittently he'd leave the Junction Hotel and return with a supply of cash. In the evening he headed for another old haunt, the Grandview Hotel. By midnight he was so full of drink he could hardly put the key in the ignition. The drive back to Mansfield Street was a typical roller coaster. Official records suggest that only one parked car in Mansfield Street served as a buffer against his driving his car into someone's front bedroom. Once in the carport he surveyed the damage to his one and only prized possession. From the days of the big white Ford, Keogh always loved his car. Dented and with its duco bleeding the car was a pitiful sight. As he collapsed on the bed, life seemed to have run its course.

A victim all his life, Keogh wondered whether he could read from Bob Vernon's script one more time. An attempt at suicide would prove what a bastard I was for pursuing him and driving him to despair. 'Max will arrive and notice the exhaust, and then, bingo.' I'm not convinced that wasn't the strategy the coward was pursuing when he went down the road and bought a new piece of hose. A new hose to confirm his intentions, and one more lie about Phil Cleary exposing him over the 0.05 charge. Now it looked for real. All was in place for the sting. Unfortunately, the plan went awry, and Max, his landlord, wasn't there to open the door and hear that final lie.

Death by carbon monoxide poisoning is death without pain. For the man who had inflicted so much pain, it was a death totally at odds with his life. Keogh didn't leave a note. On the table in his room were a number of books. A book on serial killers, one on women who kill and another bearing the title *Rites of Burial* were all he left. Ironically the books belonged to his landlord, Max Thomson.

Yet those books so consummately captured the identity of the man in the smoke-filled car with the bottle of bourbon at his side. The *Rites of Burial* tells the gruesome story of Robert Berdella, a sadistic serial killer who kidnapped, raped, tortured, and dismembered six young men over the course of four years during the late eighties. It earned the killer the title 'The Butcher of Kansas City, Missouri'. When Thomson opened the door and grabbed his drinking mate's hand, he knew he was dead. 'Stiff as a board, don't know why the ambulance bloke tried to resuscitate him,' he told the police.

Keogh was dead but it didn't seem right. I was sure that one day Perry and I would corral him, back him up against a wall and say, 'How's it feel when the boot's on the other foot, you bastard'.

It mightn't be what enlightened people are supposed to think, but too bad. Where was enlightenment when Vicki needed it?

Ten years after Vicki's murder, the federal Coalition Government's discussion paper, 'Fatal Offences Against The Person', called for an end to the defence of provocation. In a press release, the Minister for Justice, Amanda Vanstone, described provocation as an excuse for men to kill women. The discussion paper identified all the absurdities of the provocation defence, but something was missing.

Nowhere was the name Vicki Cleary or a single reference to R v Keogh. Despite everything I'd said and written over the journey, not a soul in the legal fraternity was prepared to say George Hampel's ruling had failed to take into account the requirement that Keogh must be an ordinary man and must not have induced the provocation himself. That, and an apology, was all my family wanted. Vicki deserved it. But do you think you can find one larrikin spirit among the boys and girls of the Bar to summon the courage to say that Vicki didn't get justice?

When I raised the matter of provocation with Victoria's Attorney General Michael Lavarch in the House of Representatives in 1994, he acknowledged my 'longstanding interest in the matter', and agreed to put it on the agenda. It was a slow process. Had Jocelynne Scutt been our chief lawmaker it would have been different. She's never been scared to tell the blokes what they don't want to hear.

Ask Paul Coghlan QC, director of public prosecutions in Victoria since October 2001, and you'll conclude that here have been some terrible judgements in favour of violent men such as Keogh. So maybe Coghlan's respect for a woman's rights, and Attorney General Rob Hulls' flagging of a Family Violence Court, is reason for hope. But all in all it's a disappointing tale. It's no wonder the thought that I might have been there in Cameron Street, to shout, 'Hey you', won't go away. Nothing would have been too much for my sister.

But it wasn't to be. These days Vicki writes little messages to me. I read them on the wall at night. She always signs them, 'Thanks, love you all, Vicki'. She was a gift. But I wish she'd come home. We so miss her.

In April 2002, almost a year after Keogh went belly up, Brian Sanaghan and I shared a few drinks at the Cornish Arms Hotel in Sydney Road Brunswick, and talked about everything that had happened.

'Well, Phil, one thing your family should congratulate you for, is that you got the lot of them. Freake, Watson and Keogh. You put them on notice and now they're dead. The Clearys should be happy about that. I would be.'

'Yes, you're probably right, Brian. You're probably right. Maybe that's the end of it,' I said.

But what about the bloke in the bungalow in McLachlan Street in 1963, and what about Julie McAllister's house? I thought. Will we ever get answers to those questions? On 30 June 2002, one year after a swab was taken off Keogh's corpse for DNA testing, Detective Ron Iddles told me it would be another year before we knew if he killed Maria James.

And so we wait. For the waiting never ends. There's just no end to murder.

endnotes

Many of the names used in this book have been changed to protect people's identities. Some of the sources listed below are therefore necessarily general in nature. The court transcripts and police files referred to are held at the Office of Public Prosecutions for the State of Victoria, referred to in the book by its former name, the DPP.

unfinished business

General information was obtained from conversations with Julie McAllister and photographer, Nicole Garmston.

Keogh at large

General information on the Keogh family was obtained from police files and Births Deaths and Marriages, Melbourne.

Information on Peter Keogh's crimes came from his criminal record in the police file held as part of the trial brief, R v Keogh, 1989.

Information was obtained from conversations in 2001/2002 with Marilyn Reeves, Carmel Boyce, Jackie Young, teacher, Peter Stapleton, teacher, Alex Goodwin, Kevin Chamberlain, Sergeant

Ryan, Peter Berman QC, Detective Steve White and former
Detective Jack Jacobs.

General and quoted material came from:
Court transcript, rape case before Justice Adam, April 1960.
Court transcript, rape case before Justice Bourke, 1961.
Court transcript, R v Keogh, County Court, 1976, cited at the
murder trial in 1989.
Court transcript, R v Keogh, County Court, 1972, cited at murder
trial in 1989.
Police file on 1968 assault on George Vlahos, cited at murder trial in
1989.
Police file on 1975 assault at T&G, cited at murder trial in 1989,
including Parole Officer Hobbs' Report, 1976.
Court transcript, R v Crowe, 1988.

decent women

Information came from conversations with Julie McAllister, former
detective Jack Jacobs, and police files.

murder changes everything

Information has been obtained from conversations with a former
Loddon gaol inmate who does not wish to be identified.
Conversations also took place with Kevin Chamberlain, former
Detective Frank Bellesini and the family of Judy McNulty.

'In my view, the sentence imposed in this case was a lenient
one.'(Memorandum for the Solicitor to the Director of Public
Prosecutions, from R L Langton, Prosecutor for the Queen, 15 March
1989)

Information on the Saddington Family is from Births Deaths and
Marriages, Melbourne.

Information on the sexual assault at Fyffe Street 1982 came from the
police file which included Dr Clark's 1983 psychiatric report.

Information about Jack Keogh at the Dunlop factory came from conversations with Harvey Mynott and Claude McFarlane.

Historical information on the Rubber Workers Union came from University of Melbourne Archives.

Information about the Easey Street murders was taken from *They Trusted Men*, Tom Prior, Wilkinson Books, 1996, and conversations with Tom Prior.

Information on the Thornbury Bookshop Murder came from the case file.

General and quoted material came from:
Court transcript, R v Keogh, County Court, 1972, cited at murder trial in 1989.
Court transcript, R v Keogh, Supreme Court, 1964, cited at murder trial in 1989. This file includes parole officers' reports.

killings of the intimate kind

General information has been obtained from conversations with Bob O'Brien from Moreland Auctions, Peter Stapleton, former Fitzroy High teacher, Isaac Rochwerger, former resident of McLachlan Street, Janet Benstead, colleague of Vicki Cleary, Dr Doug Wells, Pam O'Grady, Fabian Gatt and murder witnesses Bell, Docherty, Piccolo, Berlowitz and Seirlis. Information also came from conversations with Pat Cole, Kevin Chamberlain and Pam Duggan.

General and quoted material came from:
Trial transcript R v Keogh, 1989.
Trail transcript R v Keogh, 1964.
Psychiatric report by Dr Lester Walton, held as part of the trial brief for R v Keogh, 23 December 1987.
Record of Interview with Detective Jim Conomy, part of the Trial Brief, R v Keogh.
Assault in Coburg in 1970, Police file.
The *Sun*, Friday 1 July 1960.
The *Sun*, 14 November 1983.

losing one of your own

Information has been obtained from conversations with members of the McNulty family, Kevin Chamberlain and Pat Cole.

General and quoted material came from:
Transcript from Committal Hearing held at Hawthorn Magistrates Court, 1988.
Trial transcript from R v Keogh, 1964.
Police records of interviews with Chamberlain and Cole.
Police records of Keogh's crimes.
Coroner's report from 27 August 1987, presented at the inquest 8 July 1988.
Psychiatric reports on Keogh by Dr Thomas Clark, held as part of the trial brief for R v Keogh, 10 January 1989 and 26 April 1983.
Psychiatric report by Dr Lester Walton, held as part of the trial brief for R v Keogh, 23 December 1987.

the final insult

Information was obtained from conversations with Detective John Hill.

General and quoted material came from:
Trial transcript, R v Keogh, 1989.
Trial transcript, R v Dincer, 1982.
Appeal Court transcript, R v Parsons, 2000.

Dr J Wodak's report on his assessment of Keogh, 26 September 1987, was for the Legal Aid Commission, Melbourne and held as part of trial brief for R v Keogh.

Cleary Independent, Harper Collins, 1998, page 209.

Provocation is complex. For a discussion on its application, see the Victorian Court of Appeal's decision in R v Tuncay, 1988, in which the Court concluded that the issue of provocation should not have been left to the jury.

a noose around a coward's neck

General information has been obtained from conversations with members of the McNulty family, Chris Wheeler, Detective Ron Iddles, Jim Goulding (2001), Fred Tyrrell (1997) and Damien Keogh (2001).

Justice Cummin's words are taken from R v Parsons, 1999.

Information on the Thornbury Bookshop Murder is from the police file.

Keogh family history was pieced together from Births, Deaths, Marriages in Melbourne, Limerick Archives and Glenlyon Cemetery.